THE WORLD'S MOST MYSTERIOUS CASTLES

THE WORLD'S MOST

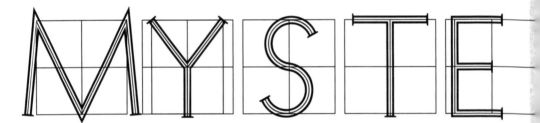

LIONEL AND PATRICIA
FANTHORPE

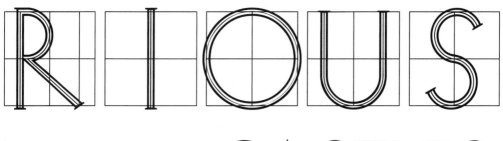

CASTLES

THE DUNDURN GROUP
TORONTO

Copy-Editor: Jennifer Gallant
Design: Andrew Roberts
Printer: Webcom

Library and Archives Canada Cataloguing in Publication

Fanthorpe, R. Lionel
    The world's most mysterious castles / Lionel and Patricia Fanthorpe.

Includes bibliographical references.

ISBN-10: 1-55002-577-5
ISBN-13: 978-1-55002-577-4

    1. Castles. I. Fanthorpe, Patricia II. Title.

NA7710.F35 2005   728.8'1   C2005-903994-9

1 2 3 4 5   09   08   07   06   05

We acknowledge the support of the Canada Council for the Arts and the Ontario Arts Council for our publishing program. We also acknowledge the financial support of the Government of Canada through the Book Publishing Industry Development Program and The Association for the Export of Canadian Books, and the Government of Ontario through the Ontario Book Publishers Tax Credit program, and the Ontario Media Development Corporation.

Care has been taken to trace the ownership of copyright material used in this book. The author and the publisher welcome any information enabling them to rectify any references or credit in subsequent editions.

J. Kirk Howard, President

Printed and bound in Canada.
Printed on recycled paper.

www.dundurn.com

Dundurn Press
3 Church Street, Suite 500
Toronto, Ontario, Canada
M5E 1M2

Gazelle Book Services Limited
White Cross Mills
Hightown, Lancaster, England
LA1 4X5

Dundurn Press
2250 Military Road
Tonawanda NY
U.S.A. 14150

The World's Most Mysterious Castles

To all the very helpful friends and guides we met while visiting and researching these castles and King Arthur's Great Halls in Tintagel — especially to the staff of the magnificent restaurant at Castle Coch in Wales who cooked such delicious food for us and served it so well.

Table of Contents

TABLE OF
CONTENTS

Foreword
by Canon Stanley Mogford, MA

ALL OF US have respect for men and women of ability. Libraries are full of clever books we can read but know we could never write. Concert pianists astound us with the brilliance of their playing. Compared to such outstanding gifts as these, the humbler talents of cartoonists may seem both ephemeral and lightweight, and yet, on occasion, the apparently facile drawings will drive home a truth the world forgets at its peril.

One such cartoon, drawn many years ago, made a considerable and lasting impression. The cartoonist arranged his drawing in two sections. The left section depicted a knight in full armour, clothed in chain mail from head to toe, his visor closed, every inch of his body protected from sword, lance, or arrow. On the right of the cartoon, he drew a similar figure but equipped for modern warfare. He, too, was covered from head to toe but now with anti-contamination clothing, the visor replaced by a fearsome looking gas mask. Every inch of his body was protected against whatever germ or gas attack an enemy could devise. The caption above the two illustrations bore just one pungent word: *PROGRESS*. Perhaps the writer of the book of Ecclesiastes, all those centuries ago, had it about right with his words: "The thing which hath been is that which shall be and that which is done is that which shall be done and there is nothing new under the sun."

Another like subject might also appeal to a cartoonist. Castles of old and houses of today have something in common. The castle, by its very nature, is something of a fortress. There might have been families making a home in it, but it was massively built of great stones, its entrance protected by an almost impregnable drawbridge, the area around circled by a deep moat. Castle designers made them as indestructible as possible against marauders and even hostile armies. Equally, at least in the so-called developed world, we have had to make fortresses of our homes. We have learnt how best to protect them with burglar alarms, security lights, double locks on all outside doors, and every window with its own protection. Like the castle owners of long ago we have had to use every ingenious device the wit of man can devise to protect our homes from all intruders. Here, too, sad to say, as with man's hostility to man, progress has been slow to come.

Protect them as we might, however, few castles and even fewer houses last forever. If intruders don't get them, the years will. Even the strongest, over time, if left untended, will show the effects of wind, rain, and vegetation. Some great castles that once stood proud and defiant are now difficult even to find, their stones slowly pirated to build nearby cottages, barns, and boundary walls. Others have been rescued in time and carefully restored, the new blending skilfully with the old. Such castles are still there for us to visit and are a focus of attention from all over the world.

Some will remember the popular artist Semprini and the words he used to introduce his repertoire of musical pieces: "Old ones, new ones, loved ones, neglected ones." Such words could equally apply to castles. Of diverse ages and differing qualities they are there for us to see. We owe a great debt to Lionel and Patricia Fanthorpe for identifying some of the more interesting of them for us. They have researched deeply, travelled widely, and written skilfully, not only about what they could still see for themselves, but also about much that must once have happened there. The stones have stories to tell, and the writers have retold them for us. As we read these tales, some of our illusions may be somewhat shattered. We tend to associate castles with chivalry and gallantry. Knights in shining armour, riding to the rescue of the hapless and the unfortunate, have provided the subject matter for many of our best novels. The people around looked to the castle and its squire for protection, to maintain order, to care for the dispossessed, and in the presence of an enemy they sought shelter within its walls. But some castles had their darker side, and our authors have spared us none of the shame of it.

Many dungeons have terrible tales to tell. The instruments of torture are in some cases still there, bearing witness to the cruelty and barbarism that went on inside those deep, dark walls. The twentieth century had to hang its head in shame when the secrets of Auschwitz and Belsen were finally exposed. We can't escape the painful fact that once, on a lesser scale, a castle's oubliette took the place of a gas chamber. Its floor opened, and the individuals plunged to the floor below, into a room from which there was no escape; their cries unheeded, they were left to starve to death. Small wonder, then, that the ghosts of tormented souls are said to roam forever within the walls that so abused them. Their suffering outlasted even the great walls that slowly crumbled round their bones. Caerphilly Castle saw many tragic happenings, but none more poignant than the tearful agony of Alice of Angouleme, who was forced to wait longingly for her lover to return, not knowing that his enemies had made sure he never would. They say she still looks over the ramparts, ever hoping but never consoled. Will Berkeley Castle ever free itself of the agonized screams of the king so savagely and brutally done to death within its walls?

Over the years it has been my privilege to commend the books of my two friends, Lionel and Patricia Fanthorpe, to an ever-widening readership. I am almost ninety-two now, and an armchair and a book replace any travelling I might once have done. The Fanthorpes have been to all these places for me and, perhaps, for you. All have been made alive for us, from the Alamo, so beloved of all moviegoers everywhere, with its legendary heroes Jim Bowie and Davy Crockett, to the fortress of Quebec in Canada where seemingly impossible cliffs were scaled by five thousand British soldiers under General Wolfe. From that side of the world, they took us to Dracula's castle in Hungary, then to the castle of Frankenstein in Germany where Shelley's monster was said to have been created. Blarney Castle of Ireland came next, and then castles of Scotland and Wales, leading on to the Tower of London. They are all there for us, well documented and vividly described. They are still there and will be for centuries to come. If some of you who read this book are inspired enough to see them for yourselves, the authors will feel richly rewarded.

Stanley Mogford,
Cardiff, Wales, U.K.
May 2005

Introduction

SINCE THE FIRSt troglodyte had the idea of rolling a boulder defensively across the mouth of his cave or piling up earth to give him the advantage of high ground when attacked, human beings have built castles and fortifications of every description.

As these structures developed with the passing centuries, gloomy dungeons and subterranean torture chambers were added. Secret passages provided escape routes in emergencies or a means by which a small party of determined defenders could sneak out silently and get into the besieger's camp to wreak havoc under cover of darkness.

Many of these ancient castles and fortresses are filled with mystery. Ghosts and spectres are reported by numerous sensible and reliable witnesses. Others, like the castles of Vlad the Impaler and the Frankenstein fortress, have left their toll of horror. In some, like Glamis in Scotland, there are legends of monsters incarcerated in secret rooms and subterranean chambers.

The heroes of the Alamo fortress in San Antonio, Texas, are said to haunt a neighbouring bookshop built over the site where their bodies were cremated. Castle Chinon in France is closely associated with the mysteries of Joan of Arc, the strange voices that guided and inspired her, and the riddle of her reappearance at Metz — five years after her supposed death in the flames at Rouen.

The elusive Camelot of King Arthur and his knights might well have been Tintagel in Cornwall, England, and the symbolic stories told of his heroes could have been an ingenious code created by the Knights Templar.

Each castle that we have visited, researched, and photographed has had its share of history and mystery, heroism and horror to impart.

But what has intrigued us most is the way in which the typical castle seems to be a projection of what goes on inside the human mind. No matter how fortunate a person is, no matter how many mental and physical advantages she, or he, might have, life is a battle — and as John Bunyan would readily have agreed after writing *The Holy War*, the defence of the castle in the mind is our first priority.

Chapter 1

An Outline History of Fortifications from
Stone Age Earthworks to Bombproof Bunkers

THE FIRST NEANDERTHAL humanoids may have dated from two hundred thousand years ago — perhaps more. They had powerful bodies, heavy jaws, and prominent eyebrow ridges. Traces of them have been found all over Europe, the Middle East, and Asia. They made and used tools and had also mastered fire. They almost certainly had more intelligence than we tend to think they had. When your technology is as primitive as theirs, you have to make up for it with extra ingenuity and versatility. Their social norms and mores included making and wearing clothes, caring for the sick and injured, and cooking some items of their food. Their religious beliefs incorporated an afterlife where tools and weapons would be needed: they buried their dead with equipment that they thought would be useful in the hereafter.

As distinct from the primitive-looking Neanderthals, the Cro-Magnon people looked remarkably like modern human beings. They first appeared some forty thousand years ago and died out roughly twelve thousand years ago. They had high foreheads and eyebrow ridges and jaws like ours. They seem to have been mainly cave dwellers from Spain and southern France. Their technology was ahead of that of their Neanderthal contemporaries, and they made better and more extensive use of the animals they hunted and killed. Skins became clothes; antlers were transformed into hooks, needles, and handles for tools. Cro-Magnons became farmers and stockbreeders.

ONE

They also drew and painted, probably for religious or magical, rather than aesthetic, reasons, and had also developed the ability to weave and build.

Archaeologists and anthropologists tend to categorize the Cro-Magnons as early versions of *Homo sapiens sapiens* — our own sub-species. They were a little bigger and stronger than most modern human beings, and their brains were about 5 percent larger. Their capacity for abstract thought and rudimentary mathematics seems to have enabled them to produce one of the earliest calendars about thirty-five thousand years ago.

Other very early species of humanity included such groups as *Homo erectus*, those who were able to walk upright, and *Homo habilis*, those who were able to make simple stone tools and implements. One group after another appeared and then gradually faded out again, leaving behind the mystery of where they had gone and why.

One possible solution turned up in 1998 in a Portuguese cave dwelling in the Lapedo Valley, less than 160 kilometres north of Lisbon. The twenty-five-thousand-year-old remains of a four-year-old boy were discovered there and analyzed: it transpired that he was almost certainly a Neanderthal–Cro-Magnon *hybrid*. If interbreeding between the different humanoid groups had led to new and more effectively survival-oriented offspring, then perhaps it was superior fertility on the part of the Cro-Magnons, rather than inferior fighting skills on the part of the Neanderthals, that removed the Neanderthals as a separate species.

Nevertheless, the remains of ancient hill-fortresses, defensive ramparts, and earthworks provide clear evidence of the hostile and aggressive relationships that existed between rival species, subspecies, groups, and clans.

Hostile relationships with their neighbours and rivals must have prompted these first humanoids to build the earliest known fortifications. It would have occurred to these primordial military strategists — probably from their knowledge of hunting — that high ground was a decided advantage. An attacker moved more slowly when trying to climb a steep slope. A boulder or spear did a lot more damage when it was hurtling downwards. The higher the hill, the greater advantage the defenders had at the summit.

There are many of these early fortifications in Canada and the United States. The excavations at Port au Choix, for example, suggest that the earliest inhabitants of that part of Canada were concerned with defence mounds and burial mounds as well as other mounds with some type of religious significance.

The Maritime Archaic Indians were apparently the earliest visitors to Port au Choix, arriving about eight thousand years ago. They were referred to as "Archaic" because they were hunter-gatherers rather than farmers, and "Maritime" because they derived almost all they needed from the sea. Their predecessors were known to archaeologists as "Paleoindians" and were in the region as much as ten thousand years ago. Found in Labrador and as far south as Maine, they were a highly intelligent and resourceful people, with a degree of craftsmanship that also applied itself to their weaponry. Their fatally sharp, polished slate spearheads and bayonets were works of military art. Warriors who created weapons like that were also capable of creating defensive positions and secure sanctuaries. They also used their daring maritime skills as a defence against land-based enemies. Perhaps for the Maritime Archaic Indians, the ice-cold seas were their ultimate ramparts.

The mysterious ancient fortresses and castles from Central and South America pose a controversial question: were they the centre from which primeval knowledge and culture spread both east and west? Theories abound to the effect that such early cultures first moved eastwards across the Pacific and were enjoyed by the peoples of Central America, who, in turn, sent their ideas both northwards and westwards again *to* Britain and Europe. Contradictory theories talk of an early culture that spread westwards *from* Europe.

The old chicken-and-egg argument remains unresolved. Who came first? One clear fact emerges: the earliest Central Americans followed the watercourses. Mounds that may have been defensive as well as religious have been found along the trail of such watercourses containing the burnt remains of animal and human skeletons. Some human corpses had been interred inside stone sarcophagi. These wise and skilful ancient peoples knew how to make cement involving ground-up seashells — ideally strong for defensive structures. They also made very effective stone axes, knives, spearheads, and tools.

Another group of very early American and Canadian peoples are referred to by archaeologists as Mound Builders. These peoples left their traces all along the valleys of the Mississippi and Ohio. It was characteristic of them never to move far from the great rivers and lakes.

What some archaeologists refer to as a chain of prehistoric forts can be found running from New York to the Wabash River. Another line connects Madison County with central Ohio. Yet more of them connect Tennessee with Kentucky. Were these ancient but able inhabitants trying to defend their river valleys against dangerous invaders? If so, who were these invaders and where had they come from?

The wider question of who took the concept of hill-forts and defensive earthworks not only along natural watercourses in the Americas but from one point of the globe to its antipodes remains a controversial one that involves theories ranging from Atlantis and Lemuria, through starting points in the Middle East, the Far East, the Pacific Islands, Europe, and Scandinavia. The Maori people of New Zealand built hill-fortresses known in their language as *pa*. They frequently took advantage of extinct volcanoes as sites for these high-level defences. Archaeological evidence abounds that Sweden alone had well over one thousand early fortifications of this type, many dating from the Iron Age — some probably much earlier.

Britain and Ireland have an abundance of hill-forts and other early defence works. Silbury Hill, near Avebury, Wiltshire, England, is one of the most impressive of these. It is generally accepted by archaeologists that Silbury Hill is the largest human-constructed mound in the whole of Europe. Supposing that one thousand workers could have accessed the site simultaneously, it would have taken them eight years to raise Silbury Hill. There are three distinct stages in the huge structure: the innermost hill is about six metres high and covered with broken chalk, the outermost structure rises to a height of forty metres, and its base covers almost six acres. Theories of its real purpose range from a tomb (although no evidence of either a burial chamber or a corpse has ever been found inside it) to a religious site, from a vast sundial or shadow calendar to a hill-fortress. It remains an enigma.

Silbury Hill near Avebury.

Not far from Silbury Hill lie the Avebury Rings. These huge stone circles have much in common with the world-famous Stone Henge, and, as with Silbury Hill, their purpose remains a mystery.

There are theories of intersecting ley lines below the henges. There are ideas about ground zodiacs. Henges may have been religious venues — or they may have been defence works. It has often been surmised that the huge monoliths were raised along sloping banks of earth, which were then removed, but what if they weren't? The vast henge stones reinforcing their earthen ramps would have provided formidable defences.

Dorset has an awe-inspiring hill-fort known as Maiden Castle, near the village of Winterborne Monkton. It covered over forty acres, and in its heyday the outer ramparts were nearly three kilometres long. The oldest part of the fortifications dates back at least five thousand years, and some twenty-five hundred years ago, during the late Neolithic era, it was extended and developed considerably. Double and triple ramparts and complex defensive entrances were added later. It was no match for the Romans, however, and under Vespasian they conquered it in AD 43. Among the exhibits in Dorchester Museum is the spine of one of the unfortunate Maiden Castle defenders — with a Roman arrowhead still lodged in it.

France is famous for Mont Beuvray and the excavated Gallic city of Bibracte. Beuvray is roughly fifteen kilometres southwest of Autun, about three thousand metres above sea level, and six hundred metres higher than Autun itself. The ancient city of Bibracte was famous for its ironworks, which brought the Phoenician traders there along with Greeks and Romans. There are traditions in the area to the effect that the Phoenicians brought house-building skills as well as trade. Prosperity is a great temptation to rival groups: Bibracte and Beuvray had to defend themselves.

Another very old French hill fortification exists at Mont Sainte-Odile near Altitona in Alsace. This has legendary connections with the mysteries of the zodiac and is said to represent the water vessel that Aquarius carries. It is argued by some researchers that the name Sainte-Odile may be a corruption of the Arabian *Al-Dalw*, meaning Aquarius.

Perhaps the most famous of all the ancient French hill-fortresses is Mont Alesia, not far from what is now the pleasant and peaceful town of Alise-Sainte-Reine, within fifty kilometres of Dijon. Over two thousand years ago the great hero Vercingetorix, an Avernian chieftain, fought there against Julius Caesar. The Roman Emperor described the fortress of Mont Alesia in his *Gallic Wars, VII, 69*: "Alesia is impregnable except by blockade. It commands a high position at the top of a hill below which rivers flow both north and south."

The indomitable Roman leader was right: although outnumbered six to one, the Romans achieved a historic victory over Vercingetorix's fearless attackers. The strategic advantages of the hill-fortress were put to the test at Alesia — and they passed with flying colours.

The Saxons were noted for their sturdy round towers — a thousand years before the almost impregnable Martello towers took advantage of the same principle. Harry Orford Mansfield, the great Norfolk teacher, writer, and historian, who was a close friend of the authors' in the 1960s, commented sagely: "The round towers of Norfolk and Suffolk are, in the majority of cases, to be found close to rivers which, in late Saxon times, were navigable for moderately flat-bottomed boats. It is therefore reasonable to assume that their primary purpose was for defence."

As with most human activities, progress in castle and fortification design was accelerated by experience and observation: over the centuries, people learnt from their mistakes. Gateways could be stormed by superior numbers with better weaponry or fiercer motivation. Walls could be scaled — especially earthen ramparts. High ground gave positive advantages but not necessarily decisive advantages. A large enough force could eventually bring down a garrison by blockades and starvation. The next significant advance in constructing fortifications was the motte-and-bailey castle associated with eleventh-century European warfare, and especially with Normans like William the Conqueror.

The Norsemen — strong and adventurous enough to fight their way across the Atlantic to Canada's eastern seaboard centuries before Columbus — had made a habit of sailing south to invade France, and French kings and nobles had responded by building castles, known as *castellums.* The common denominators of these simple, early, defensible places were a mound (the *motte*) with a fortification on top of it and a fenced-in area (the *bailey*) that offered some degree of safety. Over the years, Norsemen settled in France and eventually became the Normans. When Duke William of Normandy led his men to England in 1066 and overcame the Anglo-Saxons under King Harold at the Battle of Hastings, William was already a very effective and experienced soldier with shrewd ideas about what optimized the safety of a castle. There was a large territory to be subdued and ruled, and William's Norman lieutenants needed to erect castles as quickly as they could. The motte-and-bailey design was their answer.

In the eleventh century, people, oxen, and horses provided the power that got things done. With no steam power, diesel engines, or electricity, it was oxen, horses, and human hands that created the mottes — some of which were composed of an estimated twenty thousand tonnes of earth.

For the first two or three years after his success at Hastings, William did everything he could think of to subdue his newly conquered land by tact and diplomacy. He even allowed the Saxon nobles to retain their estates — but this softly-softly approach met with a deluge of rebellions and uprisings. William's response to these insurrections was to ride to the site of the trouble and subdue it by force of arms. He then gave the lands concerned to one of his own Norman aristocrats and insisted that a castle be built there to quell the restless local Anglo-Saxons.

When William's castle at York was sacked and burned by Saxon rebels from the north, he responded ruthlessly, and Norman overlordship was reinforced by his policy of devastating the north of England as a grim example to any other potential rebels. When William's loyal and effective ally, Roger of Montgomery, was made Earl of Shropshire, he had to erect seventy or more motte-and-bailey castles along the dangerous border territory that he governed for William. Historians have estimated that during William's reign as many as six hundred motte-and-bailey castles were erected in England. Once their work of subduing the English had been more or less accomplished — and one great asset of the motte-and-bailey design was that given enough forced labour from the subject peoples the structure could be put up very quickly — the Normans began building the sturdy stone castles that form such an integral part of medieval military culture.

Motte-and-bailey castles were frequently wooden buildings. The bailey was particularly vulnerable, and once it was taken or breached there was little to prevent the attackers from reaching the motte. Wooden buildings were, of course, highly susceptible to fire. Castle walls — whether of wood or stone — could easily be undermined. Stone walls were an improvement, and they were very fire-resistant compared to wooden walls, but they could still be undermined, and the weight of the stone made collapse resulting from undermining even more of a hazard. A big enough battering ram, wielded with enough muscle and determination, could also bring stone walls crashing down.

Castle builders, military architects, and designers worked on these problems. As new forms of attack were devised, so new forms of defence were developed to neutralize them. Moats and water defences made undermining and battering ram attacks extremely difficult if not totally impossible. One of the most significant developments was the concentric castle, like the magnificent Beaumaris Castle in Anglesey, Wales, U.K. It was the last of the castles that King Edward I raised in Wales, and it was also the biggest. Its Anglesey site was not influenced or restricted by any previous structure, and this gave its architect, Master James of St. George, freedom to exercise his genius to the full.

Beaumaris Castle, Anglesey, Wales, U.K., was the brilliant work of Master James of St. George.

The concentric structure of Beaumaris made the interior deadly for invaders. This tower commanded the inner courtyard.

James seems to have been the genius behind at least a dozen of the Welsh castles that Edward either built or reconstructed and improved during the closing decades of the thirteenth century. Concentricity was the hallmark of James's plans and designs. His characteristic walls-within-walls structures meant that the defenders could unleash lethal storms of arrows, spears, stones, and boiling oil on any attackers who were foolhardy enough to pass the outer curtain walls and make an attempt on the inner strongholds.

But James was by no means a solitary genius: more accurately, he was the leader and inspirer of teams of highly skilled artificers. There was Giles of St. George, who appeared in some ancient records as Gilet and was known to have worked on Harlech Castle in 1286. In the same year, there are records of Albert de Menz working there. He seems to have been a chimney specialist — perhaps a thirteenth-century version of a modern steeplejack. Another of the experts who served at the same time as James was Bertram, a veteran military engineer from Gascony (or Gascogne). His birthplace was associated with the proudly independent Basque people from earliest times. It was under Roman influence from 27 BC until 418, and then Visigoths and Franks exercised as much control over it as they could until the establishment of the Carolingian Empire in 719. The last Carolingian Duke of Gascony was Arnold, who was replaced by King Sancho I in 872 when Gascony became a kingdom for the next two centuries. The tides of war that flowed over Gascony for so many years carried within them a culture of courage and military experience. Bertram was an inventor, designer, and builder of siege engines, and his practical knowledge of attack and defence must have contributed significantly to the work done on the efficient Welsh castles in the closing decades of the thirteenth century.

Just as the records show that there were chimney specialists like Albert de Menz, so there were craftsmen who were expert well-diggers, such as Manasser, who came from Vaucouleurs in the Champagne district of France. Albert was on James's payroll from time to time and seems to have been responsible for carrying out about twenty metres of work at Hope Castle before undertaking his later responsibilities at Caernarfon. Philip the Carpenter was another senior craftsman in the

Welsh building team, and like many of the others he had acquired his skills doing similar work for the Counts of Savoy. To understand the intricacies and complexities of castle-building during its thirteenth-century heyday is to understand the division of labour and closely guarded "trade secrets" of the diverse experts who put the great military edifices together.

Castles possessed beauty and decoration as well as strength and military ingenuity. Stephen the Painter was another of James's team, and this same Stephen had also been responsible for the artwork in Westminster Hall for Edward I's coronation and for equally exquisite designs in Count Philip of Savoy's castle at St-Laurent-du-Pont.

When the great days of gigantic castles like Beaumaris had faded, the fourteenth and fifteenth centuries saw the compromise designs of the crenellated manor houses. The addition of battlements or other fortifications to a manor house required a royal licence. The Duke of Buckingham, Edward Stafford, began building the fortified manor known as Thornbury Castle during the early part of the sixteenth century — without royal permission. As many other prominent politicians in the sixteenth century discovered to their cost, it was never advisable to annoy Henry VIII. Buckingham was a descendant of Edward III and as such might have been seen as a rival claimant for the throne. Stafford did himself no good by promoting the cause of a group of aristocrats who were out of office and by getting on the wrong side of Henry's confidant and influential counsellor, Cardinal Wolsey. Strange charges of treason were levelled against Buckingham — including listening to weird prophecies of Henry's death and his own succession. He was also accused of trying to fulfil them by assassinating Henry, who took a personal interest in the case and interrogated witnesses himself. Not surprisingly, Buckingham was found guilty and duly executed on May 17, 1521. The fortifications at Thornbury were never completed: Henry took it over as a palace instead.

As gunpowder, cannon, and grenades became increasingly widespread and effective, so castles that had once withstood siege engines and battering rams diminished in importance. The Martello tower, however, was a very effective descendant of the traditional medieval castle that proved itself time and again. The idea reached British military strategists after two heavily gunned, state-of-the-art British warships (HMS *Fortitude* and HMS *Juno*) failed to overcome the defenders of a tower at Mortella Point in Corsica in 1794.

The basic principle of the Martello tower was that its rounded shape would tend to deflect cannon shot rather than take the worst of the impact full on. The walls were also very thick and strong so that it could withstand bombardment. It was a squat, two-storey building with a piece of heavy artillery on its flat, reinforced roof, designed to fire in any direction around the full 360-degree range. Some Martello towers had the additional protection of a moat.

With a slight change of name from the original Corsican location of Mortella — a change that was almost certainly accidental rather than deliberate — the British Martello towers were based on this very successful Corsican pattern. For the first decade of the nineteenth century, the British built Martello towers all around their southeast coasts and defended Ireland and Guernsey in the same way. Before the end of the Napoleonic Wars, England alone had over one hundred of them. The success of this rapid building program was largely due to the skilful planning of General Twiss and the energy of his trusty assistant Captain Ford: they were the early nineteenth-century equivalents of Master James of St. George and Albert de Menz.

To be *seen* to be well-prepared is an essential ingredient of an effective defence, and it was perhaps for this reason that the British Martello towers were never put to the test against a full-scale Napoleonic invasion. After the threat of such an attack had safely passed, the Martello towers met very different fates: some were demolished so that their stone could be reused; others were taken over by the Coast Guard and Revenue Services as defence against smugglers; a few were used as targets to test new artillery pieces; and some were eventually washed away by the encroaching tides. About fifty are still standing today, two centuries and more after Twiss and Ford had them built.

So effective and successful were they that the design reached Canada. One, now a very fine museum well worth visiting, stands on the Plains of Abraham, near Quebec City, overlooking the St. Lawrence River. Another excellent Martello tower museum is the

Murney Tower, built in 1846 as the Murney Redoubt on the shores of Lake Ontario. It was taken over by the Kingston Historical Society early in the twentieth century and opened as a museum in 1925. There are five more Martello towers in the vicinity of Kingston, Ontario.

Just four years after the Kingston Historical Society opened its museum, France began work on the Maginot Line. From 1929 until 1940 intensive work was carried out on state-of-the-art bunkers, connecting passageways, fortifications, and other ingenious, subterranean military systems. The idea was to protect France's borders from the Mediterranean to the Alps in the south and from the Ardennes to Switzerland in the north.

This amazing fortification, sometimes called the Great Wall of France, was named after gallant war hero André Maginot, the deservedly popular Minister of Veterans Affairs and Minister of War until 1932. It was not the blunder that many military historians think it was. It did what it was designed to do — and it did it well. It gave the French army a breathing space in which to mobilize. If only it had been longer it could have changed the course of the Second World War. The Maginot Line made it crystal clear to the Germans that it would be singularly unwise to try to attack across the French eastern frontier, which the line defended. Instead, Hitler's armies went around it. In the First World War, France had successfully held some six hundred kilometres of front line with barbed wire and trenches. How sensible and practical it must have seemed to the veteran commanders of that war to trust in a line that was modern, lethal, and infinitely more formidable than trenches and barbed wire entanglements.

It was also the Second World War that saw the characteristic "pill-boxes" — miniaturized descendants of medieval castles and Martello towers. The arrival of nuclear weapons made the so-called bombproof contemporary bunker a contradiction in terms.

So from prehistoric hill-forts to the deepest modern subterranean concrete and steel, fortifications and defensive structures have been an integral part of human culture. They have constantly changed and developed in a grim, leap-frogging race between the technologies of attack and defence. But what of the future? If threats of biological and chemical warfare are realized, what kind of defences can exclude toxic gases, lethal bacteria, and viruses? Will the force fields and electronic shields of today's science fiction play a vital role in future conflicts — will they be the castles of tomorrow?

Chapter 2
Dungeons, Darkness, and Secret Passages

THE SUBTERRANEAN DUNGEONS and passageways below the foundations of many ancient castles were more sinister and intriguing than the visible structures above ground level. A few of these deep labyrinths and hidden chambers served innocent enough purposes. They were intended for storage, for hiding places of last resort if enemies captured the castle, and for emergency escape tunnels. Tragically, many of them served savage and sinister purposes. Prisoners were thrown down into them to lie dying in the rat-infested darkness with limbs broken and internal organs fatally damaged by the fall.

The rack was a favourite torture dungeon instrument.

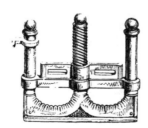

Thumbscrews were more localized than the rack but equally effective.

Captives were dragged screaming with terror into interrogation dungeons and torture chambers. These were lit by the flickering flames of threatening fires, where branding irons glowed and molten lead was prepared.

The torturers' instruments that filled these dungeons were designed to inflict maximum pain without causing death until the victim had confessed to whatever the interrogators wanted to hear — and had implicated family, friends, and neighbours in wild, unfounded accusations of witchcraft, heresy, or treason.

Various forms of bridles were used for both torture and punishment.

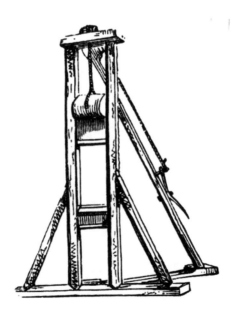

An early form of guillotine used in Scotland long before the French Revolution: decapitation could follow confession after the torturers had finished their grim work.

Victims' heads on spikes outside castle gates.

The infamous Clink Prison, now the Clink Prison Museum, occupies 1 Clink Street in London, England. It served as a prison when attached to Winchester House, which was the residence of the Bishops of Winchester from the twelfth century until the seventeenth. Religious prisoners of conscience were imprisoned there in appalling conditions during the sixteenth century. The areas around Winchester House and the Clink Prison were the centre of a curious anomaly of the law: they came under the jurisdiction of the Bishop of Winchester rather than the aegis of the City of London authorities. Rather appropriately, the area was called the Liberty of the Clink and served as a notorious red-light district. The Bishops of Winchester were often censured by moralistic historians for licensing the numerous brothels there instead of closing them down: careful thought, however, suggests that licensing and controlling the trade would have had considerable advantages in terms of reducing disease and violence to the girls. The Bishops of Winchester deserved praise for their pragmatic common sense, rather than criticism.

The Clink Prison in its heyday held a wide variety of law-breakers from the taverns of Bankside as well as other convicts. The deepest and darkest of its cells was next to the River Thames and flooded under certain tidal and climatic conditions. Prisoners confined in it at the time would have drowned like rats in a trap.

The Chamber of Horrors in Madame Tussaud's wax museum in London houses grim relics of other prison hardships, including the infamous treadmill from York Castle. Prisoners were forced to work this laborious device for hours at a time, until pain and exhaustion were added to their suffering.

Wewelsburg Castle in Germany was taken over by Heinrich Himmler, leader of the SS, in 1934. His intention was to turn the old fortress into a training headquarters for SS officers. He also intended it to become a cult centre for Nazi ideology. Nearly four thousand slave labourers worked there during the Nazi hegemony — almost fifteen hundred of them dying of exhaustion, malnutrition, and the sheer brutality of their Nazi guards and overseers.

Wewelsburg Castle in Germany.

When co-author Lionel was presenting *Castles of Horror*, also known in some places as *Bloody Towers*, the widely acclaimed Discovery Channel television series on historic castles, Wewelsburg was one of the sixty castles visited and studied by the BBC Wales television production team, of which he was a member. It was among the strangest, most notable, and most sinister of all the castles the team studied. During the middle ages, while the German witchcraft persecutions were at their worst, dozens of innocent victims were held in the grim torture dungeons below the castle and subjected to indescribable cruelties until they confessed. Confession meant death.

Lionel and the crew felt that there was a very sad, negative atmosphere in the castle. It required only a small stretch of the imagination to conclude that a combination of medieval suffering and twentieth-century suffering had left an indelible impression on the fabric of Wewelsburg. This, combined with the strange SS quasi-religious rituals that had been held there, made the team glad to finish filming and leave.

Co-author Lionel in the sinister torture dungeon below Wewelsburg Castle.

Another typical example of a castle that possesses not only a singularly gruesome and well-equipped torture dungeon but also reputedly more than its fair share of ghosts testifying to past tragedies is Chillingham Castle in Northumberland, in the northeast of England. One of the ghosts is the notorious "Blue Boy," who appears near a short tunnel cut through a wall three metres thick. Witnesses report that he cries out and moans pitifully with what they say sounds like a mixture of pain and terror. Another feature reported in connection with this haunting is the inexplicable appearance of a gentle envelope of light around a four-poster bed, on which the recumbent figure of a boy dressed in blue can be seen. It is also reported that behind the walls of this same chamber the skeleton of a young boy and fragments of blue cloth were found many years ago. The unhappy ghost of deserted Lady Mary Berkeley has also been reported by witnesses as she looks everywhere for her husband.

Chillingham's torture dungeon contains an iron maiden — a larger than life-sized steel case lined with spikes designed to penetrate the victim shut inside it — thumbscrews of various patterns, cages, chains, leg irons, various shackles, spring traps, and branding irons.

There are exciting records of strange events in Nottingham Castle during and immediately after the reign of Edward II. His queen, Isabella of Angouleme, was the sister of Charles IV of France. Despite Isabella's beauty, Edward seems to have preferred male company, although Isabella did have one son — the future Edward III — who might or might not have been Edward II's child. The passionate and dynamic Isabella wanted to share the throne with her lover, Mortimer, and, after the usual tangle of medieval scheming and plotting, Edward II was imprisoned in several unpleasant castle dungeons until he was ultimately transferred to Berkeley, where, according to the majority of orthodox historical accounts, he met his death — although there is some interesting evidence suggesting that he survived and lived for several secret years as a religious recluse in Europe.

Needless to say, his father's murder alienated young Edward III from Isabella and her bloodthirsty lover, Mortimer. There can have been little doubt that the ruthless Mortimer intended to dispose of young Edward III, marry Isabella, and become king. A secret tunnel in Nottingham fouled up his plans.

The young Edward III had been guarded throughout his childhood by a staunch old soldier who had come to love the boy as a son. This wise and sturdy old warrior — versed in medieval politics — realized that young Edward III was Mortimer's next target. This trustworthy guardian and a party of fellow soldiers who were also loyal to the boy-king learned that there was a secret tunnel connecting an inn called the Trip to Jerusalem to the interior of Nottingham Castle.

Mortimer and Isabella were in bed when Edward III's men arrived. Isabella is alleged to have screamed, "Dear son, have pity on the gentle Mortimer!" The dear son, however, had other plans! Mortimer saw the inside of several dungeons on his way to the gallows at Tyburn, where he was hanged on November 29, 1330, and Isabella spent the rest of her long life as a prisoner at Castle Rising in Norfolk. It is recorded that the experience drove her insane, and there are numerous records of witnesses who were sure that they had heard her ghostly screams echoing down the centuries.

It is interesting to bear in mind that the Trip to Jerusalem Inn is at the foot of the cliff on which Nottingham Castle stands. Some of the cellars in the inn are carved out of solid rock: if cellars can be cut out that way, why not a connecting tunnel as well? Phantom footsteps are reportedly heard there, and other witnesses have described a ghostly woman's voice crying in despair as she searches for Mortimer.

Blackness Castle in Lothian also stands on solid rock beside the Firth of Forth. It changed hands more than once during its checkered history, and Charles II had it converted into a prison for Covenanters after the monarchy was restored in 1660. Blackness has a pit-prison that is washed by the tide, and there is said to be a secret tunnel linking Blackness Castle to the House of Binns, about three kilometres away.

Another grim pit-prison reminiscent of Jeremiah's dungeon can be found at Hailes Castle in Midlothian in Scotland. The castle rests on the south bank of the River Tyne about three kilometres west of East Linton. It was built in the thirteenth century by the Earl of Dunbar.

The physical darkness of such dungeons was a reflection of the mental darkness in the minds of sadistic accusers and interrogators who imprisoned their victims there. Yet as Byron revealed with such brilliant insight in "The Prisoner of Chillon," there are powerful human spirits who can defy the worst that their enemies can do to them. His poem refers to the amazingly courageous and defiant Francoise de Bonnivard, who endured long years in the dungeon of Château Chillon on the shore of Lake Geneva, Switzerland. He was a Swiss patriot and academic historian. As Prior of St. Victor, he opposed Charles III of Savoy when Geneva made a bid for freedom. Consequently, Bonnivard was imprisoned from 1530 to 1536. After his liberation by the Bernese, Bonnivard became a Protestant, and the grateful citizens of Geneva rewarded their hero with a richly deserved pension. Byron himself spent a night in that same grim dungeon before writing his masterpiece that begins:

> Eternal Spirit of the chainless Mind!
> Brightest in dungeons, Liberty! Thou art...

Byron goes on to say:

> There are seven pillars of Gothic mould,
> In Chillon's dungeons deep and old,
> There are seven columns, massy and grey,
> Dim with a dull imprison'd ray,
> A sunbeam which hath lost its way...

The site on which Château Chillon stands today seems to have been inhabited since time out of mind and was almost certainly a Roman fortress in the days of the Caesars. It guarded the vital trade route between Switzerland and Italy, and Roman artifacts have been found there. The present building is one of the best preserved thirteenth-century castles in the world.

Grim as the subterranean dungeons of Chillon were in Bonnivard's time, not all dungeons were set deeply below ground. The modern word *dungeon* is derived from the earlier French *donjon*, which originally meant a tower. Prisoners were usually held in the castle's highest tower, although deep, dark underground dungeons were used as well.

The idea of a deep, dark, damp, castle prison is found in the *oubliette*. One grim example can be found in the Black Tower at Rumeli Hisari in

Istanbul. This was built by Mehmet II in 1452. The whole of Rumeli Hisari was completed in a few months because Mehmet employed a thousand skilled masons with two thousand labourers to assist them. It later held a garrison of some four hundred of the sultan's janissaries. In the dreaded Black Tower of Rumeli Hisari, prisoners were forced along a dark tunnel or passageway that led to a hole in the floor through which they fell into the oubliette, never to emerge.

A number of British castles had bottle-shaped oubliettes that made escape impossible. The authors examined one in the mysterious old Château Hautpoul in Rennes-le-Château, which could at one time have hidden treasure of some sort rather than incarcerated hapless prisoners.

A very interesting biblical reference to dungeons of this type can be found in Jeremiah 38, where there is a detailed account of how the prophet is not only lowered into something that sounds very much like an oubliette but also later rescued and released from it.

Dungeons such as the one where Jeremiah suffered were almost certainly intended for the incarceration of prisoners in the worst possible conditions — with the intention of causing death. But other mysterious dungeons are intriguing mainly because their purposes were unknown. The mystery of the controversial Shell Grotto in Margate, England, has never been satisfactorily resolved. Some experts think it might date right back to the Bronze Age or even earlier. Other theorists suspect that it could have a Roman connection from the first four centuries AD, when Britain was part of the Roman Empire.

Co-author Lionel exploring the mysterious Margate Shell Grotto.

One of the many strange patterns in the enigmatic Margate Shell Grotto.
Does it have astrological significance?

Hastings Castle provides another example of these curious, unexplained underground sites. A small cave is located close to the main entrance of Hastings Castle, on the south coast of England. There are two flights of steps: one leads down to a passageway, or tunnel, which ends at a small, subterranean room from which there is no other exit, while the other descends to a much shorter passage that ends in a round chamber. The most interesting mystery of the Hastings Castle cave is the acoustics. In the same way that the famous Whispering Gallery in St. Paul's Cathedral, London, conducts sounds, so does the Hastings Castle cave. Probably because of the ironstone bands in its walls, sound will travel from one part of the structure to another. Even a conspiratorial whisper can be heard clearly. Was there a sinister espionage purpose here? Did cunning interrogators plant an *agent provocateur* in one chamber with a suspect while they listened in the other? It is not too difficult to imagine the scene — especially during those centuries when the wrong religious beliefs could all too easily lead to torture and the stake: *You may trust me. We are safe here. Tell me ... I will help you to escape.* And every damning word was heard by prosecution witnesses in the adjoining chamber!

So *why* was the cave constructed? Espionage? Interrogation? A dungeon? A torture chamber? Or simply an innocent storeroom?

There are extensive medieval underground passages below the city of Exeter. Many dramatic legends surround them: buried treasure, emergency escape routes for notable historical fugitives, clandestine routes for the romantic rendezvous of nuns and monks, ghosts and paranormal phenomena. Most academic historians and archaeologists, however, prefer the more practical, mundane explanation: they were an early method of conveying clean drinking water. Religious buildings such as Canterbury Cathedral had a piped water supply as long ago as Norman times. The Bishop of Winchester was equally well equipped in the twelfth century. The dean and chapter of Exeter Cathedral had water laid on as early as 1226, and there is evidence that the St. Nicholas Priory in Exeter had a supply by about 1180. It is, therefore, always important for serious researchers to look for straightforward, everyday reasons for the existence of subterranean passages: water supply and sewage disposal were just as necessary in ancient times as they are in contemporary society.

While the medieval church was using tunnels to bring worthwhile utilities (such as pure, clean drinking water) to the places where it was needed, smugglers had other uses for secret underground passages. The Smugglers' Farm near Herstmonceux in Sussex, U.K., has what's said to be the opening of a long smugglers' tunnel that went all the way to Pevensey Marshes — a pretty safe landing place for smugglers bringing contraband goods into England. Just before the Second World War, an explorer and researcher named Frank Illingworth discovered a tunnel that ran inland from Pegwell Bay in Kent. That this was connected with smuggling seems to have been proved by Frank's discovery there of a pistol dating from the eighteenth century and a few buttons from the uniform of a customs officer.

Mysterious underground passages and secret subterranean ways that are almost certainly much *more* than innocuous water tunnels — or smugglers' hiding places — are believed by many experts on Templarism to lie concealed under Hertford in England. There is an old Templar site at Temple Dinsley, not far from Hitchin in Hertfordshire. Prior to the partial destruction of the Templars by Philip IV of France and the unwelcome attention paid to the English Templars by Edward II, who reigned from 1307 until 1327, this site was one of the most important Templar centres in the U.K. Five or six Templar knights commanded Dinsley in its prime and controlled a large staff of servants that must have included armed retainers. There was also a large number of tenant farmers under Templar supervision, and those sturdy farmers could also have been called on to support the Order in times of need.

There are records that show that King Stephen granted two mills to the Templars in 1142, and the good and generous Bernard de Balliol made a large land grant to them in 1147. Bernard himself was a former crusader who clearly knew a great deal at first hand about the vital — and often highly secret — work of Templars. But even prior to the overt formation of that aspect of their Order that did such prominent work in the Middle East, there are references to Dinsley in the Domesday Book dating from 1086. When the noble and heroic Order was notionally disbanded in 1307, Dinsley was formally handed over to the Knights of St. John, widely known as the Hospitallers.

There are strong and persistent rumours that during the Templar hegemony in Hertfordshire, they constructed amazing labyrinths of secret tunnels connecting Dinsley with important access points in Hertford itself and beyond. According to some sources, this labyrinth of tunnels centred at a point below Hertford Castle itself. Built originally in 1070, only the later gatehouse remains as an intact historical building, but although the medieval superstructure has largely vanished, the rumours and legends of Templar tunnels and secret underground hiding places persist. One version suggests that the Holy Grail is concealed there. Another hints that it is the hiding place of the Ark of the Covenant. If it's true that there's no smoke without fire, then it is remotely possible, first, that the Hertford Templar tunnels existed at one time — and may still be there — and, second, that they may contain important religious relics of one kind or another. It is not beyond the bounds of possibility that before Edward II ordered several Templars from Dinsley to be taken to the Tower of London and the remainder to be incarcerated in Hertford Castle, they hid *something vital* in the Hertfordshire tunnels. Is it possible that the secret passages beneath the castle — always assuming that they really existed — might also have provided escape opportunities for the imprisoned Templars?

There are even more mysterious tunnels and secret chambers almost certainly known to the widely travelled Templars of the twelfth and thirteenth centuries during their time in the Middle East and the surrounding areas. Egyptology is a well-developed and rigorous discipline, but there are still more secrets to be unearthed.

For example, as a boy, Mohammed Abd al-Mawgud Fayed helped with the clearing and cleaning of the Sphinx in 1926 and worked there with Emile Baraize, who was the engineer for the Antiquities Service. A tunnel entrance was discovered at the rear of the Sphinx. The young man, Mohammed, stayed with the Antiquities Service for many years and rose to become one of its overseers. When Mark Lehner and some professional academic colleagues were working on the Sphinx in the 1980s, Mohammed was able to point out the exact stone that had revealed the way into the tunnel when he was a boy all those years ago.

As recently as April 1996, an expedition from Florida State University used remote sensing techniques and reported that there certainly seemed to be tunnels and chambers inside and below the Sphinx. It's a long way from Hertford Castle, but the Templars were closely associated with *both*. Some of the secrets that might have been concealed in the strongly suspected labyrinths below the Sphinx might well have found their way to the strongly suspected labyrinths below Temple Dinsley and Hertford Castle. In this connection, references to the Grail and the Ark of the Covenant recur.

It must be remembered that the earliest legendary references to the Grail had nothing to do with Jesus or with the Christian traditions of a sacred cup or chalice. The ancient Grail of mythology was a cornucopia — a horn of plenty — something like Aladdin's lamp, able to provide whatever its owner wanted. Although this legendary cornucopian Grail was primarily a provider of magical food and drink, it could reputedly disgorge other things, too — including gold, silver, and jewels. If something ancient and mysterious *had* fallen into Templar hands after resting for millennia in a secret labyrinth below the Sphinx, what would have been more natural than for its new Templar custodians to find a similarly secure repository for it under one of *their* castles or commanderies?

Even older and more mysterious than the legends and tales associated with the Sphinx and its concealed treasure are the strange stories of an eldritch prehuman civilization concealed *inside the Earth itself*: the Hollow Earth Theory, in fact. There are a great many folktales in Asia — particularly in the region of the Karakoram Pass — that refer to ancient races dwelling inside a hollow Earth. The Karakoram Mountains extend for nearly five hundred kilometres between the rivers Indus and Yarkant. Some of the peaks in this range have summits close to nine thousand metres, and Mount Godwin-Austen is one of the highest mountains in the world. The Karakoram Pass itself is over fifty-five hundred metres high and stands on the main route from Kashmir to China. It is in this vicinity that several hollow Earth legends are widely shared by neighbouring peoples and local residents.

It is said among the indigenous peoples that tunnels and caverns exist that are so huge and extensive that it is possible to go through them and emerge in different countries. There is also widespread belief in an ancient subterranean kingdom of underground people. They are credited with being as good and as wise as the legendary Atlanteans. The legends of these awesome tunnels and subterranean passageways describe the method by which they are guarded by strange elemental spirits, who, in turn, have the power to disguise themselves as rocks. The word *gupta* associated with these legendary Asian tunnels means *secret, hidden,* or *concealed.*

From legends of labyrinths beneath Hertfordshire in the U.K. to tunnels under the Sphinx and then beyond that to legends of the Earth itself being hollow is a very long mental journey. But in order fully to understand the minds of the tunnel makers and the excavators of deeply hidden, secret underground chambers, it is important to consider where their ideas were coming from and the mysterious old cultures that had influenced and motivated them.

It was not only from Asia that the legends of the huge tunnels and vast caverns came. South and Central America also have persistent tunnel and chamber legends. They are said to run from Colombia, through Bolivia and Peru, and all the way down to Chile. The redoubtable Madame Blavatsky reported that she had heard of an enormous tunnel extending between Cuzco and Lima. The indigenous peoples of North America also have awesome legends of huge subterranean caverns from which the remote ancestors of the present human race emerged millennia ago.

What could all these widespread and persistent myths and legends mean? Does psychology have more answers to offer than archaeology or geology? Both Freud and Jung, in their respective styles, have interesting comments to make on the symbolism of tunnels: Freud is interested in the possible sexual meaning of tunnel metaphors; Jung refers to them as transition experiences — symbolizing moving from one state of being to another. There are also interesting mystical references to near-death and out-of-the-body experiences in which tunnels are an integral part of the symbolism. It seems as though there is symbolic movement through, or along, a metaphorical tunnel between the dimensions, or between the normal, everyday, *physical* life of Earth and the mystical, *spiritual* life of Paradise.

Taking all of these considerations together, is it possible that they have acted as strange, subconscious motivators for the constructors of real-life tunnels and underground passages — on various scales — all over the world?

The ruined Château Hautpoul at Rennes-le-Château. One tower was called the Tower of Alchemy.

Chapter 3
The Ruined Château of Rennes

THE MYSTERY OF Rennes-le-Château, not far from
Carcassonne in southwestern France, is one of the oldest,
strangest, and most extensive and complex enigmas known
to researchers of the anomalous. Like Dr. Who's mysterious
TARDIS, it's far larger on the inside than it appears from the
outside. Initially, a nineteenth-century village priest named
Bérenger Saunière suddenly acquired either wealth or
considerable ability to create and control the things that
wealth can provide: there's a subtle difference. From 1885
until his death from questionable causes in 1917, Saunière
was responsible for repairing and enriching the sadly
neglected church of St. Mary Magdalene, ostentatious
spending in the village, and various constructions such as
his orangery, a watchtower with a steel door, and the lux-
urious Villa Bethania. Closer inspections and years of
deeper research since our first visit to Rennes in 1975 have
provided far more questions than answers.

    The major problem with Rennes is that there are suspect
clues, dubious evidence, false theories, and paradoxical,
contradictory statements disguising the mystery and the
facts. These dense entanglements become worse when different investigators take up diametrically opposed positions
on the mystery and then proceed to defend their own
positions as if they were the *only* possible solutions —
solutions that by their very nature exclude all others. It's
part of human nature, of course, but tolerance, objectivity,
and inclusiveness are the best allies of serious professional

researchers. If theory A is correct, it doesn't necessarily mean that theories B, C, and D are wrong! Composite mysteries require composite solutions.

Religious researchers, for example, are appalled by the possibility that Jesus married Mary Magdalene and had children by her. According to this hypothesis, Mary and those children later escaped to Rennes, ultimately marrying into the French Merovingian Dynasty. Supporters of this hypothesis tend to assume that their theory automatically precludes Christ's simultaneous divinity and his unique role as the Messiah and Son of God. But logic shows that it doesn't. Marriage and human fatherhood are no obstacles to a belief in Christ's uniquely divine role. If anything, they enhance it and make it more probable. Traditional Christian theology sees Jesus as perfect man as well as perfect God, and being perfectly and completely human might well include finding a loving partner and experiencing human parenthood.

Skeptics and cynics try to belittle the mystery of Rennes, or dismiss it altogether, by saying that Bérenger Saunière made his money by selling Masses for the dead, blackmailing wealthy penitents, trading in postcards — or even that he never had any real wealth! These prosaic theories also allude to Saunière's right-wing, royalist politics and suggest that whatever money he spent was probably supplied by political supporters of that cause.

Psychics, magicians, alchemists, and other occultists emphasize the paranormal elements of the Rennes mystery and focus in particular on the effigy of the demon inside the door of what was once Saunière's church of St. Mary Magdalene. Is that statue meant to be Asmodeus, the legendary demonic guardian of buried treasure?

Templar historians focus on the various Templar connections with Rennes and ask if Saunière found treasure that the local Templars had hidden from the rapacious Philip IV when he attacked their noble Order in 1307. Enthusiasts for the Priory of Sion hypothesis — allegedly a very ancient secret society with pre-Templar roots — maintain that the mysterious priory was financing Saunière for reasons of its own.

Other melodramatic theories accuse the enigmatic priest of more than one murder. Three bodies were discovered under the grounds of the presbytery, long after Saunière's death in 1917. In April 1956, Monsieur Descadeillas, Dr. Malacan, Monsieur Brunon, and Monsieur

Despeyronat were excavating part of what had once been Saunière's garden, when they turned up three badly decayed corpses. They were all males, aged between thirty and forty. Their identities were never established with any certainty, and some theories suggested that they might have been Free French resistance heroes shot by the Gestapo in the Second World War. It is more probable, however, that they were connected with the grim and ruthless Austro-Hungarian secret police. Count Taafe seems to have been in charge of them, and if, as suggested later, Saunière had sold something of enormous value to the Habsburgs, Taafe's men might well have been sent to deal with him rather than pay him. If three Austro-Hungarian secret agents had assumed that a mere village priest would be a soft target, they had fatally underestimated Bérenger Saunière. He was a strong, athletic, determined, and ruthless man.

Was Saunière also responsible for murdering Father Antoine Gélis, the priest of Coustaussa, a village close to Rennes-le-Château? Some while before he was battered with fire irons and then finished off with an axe, Gélis had been so frightened that he would admit no one to his presbytery except the niece who brought his food and clean laundry. He always insisted that she waited on the doorstep until she had heard him bolt the presbytery door. Had Saunière killed him for refusing to disclose the information that he had acquired from some coded manuscripts that Saunière had entrusted to him to decipher at the start of the mystery? Gélis was a scholar; Saunière was not.

Another very different — but equally intriguing — theory accuses Saunière of involving his beautiful young housekeeper, Marie Dénarnaud, in strange divinations that involved blatantly sexual magic rituals. This theory suggests that Marie and Bérenger were together working a ritual known as the Convocation of Venus, which was supposed to enable participants to make accurate predictions of future events — predictions that were then sold for high prices to eager bidders.

Yet another theory suggests that Saunière had discovered a map showing where Visigothic leaders and other wealthy local nobles had been buried in the limestone caves near Rennes over the centuries. With the faithful Marie, he went on long walks to locate and systematically rob these graves. Her role was to keep watch while Bérenger removed the jewels and precious metals from the decayed corpses inside the cave tombs.

It was Visigothic custom to bury their dead leaders (along with their horses, their armour, their weapons, and their treasures) in cunningly constructed waterproof tombs below the beds of rivers. The faithful followers in the burial party would then break the dam that had made the river burial possible, and within a few days the exact location of the tomb below the riverbed would be impossible to find.

At Pontils, close to Arques, near Rennes, there once stood a tomb identical to the one in Poussin's seventeenth-century masterpiece *The Shepherds of Arcadia* — one of the pivots of the Rennes mystery. Some Rennes theorists put forward the view that below this tomb was a secret passage that led down below the riverbed and into the tomb of some great and wealthy Visigothic chieftain whose treasure had been interred there with him. According to this theory, Saunière found this tunnel and robbed the ancient tomb under the river.

Other ideas about the enigmatic priest include his having found the lost treasure of the Cathars — many of whom died at Montségur, not far from Rennes, in 1244. Four of their fearless mountaineers escaped, however, carrying with them the treasures of their faith — also referred to as *pecuniam infinitam*: unlimited wealth.

Harking back to the bodies found in 1956 under Saunière's lawn, there were further hypotheses to the effect that Saunière had an almost bottomless credit account with the Royal Bank of Austria in the days of Emperor Franz Josef. The mysterious priest of Rennes was thought to have sold the Habsburgs some priceless religious artifact such as the Holy Grail, the Ark of the Covenant, or the Lance of Longinus — also known as the Spear of Destiny. What *else* might that holy artifact have been? Had Saunière, perhaps, found the lost Urim and Thummim that the high priests of Israel had once used to ascertain what they thought of as "the will of Yahweh"? After all, there was a large and influential Jewish community in Septimania in the vicinity of Rennes.

It was even suggested that Saunière had found the mummified body of Jesus buried somewhere near Rennes and was busily blackmailing the Vatican by threatening to demonstrate that the resurrection had never taken place and that Christianity — together with the church's massive wealth and political power — was all founded on deception.

Some serious and able investigators have wondered whether Rennes could best be understood as "a gateway to the invisible." Had Saunière stumbled upon an access point to a dimensional doorway, a time gate, or a portal to other probability tracks?

Another very intriguing theory — and the one on which we concentrate in this chapter — centres on the castle at Rennes, known as Château Hautpoul.

Records are sketchy and incomplete, but it is probable that there were fortifications on the hilltop at Rennes-le-Château in prehistoric times. When we visited the château, Monsieur Fatin, the brilliant and celebrated sculptor who lived there with his sister, showed us his fascinating collection of ancient archaeological artifacts that he had found in the Rennes area.

The Celtic Tectosage — their name means "the wise builders" — were in Rennes before the Roman conquest, and the Romans were there in the second century BC. The Tectosage would certainly have created formidable defences for their hilltop settlement. They would also have had the necessary skill and technology to dig a labyrinth of tunnels and chambers.

Roman buildings and fortifications are as noteworthy as their aqueducts, roads, and villas. Undoubtedly, during their time in Rennes the Romans added to the defensive structures the Tectosage had left behind.

Early in the fifth century AD, the Visigoths took over at Rennes, which was then known as Rhédae, and it became the capital of the mysterious old Kingdom of Septimania. Saracens invaded the region early in the eighth century, but by the end of that tumultuous period, the church of St. Mary Magdalene — later to become Bérenger Saunière's church — had been built *very close to the castle*. There is evidence that another, much older, church was there long before that. This older building was dedicated to St. Peter.

According to some records, there was a Frankish invasion in the second half of the eleventh century, and Rennes was at its zenith as a royal city with some thirty thousand inhabitants. The territory later came under the control of Barcelona but was soon joined to estates at Carcassonne, under the direction of the Trencavel family. They lost most of their territory to Alphonse II of Aragon but managed to hold on grimly to Rennes itself.

There is evidence that Pierre de Voisins acquired Rennes and the estate that went with it in the first half of the thirteenth century. It was a gift to him from Simon de Montfort. When Pierre died, Pierre junior inherited it, but the fourteenth century was a bad time for Rennes. A plague of outlaws, thieves, and brigands attacked Rennes repeatedly — and they were followed by the other kind of plague, which caused even greater loss of life.

The Count of Trastamarre more or less destroyed the town in 1362, and it was then that the name was changed from Rhédae to Rennes-le-Château. The area around it was referred to as Razes from then on.

A century or so later, Jeanne de Voisins married Pierre-Raymond d'Hautpoul, and the castle stayed in their family for centuries. In the early fifteenth century, Blanche de Marquefave married another Pierre-Raymond of Hautpoul, and her dowry included Rennes-le-Château along with its mysterious old castle. In the seventeenth century, Henri of Hautpoul reacquired the title of Lord of Blanchefort. In the mid-eighteenth century, a Hautpoul-Félines married a Hautpoul-Rennes, and the castle seems to have been inhabited more or less continuously after they acquired it together.

The last of the Blanchefort males died in 1762, leaving his widow, Marie, who was known as Marie de Nègre. When she died on January 17, 1781, a very unusual tombstone was inscribed for her by Father Antoine Bigou, her chaplain and trusted confidant. After her death, in the turbulent political circumstances in France at the end of the eighteenth century, Bigou went into exile and died in Spain. The stone he carved — like the Poussin canvas and the tomb of Arques — may have carried a vitally important coded message regarding the Rennes treasure cache. Saunière defaced that stone and removed the inscription — a futile piece of vandalism, because an antiquarian had already copied it!

Co-author Lionel exploring the ruins of Château Blanchefort near Rennes-le-Château. It stands on a hill very close to Rennes — but its only inhabitants today are some rather unfriendly wild boars!

The enigmatic tombstone of Marie de Nègre, who died in 1781: Father Antoine Bigou, her chaplain, was thought to have carved a coded inscription on it. Father Bérenger Saunière, parish priest of Rennes, defaced it a century later.

As far as the Rennes mystery is concerned, theories of all shapes, sizes, and degrees of feasibility abound; facts and sequential logic are scarce.

We first visited Rennes in 1975, while co-author Lionel was teaching a course entitled "The Psychology and Sociology of Unexplained Phenomena," which he had devised for Cambridge University's Board of Extra-Mural Studies. We have been to Rennes on numerous occasions since then, and our in-depth investigations into the mystery are still ongoing. After three decades of work on the Rennes enigma, we still have no absolute and definitive solution to it. But one thing is certain: there *is* a genuine mystery in that little hilltop village between the Corbières and the Pyrenees, and it is a very old and complex mystery indeed.

One of the deepest and strangest clues to the riddle of Rennes-le-Château concerns the mysterious Dalle des Chevaliers, which, in turn, is linked with the enigma of the ancient castle of Rennes. It is alleged — probably accurately — that stonemasons doing some minor restoration and repair work on the church of St. Mary Magdalene (which was pretty well derelict when Saunière took it over) uncovered this stone lying face downwards below the floor of the church.

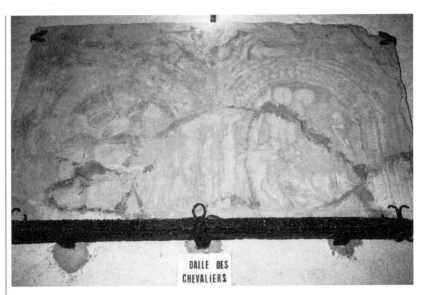

DALLE DES CHEVALIERS

The mysterious Dalle des Chevaliers, which was found below the floor in the ancient church of St. Mary Magdalene at Rennes-le-Château in the nineteenth century. Are the two arches a clue to a mystery concealed in the ancient castle at Rennes?

There are numerous theories about the date, symbolism, and meaning of this mysterious stone. The first is that it may be meant to represent a religious theme, such as the Holy Family's flight into Egypt when Herod slaughtered the children in Bethlehem. So little is now left of the carved figures and their features that it is extremely hard to identify them positively. It has also been suggested that the shared mount is a symbol of Templarism — yet the stone is far older than the widely publicized twelfth-century adventures of the Templars in the Middle East. Was the shared mount symbol (which the medieval Jerusalem knights later adopted) actually the symbol of the postulated pre-Templar Guardians, whose origins are lost in the mists of prehistory?

Another challenging theory suggests that rather than representing the well-known Holy Family — Jesus, Mary, and Joseph — the Dalle des Chevaliers actually represents the Secret Holy Family of Mary Magdalene and her children by Jesus. Persistent local traditions indicate that with help from Joseph of Arimathea, said to have been the powerful and wealthy uncle of Jesus, Mary Magdalene escaped to the Rennes-le-Château area of southwestern France. Those legends go on to relate that her children eventually married into the mysterious Merovingian Dynasty. This constitutes the famous and highly controversial bloodline theory, which features Mary Magdalene herself as the living Holy Grail — the human vessel carrying the divine, royal bloodline of Christ. Some theorists and researchers believe that unique bloodline still survives.

Another theory concerning the Dalle des Chevaliers is that it shows the fearless Dagobert II — the same mysterious king who is said to be buried at, or near, Rennes with his fabulous treasure. In this version, the stone shows Dagobert fighting off the enemies who have ambushed him, while his trusted companion gallops off to safety with his infant son. There are so many confused and conflicting accounts of what really happened to Dagobert that it is impossible — unless further evidence is unearthed — to be precise about what really became of him and where his body (and treasure) now lie.

Dagobert was married to a beautiful and courageous Saxon princess named Mechtilde, who bore him three daughters and a son. It seems probable that Mechtilde was with Dagobert when Grimoald sprang his ambush and that she escaped with their son while Dagobert fought to the death to give them the best possible head start. The Dalle des Chevaliers may, therefore, be evidence that Dagobert II's son survived.

Whoever is really featured on the enigmatic Dalle des Chevaliers, there can be little doubt that it is linked to the ancient castle at Rennes.

When Monsieur Fatin, the sculptor, showed us around his château, the close resemblance between the castle's arches and the carved arches on the Dalle des Chevaliers was undeniable. But what does this clue indicate?

Were the arches in the château older than the Dalle des Chevaliers, or had the mysterious stone been carved before the arches were incorporated into the castle? Was the original code-maker's plan to indicate the importance of the already existing arches in the castle as a vital clue to the location of Dagobert's treasure-filled tomb? Or were the arches built over the tomb *after* the mysterious carver of the ancient Dalle des Chevaliers had decided upon his symbolic, coded design?

Twin arches inside the castle at Rennes-le-Château are identical to those carved on the mysterious Dalle des Chevaliers. Is this a clue to the location of Dagobert's hidden tomb — and the treasure?

The castle at Rennes also plays a central and significant part in another of Monsieur Fatin's intriguing theories about the history of this enigmatic old hilltop village. It is quite possible, he says, that the whole of present-day Rennes-le-Château was deliberately laid out to resemble a mystical "ship of the dead," so that any researcher looking carefully at a map, or plan, of Rennes would realize that it was the burial place of some great historic king or chieftain. But, if so, who *was* he? Could it have been Dagobert II — or someone of far greater historical importance? Is it the unknown buried treasure lying beside his body that is of vital significance, rather than the identity of its silent guardian?

Researchers have tended to concentrate on the ancient church of St. Mary Magdalene in Rennes, rather than the castle itself, but the castle may well hold more keys to the mystery than the church does.

The statuary group featuring the demon Asmodeus, just inside the church door, can be shown to represent the four traditional elements of alchemical theory. Asmodeus is an *earth* spirit. Just above his head is a stoop filled with *water*; then there are salamanders (*fire* lizards), and, finally, at the top are four angels (denizens of *air* or spirit) making the sign of the cross. The whole group, therefore, can be shown to represent earth, air, fire, and water — the four elements beloved of the medieval alchemists.

This weird, alchemical statuary group connects with the castle at Rennes because one of its ancient towers was always known as the Tower of Alchemy. Certainly, the castle's dark, secret interior chambers and recesses might have witnessed almost anything during their long, sinister history. Many additions and alterations have been made to the oldest parts of the castle over long centuries. Every strangely modified stone poses two questions: why was this alteration made, and *what lay under here originally?*

It has to be remembered that there may well have been Arabian influence on the castle's structure at one time and Frankish architectural influence at another. A succession of Spanish nobility came and went. There were demolitions, repairs, additions, renovations, and expansions that went on for many years. Marius Fatin, father of Henri Fatin, the artist and sculptor, acquired the castle in 1945. Marius made an in-depth study of the castle during the remainder of his life. He and

Do these strange figures inside the church door at Rennes hint at alchemy?

Henri discovered a great deal of weird and peculiar symbolism in the crumbling château, much of which is wide open to the elements — although the Fatins still manage to maintain their living accommodation there. One of their theories was that the twelve doorways of the château stood for the twelve disciples. Other thoughts were that they represented the twelve signs of the Rennes Ground Zodiac, which some researchers feel they have discovered in the vicinity. Henri Fatin also showed us a finely drawn plan of one of the ancient doors to his old château. Under his guidance it was clear to us that this particular door had been constructed to resemble a knight's helmet from the eleventh or twelfth century. Did this indicate yet another Templar connection with the Rennes mystery?

It has been suggested by several researchers and Rennes explorers that there are tunnels and secret passageways that link the lowest levels of the Château Hautpoul to the base of Saunière's watchtower on the Rennes summit edge, the present church of St. Mary Magdalene, where Saunière once worked, and the far more ancient church dedicated to St. Peter — the precise whereabouts of which are not easy to find.

So Château Hautpoul has a significant role in the timeless mystery of Rennes. Was it an alchemist's den? Is it connected to a labyrinth of tunnels joining it to the ancient churches and the deeply hidden tomb of Dagobert II?

Rennes-le-Château, its church, its castle, and its countryside provide clues that lead in many different directions, others that lead nowhere, enigmas that are capable of strangely different solutions, and characters whose behaviour was — and is — inexplicable. Perhaps someday, someone will get to the truth of it all.

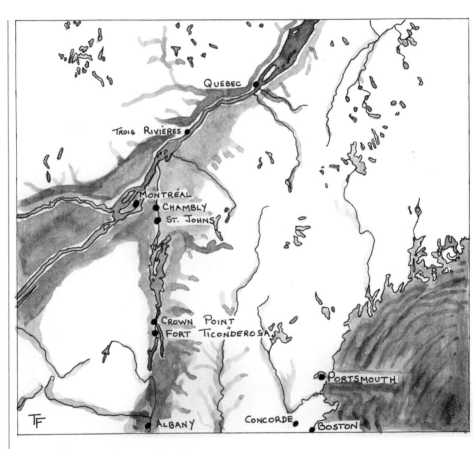

A map of some early Canadian forts.

Chapter 4
Fortresses in Canada

ONE OF THE greatest and best-known Canadian "castles" is Louisbourg, located on the Atlantic coast of Cape Breton Island. This impressive fortress guarded one of the most active harbours in the New World during the eighteenth century.

A view of the Fortress of Louisbourg.

FOUR

French pioneers reached the site of today's Louisbourg in 1713. The international politics of the time were complicated. One of the major problems was the War of the Spanish Succession, the results of which are inseparable from the history of Louisbourg. Charles II of Spain was the last of the Spanish Habsburgs. When he died childless, the succession to the throne of Spain was hotly disputed.

It is one of the lessons of international diplomacy (but one that no one ever seems to learn effectively!) that treaties that are based on unpredictable future events are likely to fail horrendously when the expected events don't materialize. The French, Dutch, and English had all happily signed a document known as the First Treaty of Partition. This stipulated that when Charles II died, Prince Joseph Ferdinand, son of the Elector of Bavaria, should inherit Spain, the Spanish Netherlands, and Spain's colonies. Spain's Italian dependencies would then be shared between Austria and France. Very inconveniently for the treaty makers, however, Prince Joseph Ferdinand died in February 1699. A second treaty had to be made — and speed was of the essence.

On June 11, 1699, the French and English signed one, and the Dutch agreed to it in 1700. Under these new arrangements Archduke Charles, second son of Leopold I, who was at that time the Holy Roman Emperor, got Spain and the Spanish Netherlands. France got Naples, Sicily, and other Spanish Italian territories. Charles's father, Leopold, refused to agree, insisting that his son get *all* of the Spanish territories: in Leopold's eyes they were a totality. In addition to Leopold's opposition, the Spanish nobles didn't like the idea either, so Charles II made a will in which he left everything to the young Bourbon, Philip, Duc d'Anjou — grandson of Louis XIV, the formidable Sun King of France. The basic political thinking here was that only the powerful Bourbon dynasty would be capable of keeping the Spanish territories intact and viable. Charles II died on November 1, 1700, and on November 24, 1700, the Sun King proclaimed his grandson King Philip V — the first Bourbon king of Spain. To make his point inescapably clear, Louis promptly invaded the Spanish Netherlands.

This triggered the formation of an anti-French alliance on September 7, 1701, consisting of England, the Dutch Republic, and Emperor Leopold. Portugal, Prussia, Hanover, and several other

German states signed up behind Leopold. To complicate an already intricate situation, Bavaria, Cologne, Mantua, and Savoy joined the French Sun King. Savoy, however, changed partners in 1703.

William of Orange, as William III of England, had no love for Louis XIV. When William died in 1702, his widow, Queen Anne, vigorously continued her late husband's anti–Sun King policies. Marlborough was Anne's man on the battlefield, ably supported by Eugene of Savoy. These two won a series of important victories between 1704 and 1709.

One of the greatest of their victories was at Blenheim in 1704, for which Queen Anne and a grateful nation gave Marlborough a stately home, Blenheim Palace near Woodstock, close to Oxford in England.

Gateway of Blenheim Palace near Oxford, England, home of the Marlboroughs.

Further military reverses for the bravely resistant French forces followed at Ramillies (1706) and Oudenaarde (1708), which ended the Sun King's influence in the Low Countries. His attempt to lay siege to Turin was also defeated by the unparalleled military skill and flair of Eugene, and this effectively ended Louis's influence in Italy and set him to steering a course for peace.

In mainland Spain itself, however, Philip V was able to maintain his power against the combined strength of England, Holland, Portugal, Prussia, Savoy, Bavaria, and Cologne.

The Sun King offered to pass the Spanish succession over to the House of Habsburg, but the British put forward the unrealistic demand that he should also use his French army to remove his own grandson from the Spanish throne. Not surprisingly, Louis said no and resumed his war against the Anglo-Dutch alliance and their supporters.

Things changed dramatically and decisively, however, in April 1711, when Archduke Charles, the Habsburg candidate for the Spanish succession, inherited all of the Austrian Habsburg territories. Britain and Holland had no intention of helping Charles of Habsburg to add Spain to his other vast and powerful holdings.

Further problems arose when Marlborough's political enemies in England edged him out of power. The old anti-Bourbon alliance fell apart, and each of the former allies now tried to make separate deals with the triumphant French. As far as the history of Louisbourg in Canada was concerned, the all-important Treaty of Utrecht was signed in April 1713. This ended the War of the Spanish Succession.

Britain slowly began to gain worldwide ascendancy at the expense of France and Spain. The French came to Louisbourg in 1713 after the Treaty of Utrecht had cost them their settlements in Acadia and Newfoundland. By 1719 they had begun building a fortified town — which was barely finished a quarter of a century later, in time for the first great siege, which came in 1745.

The Fortress of Louisbourg.

The massive fortifications at Louisbourg were tested again in the summer of 1757. John Campbell, the Earl of Loudoun, had been appointed to the command of the army (known formally as the Royal American Forces) on July 23, 1756, and soon made plans to lead an expedition against Louisbourg in June of the following year. It was Loudoun's intention to meet a powerful British naval squadron that would participate in the expedition with him. By the time Loudoun reached Halifax, however, the fortunes of war had turned sharply against him: the French fleet was already in situ in the harbour, the British squadron under Admiral Francis Holborne had been scattered by a storm, and Louisbourg itself had been significantly reinforced. Understandably, Loudoun abandoned his plans and was replaced shortly afterwards by General James Abercrombie. He was ably supported by General Jeffrey Amherst, commanding the troops who were intended to capture Louisbourg.

In 1758 Amherst, with the redoubtable Brigadier General James Wolfe, took nearly ten thousand men to Louisbourg. These ground forces under Amherst and Wolfe were ably assisted by Admiral Boscawen's very effective naval detachment. Even the awesome Louisbourg fortifications failed to hold back such a massive onslaught, and the fortress surrendered on July 27.

In view of the colossal expenditure that had been directed to the Louisbourg fortifications, it seems a little strange that even such a powerful force as that commanded by Amherst and Wolfe could have succeeded. There are expert historians, researchers, and investigators who are convinced that some of the enormous wealth that was *intended* to finance the Louisbourg defences over this lengthy period of construction was secretly diverted and hidden in the Oak Island Money Pit, off Chester, on the Atlantic seaboard of Nova Scotia.

In 1795, three teenaged Nova Scotians (Smith, Vaughan, and McGinnis) found the entrance to a very deep shaft on uninhabited Oak Island in Mahone Bay. For more than two centuries, this amazing shaft with its flood-tunnel defences has defied generations of dedicated treasure hunters. Other theories of its contents include protected graves, a pirate hoard, a repository to hold the wealth carried over the Atlantic on board the lost fleet of the Templars, an army payroll, or even secret manuscripts proving that Francis Bacon wrote the works attributed to William Shakespeare.

Of all the various Oak Island theories available, the misappropriated funding for the Louisbourg fortifications is one of the most logical and reasonable. Suppose that a large payment had been sent from France and misdirected to Mahone Bay. Is it still there in the depths of the enigmatic Oak Island Money Pit?

Furthermore, it may be supposed that when the French crown jewels went missing in 1791, they, too, found their way into the labyrinth below Oak Island rather than to Louisbourg. It is not too wide a leap of imagination to suppose that the conspirators and their descendants who were involved with hiding the Louisbourg misap-propriations at the start of the eighteenth century were also concerned with hiding the French crown jewels as the century drew to its close. The link between the history of the Louisbourg fortifications and the Oak Island mystery is a strong one.

Author and historian Reginald V. Harris in *The Oak Island Mystery* (Ryerson Press, 1958) maintains that beginning in 1713, the French built at Louisbourg a huge stronghold, which became known as the "Dunkirk of America." Harris describes how millions of French *livres* were spent on the ice-free harbour at Louisbourg, and he calls the bastions and outworks "a marvel of engineering skill, of which evidence remains to this day despite the almost complete demolition of its ramparts … in 1760, following its capture by British forces led by the redoubtable Wolfe in 1759."

Harris rightly points out that the French Treasury sent between twenty and thirty ships loaded with money and treasure during the period from 1713 to 1745, when Louisbourg was being built. This French wealth was intended to pay the skilled artisans, labourers, and contractors who were working on the Louisbourg fortifications. The finest French architectural and military engineering experts were planning and super-vising the very expensive work being undertaken to fortify Louisbourg.

The brilliant, prize-winning Canadian author William Richard Bird was born at East Mapleton, Cumberland County, Nova Scotia, in 1891. He enlisted with the 42nd Royal Highlanders and served in the First World War, where he won the Military Medal at Mons. As a gallant and very experienced soldier as well as an outstanding author, Will Bird's analysis of what happened at Louisbourg in the early eighteenth century is among the best available. One of his many books, *Off-Trail in Nova Scotia* (Ryerson Press, 1956), covers the subject definitively. Bird describes how the great military architect and engineer Vauban was responsible for the ingenious planning principles that underlay the Louisbourg fortifications.

Bird also reveals that almost anything that could have gone wrong at Louisbourg during the twenty-odd years that it was under construction did go wrong. Heavy drinking and lack of discipline were two of the major problems. Funds for the building work rarely arrived on time and were usually inadequate. According to Bird's hard-hitting account of the Louisbourg problems, soldiers were on the verge of mutiny most of the time, and officers inherited their commissions without even a month's basic training. Some soldiers worked at other jobs during the day but continued to draw their army pay. Some, apparently, had not done a guard duty for over ten years. Despite all of these gargantuan problems, the fortifications were finally completed, and highly efficient and practical Swiss mercenaries were brought in. Several hundred of the least useful members of the original garrison were dismissed from the service.

In 1745, the New Englanders raised a militia, consisting of workmen, fishermen, and farmers under the command of William Pepperrell, and attacked Louisbourg. William, who combined the talents of merchant, politician, and soldier, made a great success of this assault, and as a result was given a baronetcy by King George II of England in 1746.

History also records that a great French fleet under the command of the Duc d'Anville set out for Louisbourg in 1746 to try to recapture the fortress after it had fallen to Pepperrell's siege of 1745. Heavy storms and high winds played havoc with d'Anville's armada. Many ships were lost. Some found shelter in Chebucto Bay, which is now Halifax. Others, by dint of skilful seamanship, made their way to comparative safety among the inlets and natural harbours along the rugged Nova Scotia coast. If one of d'Anville's fleet — one of his pay ships, perhaps — had made it into Mahone Bay and found Oak Island, that ship and its crew could have been the source of the mysterious Money Pit and its precious contents.

Louisbourg is a very significant fortified site — but what of the many other forts and castles appearing on Canadian atlases? The map of Canada shows a great many settlements and sites with the word *Fort* or *Castle* as part of the name, but several of these were simply well-defended trading posts rather than full-scale military establishments, and others were beautiful mansions and stately homes built as recently as the nineteenth century.

Dundurn Castle in Hamilton, Ontario, has a great deal of interesting history to offer. Archaeologists have discovered evidence that the site was occupied in prehistoric times. In more recent years, its cellars have yielded evidence of military occupation from the wars of the early nineteenth century, and the site of an old gun platform dating from 1812 has been investigated. Archaeological work in the vicinity of Dundurn Castle provided evidence of the house that Richard Beasley had built there in the late 1700s.

Richard was a very interesting character. Born in New York on July 21, 1761, he moved to Canada in the 1790s and went to Burlington Heights — an ideal spot for shipping and trading over the lakes. His partners included Robert Hamilton, Peter Smith, and Richard Cartwright, his cousin.

Beasley became a magistrate, an important member of the government, and Speaker of the House. His military career was equally impressive. He rose to the rank of lieutenant general. But as with so many other pioneering, historic heroes, Fortune turned her whimsical back on him — and Beasley died bankrupt. Dundurn Castle remains an impressive historic landmark.

Craigdarroch Castle, situated in Victoria, British Columbia, is a beautiful nineteenth-century mansion. It was built as the home of Robert Dunsmuir, reputedly the wealthiest man in British Columbia in his day. Warren H. Williams, a brilliant architect from Portland, Oregon, was responsible for designing Craigdarroch Castle but sadly died a few months after work had begun. His partner, Arthur L. Smith, completed the work in 1890. The tragedies associated with Craigdarroch Castle, however, did not end with Warren Williams's death. Dunsmuir himself died in 1889 — before his wonderful, elegant vision was completed. His sons took over the job and completed it for their widowed mother, Joan, but when she died in 1908 Craigdarroch and its contents were sold. It now belongs to the local museum and historical society.

There are features of great beauty in the castle, including some very fine stained glass and ceilings stencilled with birds, garlands of flowers, and lions' heads.

Fort la Reine is situated west of Winnipeg on the Assiniboine River. The "la Reine" part of the title was used by several very early French trading posts specializing in furs. The main Fort la Reine was established by the dauntless frontiersman Pierre Gaultier and his indomitable sons. Originally a strongly built timber fortification, Fort la Reine became the launching point for numerous expeditions westwards across the wide Canadian Prairies to look for what those intrepid early pioneers referred to as the "Great Western Sea." Fort la Reine also did worthwhile duty as a stopping point on the trade routes up to Lake Manitoba and the northern areas. During its long history, the original timber fortifications had to be rebuilt more than once. In Portage la Prairie in Manitoba, a contemporary school is named after the proud old fortress.

Fort Erie is close to Niagara in southeastern Ontario, beside Lake Erie and the Niagara River. The original fortification there was built by the British in 1764 and fell to American troops in 1812 after a very stubborn defence. The British tried hard to recapture Fort Erie — but failed. After it was abandoned in 1814, it was blown up. Following an interval of more than twenty years, however, it was rebuilt in 1837. It grew to the status of a town in 1932 when it merged with neighbouring Bridgeburg. With a population of over thirty thousand, Fort Erie is now highly active commercially with pharmaceutical industries, a large racetrack, and steel and automotive works.

Fort Rupert was also known at one time as Rupert House and as Waskaganish. It is now both a village and trading post situated in the Nord-du-Québec region in western Quebec where the River Rupert runs into James Bay. Fort Rupert was founded in 1668 but was then known as Fort Charles. History records it as the first European settlement in Northern Canada. The French captured it in 1686 and held it until the Treaty of Utrecht was signed in 1713, and during these twenty-seven years it was known as Fort Saint Jacques. It was re-established as a trading post in 1777 and has been operating proudly as such ever since, with a population of less than two thousand.

When Sir George Simpson was general superintendent of the Hudson's Bay Company in 1830, he renamed the former Fort St. Pierre after his wife, Frances — an unusual and memorable gift. The town, with its modern population of over ten thousand, stands on the north bank of Rainy River, adjacent to Rainy River Lake. Like many other early Canadian fur-trading posts, Fort St. Pierre was primarily intended for commerce rather than a military establishment, but the early eighteenth century demanded that the rugged and fearless pioneers were able to defend themselves effectively. Fort Frances stands on the Canada–U.S. border, in sight of International Falls, Minnesota. The area grew and prospered because it was on a main trading route, and a canal was built there in the 1870s to bypass the waterfall. Currently a well-known centre for hunting, fishing, and canoeing, Fort Frances is also a thriving industrial town with ample hydroelectric power and busy mills for timber, pulp, and paper.

Jacques Cartier, the pioneering French explorer, reached Gaspé in 1534 and formally took possession on behalf of the French King Francis I of the Valois Dynasty. When Cartier arrived, the indigenous Canadian and Inuit peoples already had a history going back thousands of years. The sixteenth century in Europe was a time of mercantile expansion and far-reaching commercial adventures. It was this spirit that Cartier took with him across the Atlantic. Within just over a century of Cartier's arrival, three great historic cities had been founded: Quebec (1608), Trois-Rivières (1616), and Montreal (1642).

The formidable fortifications of Quebec and the effectiveness of the defenders were of prime importance in 1759, when the young and ambitious General James Wolfe attacked the city. The perilous cliffs overhanging the St. Lawrence River were believed to be impossible to climb — especially by soldiers encumbered with weapons and equipment — and were therefore practically undefended. General Montcalm's resolute defenders blocked one fierce frontal attack after another, so Wolfe took five thousand men down the St. Lawrence River under cover of darkness.

The Heights of Abraham at Quebec City.

Only a perilous and precipitous goat track wound its way up the cliffs, but hauling themselves from tree to tree, and from one piece of undergrowth to the next, Wolfe's men made their way as silently as ghosts up the supposedly unassailable heights. The small group of guards at the summit was totally surprised and retreated for their lives. This enabled Wolfe to assemble over four thousand men in battle-ready formation above the Heights of Abraham. Montcalm now had a hopeless dilemma: if he left his impregnable defensive position to take on Wolfe's men, he was at a grim disadvantage; if he didn't take them on, Quebec itself would fall. With heavy-hearted realism, the courageous Montcalm made the only possible choice. Having performed their "impossible" overnight climb, Wolfe's men now had every advantage. Montcalm was fatally wounded, and his gallant French regulars took very heavy casualties. Wolfe lived long enough to know that he had secured the victory, and then joined Montcalm as a victim of the battle: he was only thirty-three years old.

General James Wolfe.

Fort Chambly on the Richelieu River was another very significant military structure that played a major role in Canadian history. The first fortress on this site was built as early as 1665. It was erected in response to the urgent requests of French colonists in the area who were vulnerable to attacks from the indigenous Canadian peoples. In accordance with the religious practices of the period, this first fortification was named after St. Louis. It was a simple wooden stockade resembling the earliest defences that the Norman knights had built when William the Conqueror took England in 1066. Nevertheless, it served its purpose well. Altogether, five of these early "castles" were built at this time, designed as squares of approximately fifty metres by fifty metres. The actual palisades, or wooden walls, were between five and six metres high. By 1690, the original structure had deteriorated to such an extent that replacement was essential. Consequently, a new fortress was built on the same site but lasted only for some twelve years before being burnt to the ground one night in 1702. It was prudently decided that a wooden fortress would not be an adequate defence against hostile English cannon, so the decision was made to rebuild in stone. The work started in 1709 under the guidance of the great French engineer Josué Dubois Berthelot de Beaucours and was completed in 1711. On September 1, 1760, however, Fort Chambly fell into English hands and became a British stronghold.

The Anglo-American War of 1812 posed new dangers for Chambly, but it was not attacked. With a commendable sense of history and the need for preserving such important sites for posterity, impressive restoration work has been undertaken at Fort Chambly, which deservedly attracts many appreciative visitors today.

Fort Chambly.

In 1775 what was then the American Continental Congress decided to try to prevent a British attack from the Canadian side by sending an expedition to Canada. In August, General Philip Schuyler took part of his army to Lake Champlain and captured St. John's. Schuyler, who was born in 1733, was plagued for most of his life by a debilitating combination of pleurisy and gout, which adversely affected both his military and political careers. After his success at St. John's, Schuyler's recurrent illness forced him to hand over his command to General Richard Montgomery.

In September 1775, General Washington sent Benedict Arnold to lead a force against Quebec via Maine. Incredible hardships on the way had so weakened Arnold's troops that he was forced to wait for

Montgomery before leading any kind of assault. The attack they launched on December 31, 1775, was a disaster: Montgomery died, Arnold was wounded, and another leader was captured. Fresh British troops led by Sir Guy Carleton pushed the American forces back to Crown Point on Lake Champlain.

Although far younger than their European counterparts, the Canadian "castles" and fortresses are equally important as the sentinels of history itself. Brave men and women defended them against overwhelming odds. Men and women of courage and vision lived and died in these gaunt old fortifications to ensure a worthwhile future for their descendants. The "castles" serve today as memorials of the endurance, the fortitude, and the unbreakable spirit of those dauntless Canadian pioneers.

Chapter 5
The Alamo and Other Strongholds in the U.S.A.

AMERICAN FORTS AND defensive positions were part of the traditions of the indigenous peoples who occupied what was later to become New York State. Dutch settlers arrived there in the early seventeenth century to find that the Native Americans had systems of fortified villages on hilltops. These were built on the lines of the old Norse and Saxon longhouses and were surrounded by high, sturdy, wooden palings. The Dutch settlers referred to these indigenous American structures as castles.

These wood-encircled early forts were useful enough in skirmishes between local groups, but they proved ineffective against the incursions of the European armies. The French, for example, destroyed all of the Mohawk fortified villages in 1666.

At the start of the eighteenth century, the British built some of their early forts near the Mohawk villages. These were situated in Schoharie Valley and up on Prospect Hill.

Some forts, however, were never built for defensive or military purposes.

The world-famous Battle of the Alamo in San Antonio, Texas, took place in what had been built in 1724 as the Misión San Antonio de Valero. It had been intended to house local missionaries and those they had brought into the Church. However, there were important administrative changes in 1793, and the lands that had belonged to the five missions in San Antonio were given to the local people, who cultivated them assiduously from then on.

The Alamo, San Antonio, Texas.

A dozen or so years later, a Spanish cavalry unit took over what had once been the mission buildings. These Spanish soldiers — like most lonely soldiers posted away from home — named their new headquarters after their old hometown: Alamo de Parras in Coahuila, Mexico. The word *Alamo* itself simply meant *cottonwood*.

In December 1835, Ben Milam led a mixed group of Tejano and Texan volunteers to fight the Mexican troops who were then stationed in San Antonio. The Mexican general, Márin Perfecto de Cós, had wisely already fortified the old Alamo Mission Station before Milam's men attacked, but in spite of all their precautions, Cós's men were defeated by the Tejano-Texan alliance. The victors then took over the Alamo and used it as their central defensive point and military headquarters.

On the fateful twenty-third day in February of 1836, General Antonio López de Santa Anna arrived at San Antonio with his army of more than four thousand men. Names might play a larger part in battle determination and battle morale than is generally acknowledged. In the Second World War, the Russians defended Stalingrad with grim determination, endurance, and fortitude — until Hitler's crack regiments finally broke against those indomitable defences. Was there some strange significance in the name of the beleaguered city and the name of the Russian dictator? Was Stalin determined that, whatever the cost to his people, his city should *never* fall into enemy hands? Was *Antonio López de Santa Anna* equally determined that he would capture the fortress in San *Antonio* at whatever cost to his men?

There were fewer than two hundred Texan and Tejano heroes holding the Alamo against Santa Anna's thousands — but they held it for thirteen momentous days that left a proud, indelible record in the military history of the world.

The joint commanders of the Alamo were William Barret Travis and James Bowie, but when Bowie was crippled with pneumonia, Travis took over as sole commander. He was born in South Carolina on August 1, 1809, and had qualified as a lawyer in Alabama before going to Texas. It was his legal training and mastery of language that enabled him to write the famous appeal for reinforcements for the Alamo that began, "To the people of Texas and all Americans in the world...."

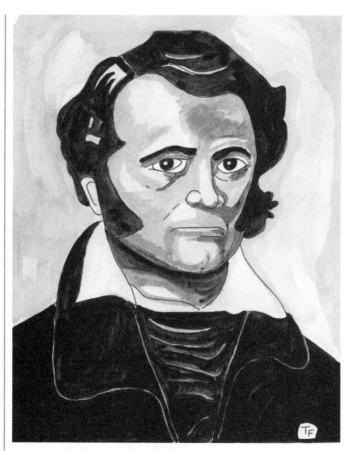

Heroic James Bowie, 1796–1836.

Born in 1796 in Kentucky, Bowie and his family moved to Missouri and later to Louisiana. Always adventurous, and a total stranger to fear, Bowie was involved in a savage fight near Natchez, Mississippi, where a number of the participants died — and even the mighty Bowie was wounded. After he had recovered in 1828, he moved to Texas.

Bowie's conspicuous courage and daring made him a great friend of many Native Americans who helped him in his long search for mysterious lost gold and silver mines that were believed to be concealed somewhere in central Texas. Some researchers think that Bowie actually found the amazing San Saba Mine — a place with the same legendary background as King Solomon's fabled mines in Africa.

Bowie's other great achievements took place during the Battle of Concepción and the famous Grass Fight not far from San Antonio. It was in San Antonio that Bowie was in command until William Travis arrived with his company of regulars.

Another of the great Alamo heroes was Davy Crockett, who was born in a log cabin on the banks of the Nolichucky River, Limestone Creek, Tennessee, on August 17, 1786. He commanded a battalion in the Creek War of 1813–14, held office in the Tennessee Legislature, and was later a congressman. He was a shrewd and thoughtful man as well as a courageous one. His motto in life was "Always be sure you are right, then go ahead." It was that wisdom, bravery, and determination that took him to the Alamo.

Heroic Davy Crockett, 1786–1836.

Because the authors are based in Cardiff, they share the natural Welsh pride in another of the Alamo defenders, Lewis Johnson from Wales, who died alongside Crockett, Bowie, Travis, and the other widely known heroes. In the Alamo chapel, along with the flags of the other states and nations represented by their fearless sons, one proud Welsh flag commemorates the gallant Lewis Johnson.

Santa Anna attacked the Alamo for thirteen days with his vastly superior numbers. During the siege, Travis sent his requests for help to all parts of Texas, and in response thirty-two dauntless volunteers arrived from Gonzales on the eighth day.

ERECTED IN GRATEFUL RECOGNITION OF THE SUPREME ACT OF HEROISM OF THE THIRTY TWO MEN FROM GONZALES WHO GAVE THEIR LIVES IN THE ALAMO IN RESPONSE TO THE APPEAL OF TRAVIS.

Memorial to the heroes from Gonzales who died at the Alamo.

Santa Anna launched his final assault on the heroes of the Alamo in the early hours of the morning of March 6, 1836. The defenders had used up nearly all their supplies and ammunition, but there was a great determination among them to make Santa Anna's inevitable victory more expensive than a defeat. Santa Anna ordered his buglers to sound the *Deguello*, which meant that no prisoners would be taken. The Mexican army of over four thousand men then attacked the Alamo from four sides — north, south, east, and west — simultaneously. Despite the incredible odds and their shortage of ammunition, the Texans and their sturdy allies hurled Santa Anna's men back with devastating Mexican losses. The attackers rushed in again — and were driven back again. The third attack concentrated on the crumbling wreckage of what had been the Alamo's north wall — and this time they smashed through.

Travis, with a bullet through his head, fell dead across the cannon he had been loading. Crocket, his ammunition gone, wielded his heavy musket as a war-club with devastating effect until he too was killed. Despite the pneumonia that had floored him, the mighty Jim Bowie was found under a pile of dead Mexican soldiers, both guns empty and his famous Bowie knife dripping with enemy blood.

The bodies of the heroes of the Alamo were unceremoniously burnt — and that gave rise to one of the strangest unsolved mysteries in San Antonio.

It is to Santa Anna's credit that despite sounding the *Deguello* he spared the lives of several women, children, and non-combatants who were in the Alamo when it finally fell. It is not to his credit that he ordered the massacre of three hundred prisoners at Goliad, who had been captured at the Battle of Coleto Creek. This, and Texan fury over the Alamo, fuelled Santa Anna's defeat.

Less than seven weeks after the fall of the Alamo, Texan General Sam Houston led a force of eight hundred furious volunteers against the Mexicans at San Jacinto. Although outnumbered by two to one, Houston's avengers were unstoppable. Their battle cry was "Remember the Alamo! Remember Goliad!" They lost only nine men and killed close to seven hundred of Santa Anna's forces. The rest surrendered.

While the authors were undertaking research in San Antonio, they came across the remarkable case of the haunted bookshop — which is closely connected with the history of the Alamo.

Brentano's bookshop in San Antonio stands over the site where the bodies of the heroic defenders were cremated by Santa Anna's men. Several witnesses whom we interviewed gave evidence that in one particular area of the shop, staff arriving in the morning found books pulled from the shelves and heaped on the floor. This has happened on numerous occasions, and one of the local theories is that the proud and defiant spirits of the freedom fighters from the Alamo were refusing to accept the primitive and disrespectful way that their mortal remains had been disposed of.

Co-author Patricia at Brentano's allegedly haunted bookshop in San Antonio.

The very dignified and respectful Alamo Memorial site, the shrine of Texas liberty, is superbly maintained by the Daughters of the Republic of Texas.

Co-author Patricia at the Alamo Memorial, San Antonio.

Fort Bowie was named after the heroic Jim Bowie of Alamo fame. It was set up by volunteers of the California Column on their way to protect the spring at Puerto de Dado in New Mexico in 1862. Fort Bowie is famous as the location where field artillery was used against the Apache nation for the first time at the Battle of Apache Pass. From 1867 until 1886 constant running battles took place against Geronimo, Victorio, Nana, Juh, Loco, and Natchez. General George Crook was appointed commander at Fort Bowie in 1871, and he stepped up the war significantly. Many of the Apache leaders made peace in 1886 and went to Fort Marion in Florida. Crook was replaced by General Nelson Miles in the same year.

Another of Fort Bowie's claims to a place in history was the heliograph signalling system that Miles set up. This was an arrangement of mirrors that could flash messages either by sunlight or moonlight. The system goes right back to the days of classical Greece, well over two thousand years ago, when the hero and writer Xenophon included the idea of signals transmitted by flashing sunlight from shields in his book *Hellenica*. The indigenous Chacoan people of what is now New Mexico seem to have used signalling mirrors made from mica some twelve hundred years ago. During the period of the British Empire in India, heliograph systems were used among British soldiers, and they were still operational in 1907. They were also used by both armies during the Boer War in Africa (1899–1902).

Heliograph signals were sent by reflecting sunlight or moonlight towards the people for whom the messages were intended, and as well as military uses, they proved very helpful for surveyors and cartographers. The beam could be switched on or off by tilting the mirror, or by placing a shutter in front of it. This made it possible to signal the dots and dashes of Morse code. The type of heliograph favoured by the U.S. Army was composed of either a mirror with a sighting rod or two mirrors fixed on a tripod. The opaque light-blocking device was then fixed to another tripod so that the signal rays could be interrupted as required. When the sun or moon was behind the transmitter, another mirror was used to redirect the rays onto the transmitter mirror, and from there, via the opaque shutter, to the receiver.

The distance over which heliograph signals could be sent was limited by the necessity of having a clear line of sight, and this was dependent again upon the curvature of the Earth itself. Mirror size was another limiting factor. Heliograph flashes could be read at fifty kilometres with the naked eye alone — and at much greater distances if the receivers had field glasses or telescopes. The size of the mirror was also critical: a rule of thumb suggested that every centimetre of the mirror's diameter would provide an additional range of seven kilometres, or each inch of diameter would give the operator an extra ten miles range. The rapid communication of vital information was of great importance to the commanders of fortifications. Was help on the way? Where were the enemy and which way were they heading? A network of heliographs linked the fortresses involved in the campaign against Geronimo and was of great assistance to the soldiers in Fort Bowie.

After Geronimo finally surrendered on September 4, 1886, Fort Bowie became more or less redundant, and after October 17, 1894, it was no longer used.

Fort Bowie, used in the wars against Geronimo.

America's largest coastal fort, Fort Jefferson, is situated on Garden Key, Florida, and contrasts strongly with Fort Bowie. Garden Key is associated with the pioneering explorer Juan Ponce de Leon, who was born in 1460 at Tierra de Campos Palencia in Spain. Beginning his career as a messenger boy in the service of the royal family, Juan graduated to the army, where he fought valiantly until 1493, when he sailed with Columbus on his second voyage. De Leon decided to settle on the island of Santo Domingo, with the as yet unknown mainland of Florida to the north of his new home.

In the fifteenth and sixteenth centuries, legends concerning the Fountain of Youth were especially rife, but the legends went back long before de Leon's day. Alexander the Great searched for it in Asia. Polynesian wise men believed that it was situated somewhere on Hawaii. An early Arawak explorer named Sequene left Cuba to search for the elusive fountain in Florida and did not return; the supporters of the Fountain of Youth legends assumed that Sequene had found it and decided to settle beside it to remain young forever. Other versions of the legend placed the mysterious stream, river, fountain, or waterfall of immortality in Bimini.

Pietro Martire d'Anghiera, better known as Peter the Martyr, was a distinguished historian and geographer who went so far as to write to Pope Leo X in 1513 on the subject. Pietro told Leo X that the mysterious water of longevity was believed to come from one of the islands north of Hispaniola, and that when combined with certain dietary requirements "it maketh old men young again." The level-headed, academic Pietro, however, added that he, himself, did not believe that the fountain existed.

Juan Ponce de Leon was said to have been searching for this marvellous water when he discovered Florida. During his travels he also found islands populated by vast numbers of turtles, which were accordingly named *Las Tortugas* — Spanish for turtles. It was on one of these, Garden Key, that Fort Jefferson was later destined to be built — although the first structure on Garden Key was a lighthouse built in 1825 to warn mariners of the dangerous shoals and reefs.

Juan Ponce de Leon, 1460–1521.

The work on Fort Jefferson itself began in 1846 and went on for thirty years. It is estimated that 16 million bricks were used — and even then the structure was never finally completed. Yellow Fever epidemics wreaked havoc on the construction workers, and there were technical building problems as well. Fort Jefferson's main purpose was to protect the American trade routes from the Mississippi out towards the Atlantic and to ensure American strategic control over the Gulf of Mexico.

The whole history of castles and fortresses all over the world has been one of progressive military technology, with each new discovery making former safe refuges vulnerable. This was eventually the case with Fort Jefferson — even those massive walls could not resist the power of the new rifled cannon. As a stronghold, Fort Jefferson was no longer viable.

At one grim period of its history, before its abandonment in 1874, Fort Jefferson became a military prison and housed army deserters from the American Civil War. It was also a place of incarceration for Dr. Samuel Mudd and some of the other conspirators accused of being behind President Lincoln's assassination. Fort Jefferson's historical association with Lincoln's death is an interesting one.

The assassin, John Wilkes Booth, was a talented actor, with several leading Shakespearian roles to his credit. He was politically inclined to support the South and blamed Lincoln for all that he felt had gone wrong for the South. Booth was obsessed by a burning desire for vengeance against Lincoln, and he wasn't alone. The conspirators included Dr. Samuel Mudd, Samuel Arnold, John and Mary Surratt (whose lodging house became the conspirators' headquarters), Michael O'Laughlen, Lewis Payne (also called Paine and Powell), David Herold, and the rather ineffectual George Atzerodt.

Their original plan was not to assassinate but rather to kidnap President Lincoln and hold him as a hostage while they negotiated the return of Confederate prisoners. The kidnapping never happened because President Lincoln changed his plans.

General Ulysses S. Grant accepted General Robert E. Lee's formal surrender at Appomattox on April 9, 1865. On April 11, Lincoln made a speech that included a reference to enfranchising black citizens. This drove the racist Booth into a frenzied anger, and he determined to kill the President the first chance he got. Opportunity knocked for Booth when he heard that Lincoln was planning to attend a performance of *Our American Cousin* at Ford's Theatre on the night of April 14. Booth laid his plans well. He paid Joe Burroughs, a lad who worked at the theatre, to hold his horse ready and waiting in the back alley. Then Booth went in through the front door just after 10:00 p.m. He made his way casually towards the box where Lincoln, his wife, and their friends Clara Harris and Henry Rathbone were watching the play. It was one of the great misfortunes of history that Lincoln's bodyguard, John Parker, wasn't there. Booth entered the president's box and shot Lincoln in the back of the head at point-blank range. Rathbone bravely went for Booth, but Booth stabbed him in the arm and then leapt down to the stage, where he broke a small leg bone as he landed. Despite the broken bone, Booth escaped into the night on the waiting horse.

The conspirators had also planned to kill Vice-President Andrew Johnson and Secretary of State William Seward, hoping the three deaths would be enough to throw the government into such confusion that the South might be able to take advantage of it. Atzerodt failed entirely in his bid to kill the Vice-President — he didn't even attempt it. Powell got a knife into Seward but wasn't able to kill him.

Booth and Herold made it as far as Dr. Mudd's house, where Booth's broken leg was professionally attended to. When the authorities caught up with them near Port Royal in Virginia, Herold surrendered, but Booth was shot dead by Sergeant Boston Corbett. The surviving conspirators were rounded up and given a military trial. Mary Surratt, Herold, Powell, and Atzerodt were hanged on July 7, 1865. Dr. Mudd, O'Laughlen, and Arnold were sentenced to life imprisonment. John Surratt escaped to Canada and then went on to Europe, where he was captured and tried in 1867. The jury could not agree, and Surratt was released.

Dr. Mudd was imprisoned in Fort Jefferson, as was O'Laughlen, who ultimately died there. Rather surprisingly, Mudd, Spangler (a stagehand from the Ford Theatre who was accused of helping Booth to escape), and Samuel Arnold were all pardoned in 1869 by President Andrew Johnson.

The greatest architectural and archaeological mystery on Newport, Rhode Island, U.S.A., is the strange old building known as Newport

Tower. There are reasonable and well-argued theories suggesting that it is of Norse origin. Other equally valid ideas suggest that it is the work of the great Henry Sinclair, one-time ruler of the Orkneys, who almost certainly brought a band of Knights Templar across the Atlantic. More daring theorists place it earlier still, suggesting that it was the work of Phoenicians, or intrepid Greek merchant adventurers who had gone out beyond the Pillars of Hercules (today's Gibraltar). Since the earliest days of navigation, Newport has had the advantage of a large, deep, natural harbour, which may well have welcomed very early mariners from the Old World. Which of those early visitors actually built the mysterious Newport Tower? That is still very much an open question.

Ancient and mysterious Newport Tower, Rhode Island, U.S.A.

The modern city of Newport was founded in 1639 by some of the settlers who had founded Portsmouth, then called Pocasset. During that turbulent and hazardous seventeenth century, Newport needed fortifications and defences, and the earliest one recorded consisted of a battery of cannons placed where Pelham Street and Thames Street are joined. It was a good tactical position for the cannons because they commanded the harbour, and any strange, unwelcome vessel would have had to answer to the Newport gunners.

During what historians refer to as Queen Anne's War at the start of the eighteenth century, a fort was built on Goat Island to defend Newport Harbour and the sea lanes that led to it. From time to time the Goat Island Fort was improved and renamed. It was originally called Fort Anne, but after 1724 its name was changed to Fort George. In 1775 it was called Fort Liberty and then Fort Washington. During 1798 its name was changed to Fort Wolcott and remained so during the lengthy period that it served as a military partner to the much larger Fort Adams. Fort Wolcott was defended and garrisoned by the Rhode Island Militia until 1794. The U.S. Army then took it over, and it passed into the aegis of the federal government. It remained an active military establishment until the mid-1830s. Just before 1870 it was transferred to the navy, a further sign of the advance of weapon technology — Fort Wolcott became one of the earliest naval torpedo stations. It continued in that capacity until as recently as 1950.

A contemporary account reports that Fort Wolcott was built of stone cemented with lime, its powder magazine constructed of brick and stone. A sally port (designed so that defenders could charge out and attack an encircling enemy if necessary) was augmented by a ditch — rather like the moat defences of older castles. The soldiers' quarters were brick-built, two storeys tall, and allegedly bombproof. There was room for ten cannons, but only five 32-pounders were actually in place in Fort Wolcott when the report was written.

In 1822, however, there was much better provision: the Army's Ordnance Department listed thirty-seven 32-pounders, twenty-five 24-pounders, thirteen 18-pounders, six 10-inch siege mortars, two 8-inch howitzers, and three 24-pounder howitzers at Newport. It seems highly likely that Colonel Crane had arranged for these.

Colonel Ichabod B. Crane, commander of Fort Wolcott, Newport, Rhode Island.

From approximately 1820 until 1825, the commander of Fort Wolcott was Colonel Ichabod B. Crane. Born in 1789, Crane took a commission in the marines when he was twenty but left in 1812 to pursue a career as an artillery officer. His more famous son, Charles, rose to become surgeon general in 1882.

The gallant and skilful artillery colonel and commander of Fort Wolcott was immortalized by writer Washington Irving in 1820, when Irving used the name Ichabod Crane for the hero of *The Legend of Sleepy Hollow*. The real Colonel Crane obtained his commission from New York State, where Washington Irving also lived. Not unreasonably, literary historians have suggested that Washington Irving named his mythical hero after a real and distinguished one: Colonel Crane went on to become commander of the First Artillery Regiment in 1843 and continued there until he died in 1857.

In 1827, 3rd Artillery Major Mann Page Lomax took command of Fort Wolcott. History records that he was both the last commander there and the longest serving commander. He was transferred from Fort Wolcott in 1836 to join the war against the Seminole Nation in Florida. When Mann and his artillery company left, Fort Wolcott was not garrisoned again.

Rather like the situation in the Crane family, Mann Lomax's son, Lunsford, became better known than his father. The Lomaxes were a Virginian family, and their son, Lunsford, was born in 1835. He served in the army until 1861 and then left to join the Confederacy. When the Civil War ended, Lunsford was a major general in the Confederate Army, commanding a cavalry division in Virginia. After peace was restored he rose to become president of a Virginian college before his death in 1913.

Fort Wolcott was overshadowed by the far larger and more impressive Fort Adams. The place where Fort Adams now stands was originally known as Brenton's Point. The earliest defence work there was only a simple earth rampart intended to protect a few guns, the largest of which was an 18-pounder. The Rhode Islanders had put these earth ramparts in place in April 1776 to protect themselves from British warships. Small as it was, however, their eighteenth-century gun emplacement was effective. The twenty-four-gun frigate HMS *Glasgow* retreated after the Rhode Islanders sent over thirty shots in her direction. Only three days later, the shore battery opened fire again, this time on HMS *Scarborough* and HMS *Cimetar*, and the British warships again withdrew. Following the War of Independence, the guns from Brenton's Point seem to have been transferred to Fort Wolcott on Goat Island.

It was later decided by the military authorities that the whole of Narragansett Bay required several forts to defend it: one on Goat Island, another known as Fort Greene in the Point section of Newport itself, Fort Dumpling in Jamestown, and another at Brenton's Point to protect the harbour. The circular tower that comprised Fort Dumpling was less than twenty metres in diameter and barely seven metres high. Fort Hamilton on Rose Island was begun in 1798 but never finished. In contrast to Fort Dumpling, Fort Hamilton had the traditional square shape of medieval castles, and the Rose Island lighthouse actually stands on one of its bastions.

The impressive Fort Adams (named after the then president John Adams) was opened with great ceremony on July 4, 1799. An appropriate salute was duly fired, and the fort's proud motto was unveiled: "Fort Adams, the rock on which the storm will beat." She carried close to twenty impressive guns and was well able to live up to her motto.

Fort Adams's first commanding officer was the adventurous and mysterious Captain John Henry, who served with a combined engineering and artillery regiment. John Henry was an early nineteenth-century equivalent of James Bond, who went from Fort Adams to Fort Sumner in Maine. His work as an espionage man and secret agent included obtaining the infamous "Henry Papers," which revealed that the British were attempting to undermine Massachusetts' state government. This information played a significant part in stirring up public opinion to such an extent that the War of 1812 followed. John Henry was next involved in undercover work in Europe — including digging up scandalous information about Caroline, the unhappy wife of the British Prince Regent, the future King George IV. There was no shortage of data to investigate.

George, the Prince Regent, rebelled flagrantly against his father, George III, in many ways. He was deeply involved with Perdita Robinson and had a four-year affair with her. Perdita's real name was Mary, and she was a talented actress, poet, and writer. Her literary work was so good that Coleridge was one of her admirers. Her early marriage to Thomas Robinson had turned out to be a total disaster for her.

However, when she appeared as Perdita in Shakespeare's *The Winter's Tale*, at a royal command performance, George saw her on stage and fell in love with her — even though she was four years older than he was. From the paintings of her by Gainsborough and Reynolds, it is clear that Mary was a beautiful woman, and young George's infatuation is understandable.

After he tired of Perdita, the Prince turned his attention to Maria Fitzherbert, a devout Catholic who refused to become his mistress and insisted on marriage. This had to be kept secret because of the terms of the 1772 Royal Marriages Act that prevented members of the royal family from marrying Roman Catholics.

Young Prince George didn't seem to improve with age and experience. His drinking became heavier, his gambling became wilder, and his pursuit of female company became notorious — even by the standards of the late eighteenth century. Before the end of the century, Prince George had debts of well over half a million, and, in order to persuade Parliament to help him out, he reluctantly agreed to marry his cousin, Princess Caroline of Brunswick. Theirs was a relationship disaster that equalled the mistake Mary "Perdita" Robinson had made when she married Thomas.

Caroline, born on May 17, 1768, was the daughter of the Duke of Brunswick-Wolfenbuttle and Princess Augusta, who was George III's sister. Caroline married Prince George on April 8, 1795, just before her twenty-seventh birthday. He described his bride as plain and unhygienic and was convinced that she was not a virgin. Caroline had an equally low opinion of George, and, predictably, the marriage did not last long.

Although the Prince Regent found his bride unattractive, there were plenty of men who didn't. If the rumours are to be believed, Caroline had affairs with George Canning, one-time foreign secretary and later prime minister, and with Admiral Sir Sidney Smith. These rumours excited Prince George sufficiently for him to have her activities investigated — whereupon she left for Europe, took up with several other lovers, and ran up debts on a scale that equalled George's! It was during her manifold misadventures and scandalous liaisons in Europe that John Henry investigated her. Perhaps he got too close to some powerful European soldier or politician — a ruthless man who was either protecting Caroline's reputation or his own. In any case, little or nothing is known of what happened to secret agent John Henry, first commander of Fort Adams, or precisely how his mysterious life ended.

When Caroline's husband became king in 1820, she came back to Britain to assume the role of queen. An attempt to take the title from her was defeated, largely because public opinion was sympathetic towards her: the general feeling was that George had treated her abominably. After her death on August 7, 1821, at the age of only fifty-three, her body was buried in Brunswick.

In 1814, after John Henry left, Fort Adams was manned by sturdy Rhode Island militia, under the command of Major John Wood. They were known as Wood's State Corps and remained at their posts in Fort Adams until the war ended in 1815.

When President Monroe made an official visit to Fort Adams and Fort Wolcott in the summer of 1817, he reported that he was "well pleased with the order and neatness" that he found there.

The tension and stress of living in close quarters with other garrison members can sometimes have tragic consequences. Fort Adams was the scene of a tragic murder that occurred when a soldier named Cornell shot another soldier named Kane. The musket ball entered the victim's leg and severed an artery: Kane bled fatally. After a trial and appeal, Cornell was ultimately pardoned by President Monroe. The reasons for both the shooting and the pardon are shrouded in the mists of history.

The construction of the later Fort Adams — the one that still stands to this day — began in 1824. A brilliant French designer named Simon Bernard was the genius behind the new Fort Adams designs. Bernard had once served as a military engineer under Napoleon. He had learnt his skills at the École Polytechnique in France and had mastered the design techniques of pioneering military engineers like Vauban and Montalembert. Another very capable member of the top team was Alexander MacGregor, a master mason from Scotland. The man in charge of much of the work, however, was Colonel Joseph G. Totten, recognized as one of the greatest military engineers and architects of the nineteenth century. So extensive was Totten's work that his Fort Adams could accommodate nearly five hundred cannons and a garrison of nearly twenty-five hundred men.

A very interesting aspect of the Fort Adams construction was the wisdom shown by the builders in advertising in Ireland for strong and able construction workers. Three hundred brawny Irish builders came over to Newport to help with the work and were responsible for establishing the significant Irish-American sector of modern Newport, along with its thriving Roman Catholic parish, originally established as St. Joseph's in 1828 but later renamed St. Mary's. Major military constructions like Fort Adams have profound and enduring effects on local communities and local economies.

Fort Adams played a leading role during the Mexican War of 1845 to 1848. It was the base from which soldiers were sent to take up frontline positions. Lieutenant Colonel Pierce, who was then in command, received urgent orders to prepare all the Fort Adams cannons late in May 1845 — but the tide of war did not actually flow that close.

When the American Civil War of 1861 to 1865 threatened, Fort Adams was prepared for action. The Confederates attacked Fort Sumter in April of 1861, and William Sprague, the governor of Rhode Island, decided that

Fort Adams.

it would be wise to defend Fort Adams in case local Confederate sympathizers, or infiltrators, attacked it. The only men he had immediately available were the famous "Old Guard." These were valiant old veterans who had been disabled in battle or were considered too old to continue with the rigours of front-line action. Proving that ageism is rubbish, some eighty members of this formidable Old Guard held Fort Adams safe until they were relieved by a force of U.S. Navy trainee officers from the warship USS *Constitution* (which also gloried in the name "Old Ironsides").

Until the war ended in 1865, Fort Adams was the headquarters for the 15th Infantry Regiment, commanded by Lieutenant Colonel John Sanderson, followed by Oliver Shepherd.

One other gallant and unselfish episode deserves to be recorded in the long and honourable history of Fort Adams. Two of its garrison, Sergeant Adams and Private McLaughlin, were in serious danger of drowning, when they were rescued by a Rhode Island version of Grace Darling. Ida Lewis was only sixteen when her father, Hosea Lewis, keeper of the Lime Rock lighthouse in Newport harbour, suffered a severe stroke. Ida carried on his duties at the lighthouse, as well as cared for him, and when he died, she was appointed keeper. In addition to saving the two soldiers, Ida saved a score of other lives during her half-century as lighthouse keeper, including two musicians from Fort Adams who were trying to walk across the ice in the frozen harbour and fell through it.

From an active, traditional military site like Fort Adams, Rhode Island, it's a long way through both time and space to Montezuma's Castle in Arizona.

About 160 kilometres north of Phoenix, these ancient cave dwellings are 30 metres above Beaver Creek, which winds its way down to the Verde River.

Montezuma's Castle, Beaver Creek, Arizona.

The ancient ruins are better described as living quarters, although their height also made them eminently defensible. The overhanging rock protects them, just as the more sophisticated of the First World War trenches across Europe had overhangs that defended their infantry-men from enemy mortar bombs and artillery shells.

The ruins are so impressive and raise so many questions about how they were constructed that it was originally believed that

Montezuma and his people must have been responsible, but modern scientific dating methods have revealed that the Beaver Creek cliff dwellings predate the famous Aztec emperor by nearly two centuries. So who did build them?

Most archaeological opinion favours the indigenous Sinagua. They were an advanced culture who knew how to grow a variety of useful crops, including corn and cotton. They travelled widely and traded extensively. Building Montezuma's Castle — and others like it — wasn't their only achievement. Not far from the cliff dwellings is Montezuma's Well, which, like the castle that bears his name, has nothing to do with the Aztec emperor.

Even the twelfth-century Sinagua people were not the first in the area. The Hohokam nation had been there millennia before, in pre-historic times, and had worked out ingenious systems of irrigation.

The mystery is what became of the Sinagua at the end of the four-teenth century? Why did they abandon Montezuma's Castle? Were they wiped out by enemies despite their formidable cliff-side defences? Did they decide that their local land was farmed out, despite their irriga-tions systems associated with Montezuma's Well?

In the next chapter, we turn from American forts and castles that were not connected with Montezuma and his Aztecs to some of the mysterious old South American structures that were.

Chapter 6
Mysterious Ruins in Mesoamerica and South America

THE STORY NOW goes on from the Sinagua cliff dwellings in Arizona, wrongly called Montezuma's Castle, to the authentic Montezuma (1480–1520), whose name in Nahuatl was Montecuhzoma. He had succeeded Ahuizotl as emperor of the Aztecs and ruler of Mexico. It was Montezuma's misfortune to mistake the dynamically successful Spanish conquistador, Hernán Cortés, for the Aztec god Quetzalcoatl, who would, according to Aztec religious traditions, one day return to his people.

Quetzalcoatl is generally thought of, and understood as, the feathered serpent-god of Mesoamerica, the area defined as extending south and east from central Mexico and including parts of Nicaragua, Guatemala, Honduras, and Belize.

Just as Quetzalcoatl appears inside a snake's skin, so this old Babylonian water god appears inside a fish skin. Is there a connection between these two ancient entities?

SIX

A remarkable carving in Yaxchilan, Mexico, showing Quetzalcoatl in the mouth of a serpent bears an uncanny resemblance to ancient Assyrian and Babylonian fish deities like Oannes and Ea inside the skins of fishes. Is it remotely possible that these curious old amphibian gods were one and the same — or were they different representatives of a highly intelligent and technologically advanced race of extraterrestrial amphibians who had visited Earth in ancient times?

Another ancient representation of a water god wearing the skin of a fish.

Although Quetzalcoatl was his Aztec name, he was far older than the Aztec period and had been known by many names in the remote past. One of his alternative names is Kukulcan, and this raises another interesting theory. The pre-Christian Irish pantheon included a superb warrior god named Chuchulain (spellings vary) who was unbeatable in battle.

Was this ancient Babylonian fish-god, known as Ea or Oannes, connected in any way with Quetzalcoatl?

Ancient statue of the head of Quetzalcoatl, the feathered serpent-god, emerging from a snake. Could this Mesoamerican serpent-god be linked to Ea, who is often seen emerging from a fish?

Were the Mesoamerican Kukulcan and the Irish Chuchulain one and the same ancient hero, whose prowess glided from historical fact into religious legend in both cultures? Did early Irish merchant adventurers cross the Atlantic and reach Mesoamerica? When the real, historical Quetzalcoatl (alias Kukulcan or Chuchulain) sailed to the east towards Ireland did he fully intend to return to his people in Mesoamerica?

The history of Mesoamerica and South America goes back a very long way indeed. There are archaeologists who would argue that the earliest evidence of prehistoric human occupation goes back many thousands of years. The most cautious academic archaeologists would accept that the earliest indigenous Americans were occupying the continent by 10,000 BC; more daring theorists suggest that there were people living there thirty thousand years ago. There are scholars who believe that members of the Clovis and Folsom cultures from New Mexico made their way down into Mesoamerica and South America twelve thousand years ago. These ancient peoples were highly skilled craftsmen who could knap flints expertly and leave a central groove or flute to which a handle could be fixed.

These stone weapons have been found over huge areas with the bones of mammoths and mastodons, indicating that their users were dauntless and successful hunters. Clovis burial sites have also been found, where the remains of the bodies showed traces of red ochre. The practice of sprinkling the dead with red ochre was common in Europe and Asia as well in these ancient times, and this raises awesome questions about the *origins* of the ancient Clovis people and the oldest inhabitants of South America. Did the adventurous men and women of the Clovis culture cross the Atlantic or the Pacific? Or had they come *from* ancient cultures in the Old World or the Far East? Corpses marked with red ochre decorations found so far apart raise the spectres of legendary lost continents and shared ancestry: Atlantis or Lemuria? *Or somewhere stranger still?*

Did the most daring members of the Clovis culture venture as far south as the southern tip of South America, where traces of similarly advanced paleolithic people were found? Or was it the other way around? Did fearless members of the ancient cultures of South America wend their way over mountains and rivers as far north as Clovis in New

Mexico? As well as these very early mysteries of origin, the ruins of Central and South America house the secrets of the Mayans, Aztecs, Toltecs, and Olmecs.

The Valley of Mexico — a massive, egg-shaped basin twenty-five hundred metres above sea level — became the home of the Aztec people, with their capital, Tenochtitlan, the largest city in their empire. Little or nothing is known of the real origins of the Aztecs, but their rise to power was little short of incredible. At one time they seem to have been a group of poor — almost powerless — nomadic people who trudged wearily into the Valley of Mexico. By the time the Spaniards arrived in the sixteenth century, however, the Aztecs were the most powerful people in the whole of the Americas.

Their earliest ancestors kept no written records. Whatever history they did retain was a matter of oral tradition: they believed that they had come from an island named Aztlan, which seems to have meant the "Land of the Herons" or the "White Land." There were supposed to have been a number of temples on this White Island, and the Aztecs thought of themselves as the Special People, or the Select People, of their god Huitzilopochtli. They thought of him as a fearsome war god who guarded and guided them; they believed that he was leading and inspiring them — his Faithful People — in their search for a Promised Land. Tenoch, their chieftain, thought that Huitzilopochtli had ordered them to build their great defensive citadel in his honour on a marshy island in Lake Texcoco.

In one sense, the choice of swamps and marshes was in itself an effective form of defence: a citadel surrounded by treacherous fens could not be penetrated easily. The dangerous wetlands all around Ely in East Anglia in the U.K. kept Hereward the Wake and his followers safe from Norman pursuit.

The modern city of Texcoco, with its population of 110,000, lies to the east of Mexico City, 2,250 metres above sea level. When Texcoco was founded in the twelfth century, it enjoyed independent status as a Nahuatl city state — very much along the lines of the ancient Greek city states, which were known as *polis.*

Its rulers were astute politicians who allied themselves with Tenochtitlan, thus making Texcoco the second most important city in the vast Aztec Empire. But Texcoco was more than a powerful city: it was also a centre of ancient learning. Many priceless old Mesoamerican books were stored and studied there at one time. When they were lost, it was as great a tragedy as the loss of the ancient library at Alexandria in Egypt. The ruthlessly effective conquistador, Hernán Cortés, took Texcoco in 1520. He killed King Cacamatzin and used Texcoco as his base for perfecting the forthcoming attack on Tenochtitlan.

When Tenoch and his early Aztec followers began to build the city on their marshy island, it was hard going. Tenochtitlan had to be defended against the constant attacks of its aggressive neighbours. Because of the nature of their site, buildings — especially heavy structures like temples and the simple fortifications that would have been essential to withstand the attacks of their enemies — tended to sink. Other structures were often placed over those that had gone down.

Towards the end of the fourteenth century, the Aztecs decided to appoint Acamapichtli their emperor: his ancestors went all the way back to Quetzalcoatl, believed at one time to have been a great Toltec ruler — prior to his Aztec connections — as well as being a god, and the Aztecs realized that having Acamapichtli as emperor would bring them great prestige. Through Acamapichtli they would be able to claim a nexus with the Toltecs, who had ruled much of central Mexico during the tenth, eleventh, and twelfth centuries. They were the dominant Mesoamerican power before the arrival of the Aztecs, and the Toltecs themselves had inherited much from the even earlier Mayan culture.

The Mayan civilization seems to have originated in the Yucatan Peninsula around five thousand years ago. El Castillo, one of the many Mayan pyramids, can be found among the other fascinating ruins in Chichén Itzá. It has very accurate astronomical alignments and is built over the remains of a far older pyramid. Like the equally mysterious pyramids of Egypt, El Castillo has a passageway inside it. Did these mysterious ancient pyramids serve as fortifications as well as religious buildings? Did their hidden tunnels provide emergency exits for priests and rulers if the worst came to the worst?

El Castillo, the ancient pyramid of Chichén Itzá.

The Mayans were masters of astronomy, calendars, and hieroglyphics. They built temples, pyramids, palaces, and defensive structures. Some of their most notable ruins are to be seen in Chichén Itzá, and one of the most significant of these is known as the Temple of the Warriors. It stands beside the Temple of the Jaguars.

The impressive Temple of the Warriors at Chichén Itzá.

In addition to their military prowess, they were expert farmers with elaborate systems of irrigation and subterranean reservoirs. They established communication systems and roads of a kind that would have done credit to the Romans; they were also expert potters and weavers. For all their ability, however, the Mayans had inherited a great deal of their cultural attributes from a still older civilization — that of the Olmecs.

It is possible that this Olmec civilization was one of the oldest — if not the very oldest — in the Americas. It was primarily agricultural but was divided into two distinct groups: the elite and highly cultured townspeople, who enjoyed luxuries and extensive trade, and the rural folk who did the agricultural work on which the elite urbanites seem to have lived. The greatest mysteries the Olmecs have bequeathed to posterity are the very strange stone heads that dot the landscape in and around Veracruz, where they once lived. These massive heads — up to three metres high and weighing as much as twenty tonnes each — are believed to be portraits of their rulers. Was their motivation similar to that of the ancient peoples of Easter Island, who might well have surrounded their island with vast stone heads as a form of defence?

Were these stone guardians meant to be a "psychic fortress" around Easter Island?

Detail of one of the strange faces guarding Easter Island.

Not all fortifications are physical. Some deeply religious peoples from ancient times apparently believed that their idols, carved of wood or stone, possessed magical powers that would frighten their enemies away — or, perhaps, that such idols acted as psychic energy transmitters, somehow enabling the *thoughts* of the defenders to be directed against their attackers. Egyptian tombs were protected by curses to discourage grave robbers — perhaps, in a few cases, mere threats were a sufficient deterrent. Did the Olmec heads serve the same purpose? Were they, perhaps, representations of their kings or champion warriors? The dramatic and powerful features carved on the great Olmec stone heads look African rather than Mesoamerican or South American. Is it possible that African adventurers, traders, or merchants reached the Americas when the Olmecs were flourishing? Did such visitors impress the Olmecs so much with their strength, courage, and fighting ability that they were hired as guardians of the urban elite? After they left again for their distant homeland, did the Olmecs carve representations of their heads in stone to deter any potential invaders?

Olmec stone head.

The Olmecs seem to have disappeared from history around 300 BC. The mystery of what happened to them, or where they went, is as intriguing as the powerful stone heads they left behind.

Between the First and Second World Wars, when airliners began flying over the Peruvian desert, they noticed strange geoglyphs — drawings on the Earth's surface — between Nazca and Palpa in southern Peru. From the air these very large figures resemble birds, insects, and other life forms. The generally accepted theory is that they had some sort of religious significance for the people of the old Nazca (also spelled Nasca) culture, which dates from about 200 BC. Some researchers have suggested that they might have been constructed for the benefit of visiting astronauts, but others have demonstrated that the lines could have been made without the advantages of getting high above them. The construction technique was simply the removal of lines of pebbles covered in iron oxide, exposing lighter coloured material underneath.

Were the Nazca lines intended to be some sort of magical defence, or protection, like the Olmec stone heads? If so, against what? Were the people of Nazca afraid of the usual human enemies, or did they know of something worse? One of the many theories concerning the mystery of these enigmatic lines suggested that they may have been meant to be seen and decoded *from the air.* If so, their creators may have felt that dangerous intruders with the powers of flight needed to be deterred with magical symbols that could be seen from a great distance away and from a higher altitude.

No survey of fortifications in Mesoamerica and South America would be complete without including the achievements of the Incas. Their great fifteenth- and sixteenth-century empire ran much of the way down the west coast of South America from Ecuador in the north to Chile in the south and included parts of modern Bolivia and Argentina. The empire's real founder and great military tactician, Pachacuti, extended his huge territory north and south from Cuzco.

The Inca language was Quecha, and in their own language they called their land Tawantinsuyu, which meant "the territory that has four parts." These four parts were Collasuyu in the southeast, Condesuyu in the southwest, Chinchasuyu in the northwest, and Antisuyu in the northeast.

Like the Romans before them, the Incan emperors realized that roads were of vital importance in controlling a vast empire like Tawantinsuyu, and they built and maintained an incredible road network extending over a total of nearly twenty-five thousand kilometres. This enabled their large army to travel anywhere in the empire and to get there fast. Ravines were ubiquitous in the steep Andes, and the Incas spanned them with suspension bridges.

Their skills were by no means confined to roads and bridges, however. Their surviving architecture still pays tribute to their amazing building abilities. Their impressive stonework is renowned for its perfect fit; the ponderous blocks of stone fit together so accurately that even a fine knife blade cannot be inserted between them. Examples of this high-quality work can be seen in Cuzco itself and in Machu Picchu.

The nearest thing to an impregnable fortress that the Incan culture possessed was Machu Picchu, more than twenty-six hundred metres high in the lofty Andes Mountains in what is now Peru, and some sixty kilometres from Cuzco. Machu Picchu stands on a ridge that conceals it from the awesome Urabamba gorge far below. Broadly translated, the name Machu Picchu means the "Masculine Summit" or the "Mountain of Men" and the structures there were either defensive, a special sacred place for religious ceremonies, a royal residence — or a combination of all three.

There are some two hundred buildings in Machu Picchu. At its height, it accommodated well over one thousand inhabitants — many of whom were women, their children, and numerous priests. Its polygonal masonry — typical of Incan architecture at its best — was mainly granite and blends well with the surrounding landscape.

The hidden fortifications at mysterious Machu Picchu.

A very strange feature in Machu Picchu is the *intihuatana*, which rises from a huge stone base and is widely thought to have been an essential component of ancient Incan worship. It is generally believed that its name means "the stone to which the sun is tethered"; the Incas seem to have thought that as the days shortened with the approach of the winter solstice, it was essential to fetter the sun in case it vanished altogether.

Although its altitude and massive stone defences safeguarded Machu Picchu to some extent, its greatest protection was its secrecy: outside of the rulers and their priests, very few people knew of its existence. Civil war and smallpox eventually wreaked havoc among Machu Picchu's inhabitants, and it became a truly forgotten city. Before Pizarro conquered Cuzco, Machu Picchu had faded from the minds of most of the Incas.

It was resurrected in 1911 by Hiram Bingham — a real-life Indiana Jones. Bingham was an adventurous professor from Yale who set out to find Vilcabamba, the Incas' last citadel. What he found was Machu Picchu, which he identified with the legendary Vilcabamba. Some researchers agree with Bingham and think that Machu Picchu and Vilcabamba were one and the same; other scholars are not quite so certain.

The curious ancient stone structures of Mesoamerica and South America served as religious centres, observatories, calendars, and places of defence. Who inspired their architects? Or were their own widely travelled architects responsible for inspiring others far across the world? Most intriguing of all is the possibility that some highly advanced culture like Atlantis or Lemuria inspired many other cultures, including Mesoamerica, South America, Egypt, India, Asia, ancient Babylonia, and the Chaldeans. Who were those ancient Wise Ones, and were some of them — Quetzalcoatl, Oannes, and Ea — really extraterrestrial amphibians?

Caerphilly Castle in South Wales.

Chapter 7
The Castles of Wales

A BROAD OVERVIEW of Welsh castles suggests that they can be placed into three categories: Norman castles, Welsh castles, and Edward castles.

The Norman castles were built after 1066 in an attempt to extend and consolidate William the Conqueror's newly acquired realm. These are found mainly in South Wales along the English borders — the area known as the Welsh Marches, home of the fierce Marcher lords. Chepstow, Pembroke, and Caerphilly castles all belong in this group.

Historians refer to those castles built by local Welsh rulers as the true Welsh castles. A fine example may be seen at Criccieth, and there's another excellent one at Carreg Cennen.

The Edward castles were built by the powerful and ambitious king Edward I of England, who reigned in the thirteenth century. He was determined to exert his power and authority over the native-born Welsh princes, and consequently his castles are usually larger and more imposing than those in the first two categories. Impressive examples of Edward castles can be seen at Caernarfon, Conwy, and Harlech.

There are one or two other types outside the three main categories: a few very old Norman motte-and-bailey castles are still around along the border between England and Wales. There are also the interesting remains of elegant fortified manor houses, built more for comfort and artistic architectural style than for defence. Weobley Castle on the Gower Peninsula near Swansea provides an example of these later semi-castles, or residential castles.

William the Conqueror's leading nobles and supporters were at first too busy establishing their grip on England to do very much about Wales, but what had begun as a defence of the English borders against their dynamic and aggressive Welsh neighbours soon became a desire to conquer and consolidate these interesting new territories to the west. More than one historian with an interest in psychology and national cultural characteristics has regarded William and his Normans as aggressive, ambitious, and bellicose. There are more than enough "control freaks" around in our own twenty-first century, and an analysis of eleventh-, twelfth-, and thirteenth-century Britain soon reveals that this singularly unpleasant and unwelcome characteristic was a besetting sin of the Normans as well.

The castle is typical of this desire to expand your territory and to subdue and control the people who were living there before you invaded them. The Normans succeeded because they brought three very effective ideas together: castles and fortifications; feudalism, where the right to grow crops on fertile land was offered in exchange for military service when required; and the deployment of mounted soldiers protected by moderately effective armour.

The French word *marche* originally meant an edge, a border, or a frontier, and it is from this word that the Norman Marcher lords were named. Caerphilly, Cardiff, Chepstow, and Kidwelly all had impressive Marcher lord castles during their long and turbulent history.

William the Conqueror was profoundly grateful to his friend and loyal ally, William Fitz-Osbern, and entrusted him with taking charge of the southern end of the Welsh Marches. Fitz-Osbern's magnum opus was the great castle at Chepstow, starting point for many of his military expeditions westwards into Wales.

Before the end of the eleventh century, two more of William's trusted henchmen, Robert of Rhuddlan and his cousin Hugh d'Avranches, had set themselves up firmly on the eastern banks of the River Clwyd. They were successful in their battles against Welsh hero Gruffydd ap Cynan and set up castles at Bangor and Caernarfon. These were not the magnificent stone edifices that can be studied there today but the quickly erected Norman wood and earth types. A mound of earth, called a *motte*, was surmounted by a defensive structure, or keep, made from sturdy timbers. Around the outside were an earthen bank and a ditch — the bailey — enclosing the area around the keep.

The Norman grip on north Wales came to an abrupt and bloody end when Gruffydd ap Cynan broke free again. He called on his Irish relatives for help — and got it in abundance. This formidable Welsh-Irish alliance disposed of the Normans, and for nearly one hundred years Gruffydd and his son Owain Gwynedd reigned over a peaceful and independent north Wales.

Before the end of the twelfth century, the powerful Prince Llywelyn ap Iorwerth had constructed sturdy stone castles around the area of Snowdonia. Some were straightforward towers for observation and defence; others were more advanced, including Dolbadarn and Castell y Bere.

These castles were needed when the unreliable and petulant King John attacked Wales in 1211 — despite the fact that Llywelyn was his son-in-law.

Documentary evidence for one of the earliest Welsh castles — actually built by a Welshman — dates all the way back to 1116 and describes a motte constructed by Uchdryd ab Edwin at Cymer, not far from Dolgellau.

Finance in the Middle Ages was just as serious a problem as it is in our own twenty-first century, and building a castle was a very expensive undertaking. Largely because castles were so incredibly expensive, it was essential for the ruler who was ordering them to have the best architect he could find, and Master James of St. George was the man every king and prince wanted to hire as his castle builder. He had acquired the reference to St. George in his name because he was one of the leading architects and designers working on the castle of St. George d'Esperanche on the turbulent borders of Italy, Switzerland, and France. Master James was an acknowledged genius in the field of military science. He knew that concentric walls offered the best defence. These provided a "killing ground" onto which the defenders could pour rains of stones, boiling oil, lethal arrows, and crossbow bolts. Master James designed barbicans, portcullises, murder holes, and arrow slits. Beaumaris is one of his greatest achievements. In building it he employed six hundred masons and labourers and used one hundred carts and thirty ferries. There were another two hundred men working in the quarries.

When Edward I laid eyes on the site for the first time in 1283, he planned to make it the capital of Wales. In order to achieve that ambition, he first had to relocate the entire population of Llanfaes to Newborough, so that Master James could have a clear, open site on which to work. Not only is the site of Beaumaris flat, clear, and open, it is also marshy. The Norman French word from which its name comes actually means "the fair, or attractive, marsh."

By any standards, Beaumaris is vast. The inner defensive area, which is almost an acre, is protected by six towers. There are two impressive gatehouses situated at the north and south, and each had provision for three portcullises. The outer wall is punctuated by sixteen towers, and beyond that is a moat twenty feet wide. Beaumaris even has its own miniature harbour — a stroke of genius that was a great help to defenders. Supplies, relief soldiers, and reinforcements could arrive by water — and, if the worst came to the worst, the defenders could escape by water. Almost as an afterthought, Master James had built in yet another sturdy defensive wall to protect this miniature harbour.

As Robert Burns, the great Scottish poet, points out, "The best laid plans o' mice an' men gang aft agley" — our most carefully prepared plans all too often go wrong. It was true for the magnificent schemes Edward I and Master James had for Beaumaris: the superb structure was never completed. Perhaps it was because the battle-hardened veterans of the Welsh wars were all too aware of how formidable Beaumaris was that no great engagements ever took place there. The first time a shot was fired in anger at Beaumaris was during the Civil War between the Royalists and Cromwell's Puritans in the seventeenth century.

One of the most magnificent castles to be found anywhere in the world is Caerphilly Castle, just a few kilometres from Cardiff, the capital city.

Nearly two millennia ago, a small force consisting of just a few hundred Roman cavalry built a simple but effective set of defences at Caerphilly. It was only a very basic timber and earth fortification — not unlike the Canadian and American frontier forts of the eighteenth and nineteenth centuries. The Romans stayed and defended their Caerphilly base for about one hundred years and then abandoned it.

Nothing much seemed to have happened there for about one thousand years after they left.

However, after William the Conqueror's success in England in 1066, he seems to have negotiated a treaty with a very powerful Welsh overlord named Caradog ap Gruffudd, who was King of Morgannwg in the late eleventh century. When the formidable Caradog died in 1081 — some six years before William — the Conqueror felt that it was essential to maintain the grip on South Wales that the mighty Caradog had exercised on his behalf. William's first move was to establish Cardiff and erect a castle there.

Under the Conqueror's son, William Rufus, who reigned from 1087 until 1100, Robert fitz Hamo, one of Rufus's men, was authorized to extend Norman rule at the expense of the fierce and defiant Welsh. Robert had already been given large estates in Gloucester, which put him adjacent to the area that Rufus wanted to acquire. Fitz Hamo established his headquarters at Cardiff and set about doing his best to obey Rufus's orders. He made some significant progress in the lowlands, but the highland Welsh from the mountains known as the Brecon Beacons were too strong for him.

A later chief of these dauntless Welsh mountain warriors was the indomitable Ifor ap Meurig, known as Ifor Bach. Fitz Hamo's grandson, William, Earl of Gloucester, made the serious error of trying to occupy territory belonging to Ifor Bach. This led to the famous raid of 1158, when the dauntless Ifor and his men climbed silently over the defences of Cardiff castle — much as Wolfe's men many centuries later scaled the Heights of Quebec. Ifor's men abducted William of Gloucester, along with his hapless wife and son, carried them all off to one of their mountain hiding places, and duly held them there until all Ifor's territory had been restored.

The powerfully free and independent Welsh rulers of the Morgannwg uplands continued to exert their strength for the best part of a century after Ifor's daring raid on Cardiff Castle. First Rhys and then Llywelyn led, guided, and protected them successfully.

From the Welsh point of view, things took a turn for the worse in 1217 when the de Clare family became Earls of Gloucester. The earlier de Clares had been among William the Conqueror's followers in 1066 and had been richly rewarded by him for their contribution to the Norman victory. They were among the strongest and most resolute of the Norman overlords ruling England in the thirteenth century, and they were not the kind of men to take no for an answer. The three most formidable de Clares during the thirteenth century were Gilbert, Richard, and Gilbert the Red. The small Welsh kingdoms went down one by one to the determined and systematic advances and territorial consolidations of the de Clares — whatever genes had made their ancestors such an asset to William the Conqueror two centuries before were still very much in evidence. The strongly independent Welsh warriors finally lost because in addition to their determination, the de Clares had vast wealth and, consequently, the massive military resources that wealth could buy. Senghennydd alone still held out against the de Clares — and it has to be remembered that Senghennydd's rulers were descended from the great Ifor Bach.

There was, however, a great deal of political disturbance among the English barons at this time. Simon de Montfort, Earl of Leicester, led a reforming party, which had the half-hearted support of the de Clares for a while — until de Montfort made a deal with the great Welsh Prince Llywelyn that did not suit the de Clares, whose territories would be involved. Accordingly, they changed sides and went to the aid of the future King Edward I. On August 4, 1265, the Battle of Evesham was decisive: de Montfort was killed in action, the cause of the reforming barons more or less died with him, and his son and supporters galloped off to the relative security of Kenilworth Castle as fast as their exhausted horses could get them there. Gilbert de Clare was a keen observer of what happened at Kenilworth. The castle's impressive water defences made a lasting impression on him.

The de Clares of this turbulent period of history were as mobile as political weathervanes. The king's cause owed them everything but gave them very little. The rebel barons — known as the "Disinherited" — had been treated unjustly in de Clare's opinion, and he now switched sides again and marched on London with them. The citizens were sympathetic to de Clare and his protégés and rose to support them. Terms were negotiated: the Disinherited got their estates back, and the only remaining problem for the de Clares was the formidable and implacable Welsh Prince Llywelyn. Red Gilbert launched the construction of Caerphilly Castle on April 11, 1268.

The work on Caerphilly Castle began in 1268.

Llywelyn attacked and burnt the early stages of the fortifications. Gilbert counterattacked and then did more building. The gentle, peaceful, deeply religious — but politically and militarily ineffectual — King Henry III sent a pair of well-meaning bishops to try to negotiate peace between Llywelyn and Gilbert de Clare. The bishops' men nominally took over Caerphilly Castle, while Gilbert bided his time and thought up a plan to recover it. The plan was simpler than Ulysses' wooden horse ploy, but just as effective.

The constable of Cardiff — one of Gilbert's loyal supporters and an effective fighting man — turned up at the gates of Caerphilly Castle with (as far as could be seen) only two knights to support him. Politely requesting permission to conduct a simple, routine inspection of the arms, ammunition, stores, and other essentials in Caerphilly Castle, they were freely admitted by the bishops' naïve gatekeepers. Once inside, the three of them easily overpowered the small force at the gate and promptly admitted forty powerful and efficient men-at-arms who had been concealed nearby. They rapidly ejected the bishops' men and repossessed the castle for Gilbert.

When the King began to enquire into the whys and wherefores of the matter, Gilbert pretended to know nothing whatsoever about it, and his protestations of ignorance were so persuasive that no unwelcome consequences ensued.

Gilbert's cause was also helped by the quarrel between Llywelyn and Humphrey de Bohun over which of them was the Lord of Brecon. Llywelyn's downfall began when the powerful and vigorous Edward I came back from the Crusades in 1274. On no fewer than five occasions, the proud and independent Llywelyn failed to appear when ordered to pay homage to the English king. For a man with a temperament like Edward I's this was intolerable. He threw the whole of his considerable power against Llywelyn, who finally retreated into the wilder and more distant parts of Wales. This meant that the massive and practically impregnable Caerphilly Castle was no longer in the front line.

How, exactly, had the massive construction been undertaken? A huge amount of work was done there between 1268 and 1271. More was carried out during the next twenty years, but practically nothing further was done after Red Gilbert died in 1295. Water defences were of prime importance to Gilbert after what he had learnt at Kenilworth, so the stream called Nant-y-Gledyr was dammed to create the lake that is vitally important to Caerphilly Castle's defence system.

Siege engines like these on the parapet at Caerphilly Castle could throw very heavy stones with surprising force and accuracy.

When Red Gilbert died in 1295, he left three daughters, the eldest of whom, Eleanor, married into the Despenser family, taking much of her late father's lands with her. The king by this time was the highly controversial Edward II, who depended upon the Despensers and gave Eleanor's husband, Hugh Despenser, the important role of court chamberlain. Hugh was Machiavellian to the core: unscrupulous, selfish, ruthless, cunning, and avaricious. He grabbed Cardiff and Caerphilly, which went with Eleanor's dowry and were part of the Lordship of Glamorgan. His brutal cruelty to Welsh hero Llywelyn Bren, who had surrendered in the belief that he was dealing with a man of honour, infuriated both Welsh and English alike. The Marcher lords rose against the Despensers and succeeded in destroying some of their property. Complaints about them were made to Edward II, and for a short time they were banished. As soon as they returned, Edward attacked the barons who had attacked the Despensers and smashed the opposition at Boroughbridge. From then on, the younger Hugh Despenser, Eleanor's husband, virtually ruled the country via Edward II. During this period of his great power and prosperity, he spent a fortune on the great hall of Caerphilly Castle, which rivalled any royal court of the time.

Hugh Despenser spent a fortune on the great hall at Caerphilly Castle — just behind these sturdy walls.

Roger Mortimer, one of the leaders of the barons who had opposed the Despensers and Edward II, managed to escape from the Tower of London. He and Queen Isabella (the disappointed and disillusioned wife of Edward II) began an affair and staged a rebellion against Edward and the Despensers. Mortimer and Isabella were amazingly successful due largely to the massive unpopularity of the Despensers and Edward II. Hugh the younger and the King fled from London and tried to find safety in Caerphilly Castle. Their great mistake was to leave it and then try to return. Because of their unpopularity, they were betrayed and captured near Llantrisant.

Barely one hundred men loyal to the King managed to defend Caerphilly Castle against a vast force led by Lord William Zouche acting for Queen Isabella. So strong was the castle that it refused to surrender until Hugh Despenser's son — yet another Hugh — was offered a free pardon. At the time of this surrender, the castle was listed as containing nearly one thousand lance shafts, over one thousand crossbow bolts, and a number of Danish axes. There were also huge quantities of beef, mutton, ham, and fish. In terms of treasure — vital in war for paying mercenaries — there were hundreds of silver goblets and cups and a treasure of about £14,000: millions at today's values.

Very curious dynastic and political machinations followed. Eleanor de Clare (Hugh Despenser's widow) married Lord Zouche — after he had abducted her — and they tried to take Caerphilly Castle in 1329. In 1330, Edward III proved that he was a far stronger man than his father (who had by this time *allegedly* been murdered in Berkeley Castle, although he may well have escaped to France). Mortimer and Queen Isabella fell from power. William and Eleanor were given the Lordship of Glamorgan, including Caerphilly Castle, and it eventually passed to the youngest Hugh Despenser — son of Eleanor.

From the mid fourteenth century onwards, Caerphilly Castle was only partly occupied, but it came to prominence again in 1400 when the great and powerful Welsh hero Owain Glyn Dwr led a very effective uprising. By the fifteenth century, Isabel Despenser had married into the Beauchamp family and with her new husband did much to restore and refurbish the castle.

Another great historical figure, Richard of Warwick — often called Warwick the Kingmaker — was closely involved with Caerphilly Castle.

There was sad neglect and decay of the castle in the sixteenth century, and by the time travel writer and historian John Leland got there

The strongly fortified entrance to Caerphilly Castle.

(sometime before 1550), he described it as having "ruined walls of a wonderful thickness."

There is some uncertainty about whether the amazing leaning tower of Caerphilly was dealt with by Cromwell's Ironsides, who had a tendency to "slight" castles — as they called the damage they did to wonderful old buildings — or whether it just started to lean of its own accord when neglect affected the water defences and caused the ground to shift.

Fortunately for Caerphilly Castle, John Stuart, the first marquis of Bute, was a very caring restorer and preserver of significant old buildings and he did a great deal to protect and save the Caerphilly Castle ruins. The third marquis did even more preservation and restoration work, not only on Caerphilly, but on Cardiff and nearby Castle Coch as well. It was this third marquis, John Patrick Crichton Stuart, who employed the brilliant architect William Burges to undertake the work.

The government took over the castle in 1950 and did much important restoration work. It is now maintained by Cadw, which looks after many other Welsh historic monuments.

In addition to its long factual history, Caerphilly Castle has two persistent ghost stories — one benign, the other sinister. Red Gilbert, who built Caerphilly Castle, was married to the exquisitely lovely Princess Alice of Angouleme. Despite his wife's warmth and beauty, Gilbert neglected her because he was frequently away fighting. In Gilbert's absence, Alice fell in love with a handsome and romantic Welsh prince, Gruffudd the Fair, from Brithdir. Troubled by his conscience, Gruffudd made the fatal mistake of confiding in a monk who he thought was a trustworthy confessor. He wasn't. He betrayed Gruffudd to the highly dangerous Red Gilbert, who immediately sent Alice back to Angouleme in disgrace. Gruffudd found the treacherous monk and hanged him in a place now known as Ystrad Mynach, meaning Monk's Vale. Unfortunately, Gilbert's men found Gruffudd and hanged him too. When the news of her lover's death reached Alice, she died of a broken heart, and her ghost sped to Caerphilly, where she and Gruffudd had once known such great happiness. Her verdant appearance as the Green Lady, flitting from tower to tower and battlement to battlement, is said to be caused by the bitter, green jealousy of her vengeful husband. She is said to stand looking northwards from Caerphilly towards Brithdir, waiting for her lover. Reports of her appearances are too numerous to be ignored and have attracted the attention of several organizations with serious investigative interests in the paranormal.

The other Caerphilly Castle ghost is known as the Moat Hag. Ancient legends and traditions seem to indicate that this is a demoness, or evil spirit of some sort, rather than the spectre of a departed human being. The Moat Hag is described as hideously ugly and malevolent. It emerges from the moat and utters blood-curdling screams as it wings its way towards its victim's house, where it is a harbinger of death. In this respect — as a premonition or bringer of death — it may have something in common with the Irish banshee legends. It may also have links with the legends of Lilith, Adam's first wife. A psychic being, Lilith was unable to accept Adam's need of physical love and fled from him on their wedding night uttering wild screams and howls. In the legend, she became a "night-haunting vampire and demoness" preying on the children she could never have as they lay asleep on the flat roofs of their homes in the Middle East. It would seem logical to associate the legendary

Lilith with a variety of screech owl that was thought to have swooped on small, vulnerable children asleep on rooftops.

But what was a Middle Eastern legend of a flying demoness doing in thirteenth-century Caerphilly? The eleventh, twelfth, and thirteenth centuries saw a great deal of British involvement in the Crusades, and there were Templars in Wales who would have made several journeys to and from the Holy Land. Medieval soldiers often brought strange stories home from the Middle East — possibly including the tale of the demonic Lilith. The de Clares had spilled a lot of brave Welsh blood, and the thought of a vengeful power emerging from the moat of their castle to bring death to them would have had considerable popular appeal at the time.

Caernarfon town with its impressive castle is located at the southern end of the Menai Straits, which lie between Anglesey and North Wales, and Bangor is less than fifteen kilometres to the northeast. From Edward I's point of view during his wars with Wales, Caernarfon was a very suitable site for a castle. The soil of Anglesey was fertile, and the Menai Straits gave Edward access to almost anywhere he chose by sea. It was especially valuable strategically because it allowed him to reach his other strongholds at Harlech and Aberystwyth.

Caernarfon Castle: part palace, part fortress.

Caernarfon Castle itself stands more or less on the site of the old Roman fortress once known as Segontium, the same site where Earl Hugh of Avranches created an early motte-and-bailey castle in the late eleventh century. When Edward I built the present Caernarfon Castle, it was intended to serve him as a mixture of fortification and palace. The castle saw action in 1294 when Madoc ap Llywelyn made a vigorous onslaught and burnt down everything that was combustible. Despite this, it was all repaired and restored by the end of 1295. At this time, interesting defensive improvements were made to the Granary Tower that enabled three archers to use arrow slits at the same time and to fire in different directions.

The maritime access was of vital importance during the building stages: almost everything that Master James needed was brought in over the water.

The dual purpose palace-castle had ample accommodation: Black Tower, Eagle Tower, Chamberlain Tower, and the Queen's Tower. In this deeply religious era, it is scarcely surprising that there were chapels on nearly every storey of each tower. The idea was originally that the castle would provide accommodation for the Prince of Wales, his courtiers, and his family. It also had to accommodate the castle's constable and his garrison.

Caernarfon Castle was believed to be invincible.

Architectural historians have often wondered whether Edward I was emulating the style of the towers from Constantinople, today's Istanbul.

There were double defences for Caernarfon — its own town walls, with the moats that protected them, and its awesome castle with walls twenty feet thick. Seven towers lined the castle's walls, and from those formidable towers arrows, crossbow bolts, and other lethal projectiles could be hurtled down on any attackers caught there. When antiquarian John Taylor wrote about Caernarfon over three centuries ago, he concluded that, provided it was well garrisoned and the garrison was well supplied, the castle was invincible.

Conwy Castle is yet another of Edward I's military masterpieces in Wales. Having recently conquered Dolwyddelan, Edward set his sights on building a vast fortress at Conwy in 1283, and the highly favoured Master James of St. George was again entrusted with the enormous task. The older fortress at Deganwy was now a crumbling ruin, and Edward's men finished it off. Much of the stone in Conwy came from the wreckage that had once been Deganwy. The indefatigable Master James had it practically ready by 1287. In 1294 Edward was very glad of its protection when Prince Madoc attacked, and Edward was also glad to be able to escape by sea from his stronghold at Conwy.

Conwy Castle.

During the long and stressful Wars of the Roses, Conwy was a Yorkist stronghold, and one of its most powerful defenders was the famous Welsh Strongbow, Llewelyn of Nannau. Even allowing for a few metres' exaggeration in the medieval measurements, Llewelyn shot an arrow that killed a Lancastrian enemy, Rhys ap Gruffydd Goch, at a distance of eight hundred metres. During the Civil War, Conwy held out for the King against the Parliamentarians. Sir John Owen fortified the Conwy town walls and defended the mighty castle for Charles. Cromwell's man, Mytton, attacked and overcame the town in 1646, but even the Puritan artillery had little or no effect on the sturdy old castle. Bishop John Williams did a great job in securing honourable surrender terms for Sir John Owen and his men, who marched out with their military honour intact having held the fort against Mytton from August until November.

Co-author Lionel exploring Conwy Castle.

Harlech Castle is associated in mythology with the tragic legend of the beautiful Branwen, sister of the powerful and gigantic King Bran. In the story, Branwen married Matholwch, king of Ireland, but the wedding celebrations were spoiled by Evnissyen, Bran's evil half-brother. He was angry because he had not been consulted about the arrangements for the marriage. In jealous, spiteful rage, he crippled the horses belonging to Bran's Irish guests. The good and generous Bran replaced them with equally fine steeds and heaped many generous gifts on Matholwch and his noble companions by way of compensation and reconciliation. He also gave the Irish a priceless magical cauldron that could restore the dead to life.

Branwen went to Ireland with her royal husband and in due time bore him a son, Gwern. Most of the Irish loved their new queen, who was kind, gentle, and loving, as well as beautiful.

There were some courtiers, however, who were still unable to forgive Evnissyen's insult and the damage to their fine horses. They decided that innocent Queen Branwen should suffer for what Evnissyen had done. A party of powerful Irish nobles confronted Matholwch and told him to choose between his bride and his kingdom. Any husband worthy of the name would either have fought them to the death or told them that he counted the kingdom as less than dust compared to the happiness of the woman he loved. Matholwch was not the man for so heroic an act: he capitulated and expelled Branwen from the royal chambers, demoting her to work as a kitchen servant. The kind and gentle girl made friends with a bird — a raven in some versions — that came regularly to the kitchen for scraps, and at last she sent it with a letter to her brother, the mighty and invincible Bran.

Bran raised a huge army and attacked Ireland. When the Irish destroyed a bridge to try to stop the invaders, Bran simply lay down across the river and his men marched over him. Peace was made, and Gwern, the son of Branwen and Matholwch, was proclaimed king of Ireland. The evil Evnissyen promptly flung the child into the fire and killed him. All hell broke loose, and there were few survivors. Evnissyen died destroying the cauldron, and Bran was fatally wounded by a poisoned arrow.

The legend then becomes very strange indeed. The fatally wounded Bran instructed his followers to cut his head off and take it home to Wales with them. The miraculous head failed to decay, and Bran continued to chat cheerfully with his people in Harlech as they enjoyed a feast that lasted nearly a century. To what extent does this Harlech legend of a supernatural talking head tie in with the Templar legends of talking heads from which those fearless warrior priests supposedly received their instructions? Does Bran's talking head at Harlech provide a coded reference to Templar influence at Harlech?

There is another version of the legend, however, that records how Bran's miraculous head was taken to the Tower of London, rather than Harlech, and that there it is guarded by his faithful ravens, which must never leave the Tower.

Is there also a cunningly coded and symbolic link with the Arthurian tale of Sir Gawain and the Green Knight, who retrieves his head after Gawain has severed it? A number of researchers believe that the Arthurian legends circulated during the twelfth century were inspired by the Templars and are actually camouflaged vehicles for various Templar codes and secrets.

The legend of Bran's head and the long feast at Harlech becomes stranger still. Towards the end of the feast at Harlech, someone opened the sinister *forbidden door*, which, like Pandora's box, released all the world's troubles. The protracted celebrations ended, and Bran's head was duly transported to London, where it was buried below what was to become the future Tower of London. Is this time in London another coded reference to powerful Templar influence?

Harlech Castle on its commanding rock.

Harlech Castle was a component of Edward I's famous "Iron Ring" of castles intended to encircle the area between Snowdon and the coast. They stretched all the way from Flint to Aberystwyth. The concentric Harlech was another of Master James's masterpieces, a great tribute to his industriousness and amazing organizational ability. At the height of the Harlech work, he employed nearly one thousand workers on the site and in the quarries.

The siting of Harlech was in itself a stroke of military defensive genius. It could be attacked only from the eastern side because of the huge castle rock and the precipitous cliff. The vulnerable eastern side was defended by a colossal gatehouse and three heavy portcullises. Perhaps the castle's greatest asset — another sign of Master James's providential wisdom and forethought — was the heavily protected route connecting it to the sea. Stairs here went down very steeply for over sixty metres so that, whatever problems the defenders had on the landward side, boats could always reach them to replenish vital supplies and bring in reinforcements. This access to the sea was of inestimable value to the garrison when Madog ap Llywelyn attacked in 1294 and 1295.

There was ample domestic provision at Harlech in addition to its guardrooms: a well-designed kitchen, a bakehouse, and a granary. There

Harlech was a very difficult castle to conquer.

was also plenty of comfortable accommodation, and from 1290 until 1293 the constable of the castle was Master James himself — making the most of what his architectural genius had produced.

Owain Glyndwr succeeded in capturing Harlech Castle after a long and difficult siege in 1404. He realized its strategic and tactical value and held on to it as his cherished headquarters and residence until 1408, when the English under Harry of Monmouth recaptured it: Harry was the future — truly redoubtable — Henry V. Born in 1387, son of Henry IV and Mary Bohun, Harry was still a teenager when he fought — and defeated — Owain's formidable Welsh army.

Still in his teens, he was in command of the English forces at the Battle of Shrewsbury. He successfully quelled Lollard insurgents and smashed an assassination plot levelled against him by aristocrats who preferred Richard II. He also showed his mettle over the question of his marriage to the lovely Princess Catherine, whose father was Charles VI of France. Nothing if not ambitious, Henry told Charles that he wanted the old Plantagenet lands (in Normandy and Anjou) as his young queen's dowry. When his future father-in-law refused, Henry declared war. With the power of bowmen like Llewelyn of Nannau, one of the redoubtable Welsh Strongbows, the English archers destroyed the flower of the French cavalry at Agincourt, and Henry went on to capture much of the Ile-de-France, Picardy, and Normandy. Charles readily signed the Treaty of Troyes that named Henry as heir to the French throne. When Henry died in 1421, he left his only son, an infant, the future Henry VI, and a reputation that Holinshed the historian reckoned to be second to none. Holinshed, an excellent judge of character, said that Henry was "A King without spot; a Prince whom all men loved." Such was the man who reclaimed Harlech from the tough and tenacious Owain Glyndwr.

During the Wars of the Roses, Harlech was defended by the Lancastrians, until Lord Herbert of Raglan finally succeeded in taking it for the Yorkist cause. Traditionally, it was during this long and bitter siege that the famous war song "Men of Harlech" was first heard.

The mighty stones of Harlech changed hands more than once — but the massive strength of Pembroke Castle never fell to the Welsh heroes, despite their best efforts. Pembroke stood on a dominant ridge with tidal inlets on either side. Roger of Montgomery founded it towards the end of the eleventh century, and before the end of the twelfth century, Pembroke was under the aegis of William Marshall, who spent thirty laborious years transforming it from soil and wood into defiant and enduring stone. The enormous round keep — over seventy feet high, with walls twenty feet thick, and boasting a very unusual roof dome — was the first part of the transformation to be completed. An outside stairway led to the first-floor entrance; there were four storeys in all. These were linked by a spiral staircase that also connected with the defensive positions on the battlements. Another very useful feature at Pembroke Castle was a wooden battle platform, sometimes referred to by military historians as a *hoard*. When extra defences were needed, this hoard would be fitted outside the battlements themselves. Arrows, crossbow bolts, stones, and boiling oil could be jettisoned from this battle platform on to any attackers who were rash enough to get that close.

Other defences included a large stone-throwing catapult, or trebuchet, which stood on a sturdy platform facing the sea. An enemy ship approaching from that direction would be shattered by just one stone from that deadly weapon: the medieval trebuchet men, whose skills rivalled those of the best Welsh archers, achieved a remarkable degree of accuracy.

One of the deep, dark mysteries of Pembroke is Wogan Cavern, the vast cave in the rock below the castle. Probably used as a storage area

Pembroke Castle.

and boathouse, it nevertheless attracted several strange myths and legends. A spiral staircase leads down from the castle to the cave, and there's also a water gate within it to keep back the tide — and any invaders who mistakenly regarded the Wogan as a way into the castle. Archaeologists have detected the remains of Stone Age artifacts in its depths, and, well before the Norman Conquest, Vikings and pirates attacked Pembroke regularly.

The castle came into the possession of Jasper Tewdwr (1431–1495) when he was Earl of Pembroke. Jasper was the son of Owen Tudor and Catherine of Valois, who was the widow of Henry V. This made him half-brother to Henry VI. Jasper was also the brother of Edmund Tudor, the father of Henry VII, who was actually born in Pembroke Castle.

Like several of the other magnificent old Welsh castles, Pembroke played a significant role in the Civil War of the seventeenth century. It made its stand for the Parliamentarians, but John Poyer, who was then mayor of Pembroke, was far from happy at Parliament's failure to offer him and his men anything like the rewards he felt they had earned. In 1648, Poyer joined another group of disaffected Puritan soldiers who were reluctant to be demobilized. These sturdy veterans defended the castle against Cromwell himself for nearly two months.

When it finally fell, Cromwell was determined that it would never be used against him again. He destroyed the barbican and blew the fronts off the towers.

In addition to the main fortification of Pembroke Castle, the town is also defended by Barnard's Tower, an impressive three-storey building with its own portcullis and gate. It seems to have been intended to function as an independent defensive unit because it's a good eight hundred metres from the castle.

Pembroke has famous literary connections, too. Daniel Defoe (1660–1731) — famous for *Robinson Crusoe* — visited the town and commented on its great prosperity, and some scholars believe that Shakespeare used the famous Wogan Cavern below Pembroke Castle as a model for one or more of the caves in his plays. In *Cymbeline*, for example, Shakespeare uses the Cave of Belarius in several important scenes. Is the fictional Cave of Belarius *really* the Wogan Cavern under Pembroke Castle?

The name Oystermouth is a brave attempt to anglicize the Welsh name Ystumllwynarth, and Oystermouth Castle bears its name proudly. It stands on a small hill above the resort town of Mumbles and the general area known as the Mumbles in Swansea Bay. Oystermouth Castle was the twelfth-century work of William de Londres, who was established at Ogmore Castle only a few kilometres away.

These were troubled times between the Normans and the local Welsh, who burnt Oystermouth twice — once in 1116 and again in 1215. Henry I, who reigned from 1100 until 1135, had awarded the whole Gower Peninsula — which includes Mumbles and Oystermouth — to Henry, Earl of Warwick, but by the thirteenth century the de Braose family was in control there, and they rebuilt the castle as a formidable stone fortification.

Oystermouth Castle, Mumbles, Swansea Bay, Wales.

Their impressive curtain wall is still very much in evidence, as is the tower. Two semicircular towers guard the southern entrance to the castle. At the rear of the keep is a small room with a fireplace and narrow windows. The commander's private quarters, also known as a solar, could be reached by a private staircase and were located above this room with the fireplace. A very interesting passageway is situated in the southeast corner of the castle. The light there is very dim, as it is admitted only through narrow slits — wide enough for an archer to use. This strange and sinister passageway wends its way around a spiral staircase, and a small guardroom lies to the west of the keep. The west range is bound on the north by a three-storey residential building, which has large fireplaces and what are known politely as *garderobes* on each floor: they were actually lavatories, and were frequently designed to allow waste material to fall into the moat — as a further deterrent to would-be attackers. At the south side steps lead down to a pair of barrel-vaulted cellars, basements, or dungeons.

Detail of the gaunt ruins of Oystermouth Castle.

Alenora, the pious and devout wife of Lord John Mowbray, added a beautiful chapel in the fourteenth century. Its east window is still impressively beautiful. Lady Alenora's chapel was used for only a small fraction of the castle's history. By 1331, the Lords of Gower had moved out of Oystermouth Castle, and before the seventeenth century dawned, it was largely ruined.

As the visitor can admire it today, Castle Coch (the Red Castle) is the work of John Patrick Crichton Stuart, the third Marquis of Bute, and his brilliant architect, William Burges. When the Marquis found out that he had inherited the ruins of a genuine medieval fortress at

Tongwynlais near Cardiff, he set out to turn his and Burges's dreams into reality. Historians are of the opinion that there was an early Norman motte-and-bailey fortification on the site and that Red Gilbert de Clare later erected a strong stone castle here because this part of Tongwynlais commanded the important communication route along the River Taff.

Castle Coch — the resurrected medieval fortress at Tongwynlais in Wales, U.K.

Gruffydd ap Rhys and other indigenous Welsh princes resented the Norman intrusion into their land and took action against them accordingly. The Norman lords, including Red Gilbert, responded by building fortifications such as Castle Coch — the Red Castle of Tongwynlais. It was the local red sandstone that gave the castle its name, rather than Gilbert's legendary red hair.

Just as the sinister fortifications at Wewelsburg were triangular, so was Castle Coch, but work on the original medieval castle was interrupted when it was burnt and undermined — and it seems to have been reduced to rubble in the fifteenth century. That rubble was nevertheless sufficient

The defiant walls and towers of Castle Coch as rebuilt by Bute and Burges.

to show Burges and the Marquis what the original ground plan of Castle Coch must have been like.

Co-author Lionel with the windlass that operates the drawbridge and portcullis.

Bute and Burges created a drawbridge that actually worked, a portcullis, and the deadly murder holes, or machicolations, which were traditional components of medieval castle defences. Burges, despite his vivid and colourful imagination, kept faith with the original designs as far as he could. He gave the rebuilt towers splayed plinths at their bases: the original purpose of such plinths was to discourage and limit the effects of any undermining by attackers. The walls were three metres thick and had arrow slits in them just as their predecessors would have had.

A medieval roof tile was found among the ruins, and the new cone-roofed towers that Bute and Burges had built in the late nineteenth century were roofed with exactly similar tiles. The medieval touches continued with the cobblestones in the courtyard, around which were the functional and residential rooms, including the kitchens and toilets.

Burges died in 1881, a decade before the rebuilding and refurbishment of Castle Coch was completed. The loss of his kaleidoscopic imagination and design genius was a serious blow to the project, but the work continued along the colourful lines he had laid down for the Marquis. There is a very real sense in which the reconstructed Castle Coch is Burges's memorial.

A flight of enclosed steps on the left as you enter the castle goes up to the large banqueting room, which goes all the way from the kitchen tower to the keep tower. The ceiling is one of the most beautiful and decorative in any castle anywhere in the world, and the murals immediately below it are no less artistic. Sensitive visitors might find some of these realistic scenes of Christian martyrdom rather disturbing — but the age of persecution was a violent one, and the martyrdoms are shown in a realistic way.

Saint Lucius was pope from June 253 until March 254 and was exiled to Civitavecchia by Roman Emperor Gallus. Valerian, who fol-

Saint Lucius above the fireplace in Castle Coch.

lowed Gallus, gave Lucius permission to return. Lucius was a good, kind, generous-hearted, and merciful man who understood the fears of those who had denied their faith when threatened by the savage persecution of Emperor Decius, and he readmitted them to the fold. His death in 254 was probably the result of the Valerian persecution, but there is no absolute historical proof of this. Saint Lucius is venerated in Denmark and is the patron saint of Copenhagen. His image also looks down from the hood over the fireplace in the banqueting room at Castle Coch.

It is the keep tower, however, that is the most breathtaking feature in Castle Coch. Is it remotely possible that Bérenger Saunière had some strange and hitherto unsuspected contact with either Burges or the Marquis of Bute? When Saunière acquired his mysterious wealth in 1885, he spent a fortune on the lavish interior of his Church of St. Mary Magdalene at Rennes-le-Château.

There are critics of his taste in statues and pictures who would say that, in their opinion, Saunière's work in the little Rennes church went a long way over the top. Such critics would not likely approve of the amazing work that Burges and Bute carried out together in Tongwynlais. The Coch colours are bold and dazzling as they set off the brilliant, imaginative work of the Marquis and his gifted architect.

Bérenger Saunière created this colourful mural in his church of St. Mary Magdalene at Rennes-le-Château in southwestern France. Like the paintings at Castle Coch, it contains strange codes and symbols. Bute and Saunière were contemporaries. Did they know each other?

An assortment of birds and animals on the colourful walls of Castle Coch.

Flowers, insects, animals, and birds; scenes from Greek mythology; and deep symbols indicating death and the meaning of life are all there — along with the folk wisdom to be found in Aesop's fables.

Aesop's fable of the Frogs and the Heron on the wall of Castle Coch.

What was once Lady Bute's bedroom right at the top of the tower is brightened by mirrors that reflect the monkeys, squirrels, and strange creatures from mythology that look back from the walls.

Part of the Marquis's purpose in resurrecting Castle Coch seems to have been his desire to imagine himself as the commander, or constable, of the fortification. His own bedroom was placed right over the gatehouse — just where a medieval commander would have been situated. Right next to his room was the powerfully geared mechanism, a very serviceable windlass, for raising and lowering the drawbridge and portcullis when required. It is said that, unlike the real medieval commanders, the Marquis disliked the noise and vibrations that occurred when the windlass was used and had it moved farther away from his sleeping quarters.

There was a sad irony about the death of Burges the architect before this great restoration work at Castle Coch was completed, and also about the death of the Marquis himself in 1900. He did, however, have some nine years to make the most of his castle and enjoy it to the full after the work was completed in 1891.

It remains an interesting but unresolved speculation as to whether John Patrick Crichton Stuart ever had any contact with the mysterious Father Bérenger Saunière, parish priest of Rennes-le-Château. Their ideas about lavishly ornate historical buildings and strange, mystical symbolism — like the three Greek Fates in Castle Coch — were remarkably similar and very, very different from those of most other men of their time.

Alongside their great achievements at Castle Coch, Bute and Burges were also largely responsible for Cardiff Castle as it stands today: a piece of living history in the centre of the thriving, ultra-modern capital city of Wales, with its well-deserved international reputation.

Two thousand years ago the Romans had a fortress on the site of Cardiff Castle, which also served them as a busy and prosperous trading post. When William the Conqueror's men arrived a thousand years later, they erected a motte-and-bailey castle to secure their interests in South Wales. This Norman building work took place throughout the eleventh and twelfth centuries, when Robert, the second Lord of Glamorgan, raised the great stone keep in response to the Welsh

Castle Coch contains this representation of the sinister Greek Moirae, or Moirai, the three goddesses of Destiny or Fate. Clotho spins the thread, Lachesis decides its length, and Atropos severs it when life ends.

The third Marquis of Bute, John Patrick Crichton Stuart (1847–1900), who achieved so much at Castle Coch and Cardiff Castle.

uprising that occurred after the death of Henry I in 1135. Robert Curtose, elder brother of Henry I, was imprisoned in Cardiff Castle for eight years before his death in 1134.

Cardiff Castle's great stone keep on top of its motte.

Despite its effective military design and formidable strength, the keep was no match for the ingenuity of the great Welsh champion Ifor Bach, who got the better of it in 1158, as did Owain Glyndwr, who sacked the castle and burnt the city of Cardiff in 1404.

During the thirteenth and fourteenth centuries, the Black Tower was added, linked by a strong wall to the imposing keep on top of the motte. In the first half of the fifteenth century, Richard Beauchamp, the Earl of Warwick, created the hall and the Octagon Tower.

Henry Holland, employed there by the first Marquis of Bute, was responsible for the late eighteenth-century work on the residential areas, but it was the brilliantly imaginative third Marquis, ably assisted by Burges, who made Cardiff Castle unique with his Gothic Revival style.

Cardiff Castle gateway and tower.

The great Raglan Castle can be found northeast of Newport, in the Welsh county of Gwent, and a few kilometres southwest of Monmouth. Beautiful Tintern Abbey and the formidable Chepstow Castle lie to the southeast of Raglan, which commands the land between the valleys of the River Usk and the River Wye. Both flow south through picturesque countryside to join the broad Severn Estuary separating England from South Wales.

Going all the way back to William's Norman conquest of England following his success at Hastings, William fitz Osbern, the Earl of Hereford (who died in 1071) was in charge of this area, and it was fitz Osbern who created early fortifications at Chepstow and Monmouth. It seems highly likely that he built an early motte-and-bailey castle at Raglan as well.

Almost a century after fitz Osbern died, Earl Richard de Clare — yet another warrior who had acquired the respectful title of Strongbow — granted Raglan to Walter Bloet (or Bluet — spellings of medieval names varied considerably). Walter had done valiant service in Ireland, and

Raglan was his reward. The rent he would have had to pay for Raglan in those days was to provide his lord with the service of one knight when called upon to do so in times of war. That may sound remarkably cheap, but *it wasn't!* To put a fully armoured knight into the field complete with his horse, or horses, and all his formidable weaponry (lances, axes, swords, daggers, mace and chain) was an expensive undertaking. Provided that he didn't fall prey to the archers before he could get in among the enemy infantry, a knight in the twelfth century was the equivalent of a light tank, or gun carrier, in the modern army. Riding a heavy, armoured horse through inadequately equipped men at arms on foot would wreak havoc. Such a knight, if totally loyal to his lord and determined to do his best for him or die in the attempt, could carve a bloody path to threaten the commander of the opposing forces — and if that commander could be brought down, or forced to surrender, the knight was worth his weight in gold. Such was the rent demanded for Raglan, which William Bloet gladly paid.

Raglan Castle, held by the Bloet family in 1172.

The Bloets of Raglan rendered their lord sterling service for many years until Sir John, last of the Bloet male line, died in the fourteenth century. His only daughter, Elizabeth, married Sir James Berkeley, who then became lord of Raglan. He died in 1405 or 1406, and the widowed Elizabeth then married William ap Thomas. He it was who began the construction of the magnificent Raglan Castle, which has survived through many vicissitudes into our own twenty-first century. Elizabeth, who had given him Raglan via this, her second marriage, died in 1420, and William himself then married again. His tomb in the Benedictine priory Church of St. Mary's in Abergavenny shows him alongside this second wife, Gwladus, daughter of the gallant Dafydd Gam who fell at Agincourt. Gwladus herself was a widow when she married William ap Thomas. Her first husband was Sir Roger Vaughan of Bredwardine, who, like her father, had been killed at Agincourt. William ap Thomas himself died in 1445, but Gwladus lived on as the lady of Raglan until 1454.

William ap Thomas's son, William Herbert, rose to greater prominence than his father, and became one of the wealthiest and most influential men in South Wales. Part of his strategy was to claim that he was entitled to his choice of name change to Herbert because he was descended from the illustrious Herbert ap Godwin, an illegitimate son of King Henry I. There was a learned enquiry into these claims in 1461, and William Herbert's case was upheld. Some academic historians have disagreed with the findings. Four of the "most learned men in South Wales" were charged with examining the genealogy, and they pronounced in William Herbert's favour. It is of some significance that the report that emerged from this enquiry was written in Latin, French, and Welsh as a mark of its international importance.

As a reward for his loyal services to the king, Edward IV gave William Herbert the title of Baron Herbert of Raglan. Herbert certainly knew how to enjoy life, if accounts showing the food that went into Raglan are any indication. The occupants, under Baron Herbert's leadership, consumed vast quantities of calves, pigs and piglets, poultry, spices, and salt — then an expensive and essential commodity.

Herbert was made a Knight of the Garter in 1462, and became the chief justice of North Wales in 1467. So important and influential had Herbert become by this time that he was entrusted with the protection and upbringing of young Henry Tudor — destined to become King Henry VII after his victory over Richard III at Bosworth on August 22, 1485 — and, accordingly, the future Henry VII was cared for at Raglan.

William Herbert achieved outstanding military success by capturing Harlech Castle in 1468, which greatly pleased King Edward IV. As a reward, the King created him Earl of Pembroke — a title that he did not enjoy for long. Despite his great success at Harlech, which was indicative of his military skill, Herbert and his brother Sir Richard fared very badly against Warwick the Kingmaker, Richard Neville, the Earl of Warwick, when their forces met at the fateful Battle of Edgecote, fought in July 1469. Herbert and his brother were captured and promptly executed by Warwick. The unhappy Earl of Pembroke was duly interred at Tintern Abbey, not very far from Raglan.

William Herbert had married Anne Devereux, and their son, also called William, was only fourteen when Herbert was executed on the orders of Richard Neville. Anne took charge of Raglan until her son came of age and then retired to Chepstow Castle, which had been left to her in Herbert's will. Young William married Mary Woodville, who was the Queen's sister. When this William died in 1491, his younger brother, Walter, took over Raglan. He was an astute politician and strategist — in the fifteenth century that was an important aid to survival — and although he had been a Yorkist, he swiftly changed sides after Henry Tudor (the future Henry VII) landed at Milford Haven. In 1502, the Queen came to stay at Raglan, a mark of the royal favour that Walter had acquired.

When he died in 1507, the King granted Raglan to his widow, Anne, but she married again in 1508. This led to Raglan being given back to Elizabeth, daughter of William Herbert, who had married Sir Charles Somerset in 1492. He was a staunch supporter of Henry VII and Henry VIII and did excellent military service in France for Henry VIII, for which he was duly rewarded with the title Earl of Worcester. His descendants did much of the later work at Raglan Castle, making both the buildings and gardens things of great beauty and elegance.

Edward Somerset, the second Marquis of Worcester, was an inventor who is remembered for his mysterious "water machine." There are some historians who credit him with inventing an early type of steam engine before Thomas Savery (1650–1715), Thomas Newcomen (1663–1729), or James Watt (1736–1819). Somerset referred to his invention as a "water commanding machine," and it may well have been a precursor to the later engines that were designed to get water out of mines. Between 1630 and 1640 Somerset built his machine either in the keep or perhaps in a hidden chamber covered by the moat. What makes it more mysterious is that no trace of the mechanism has been found by contemporary researchers. It is known, however, that its power was sufficient to hurl a jet of water as high as the top of the tallest tower at Raglan, and it was used with good effect on one occasion during the 1640s when a group of insurgents attempted to attack the castle. They were demanding weapons and ammunition, and Somerset hadn't enough retainers to defeat them by force. He turned on his strange water machine and convinced the insurgents that the noise they could hear was the roaring of his lions that guarded Raglan Castle. (No such lions existed, of course!) The water machine's roar was loud enough and frightening

Co-author Patricia examining the well inside Raglan Castle.

enough to persuade the rebels that entering the castle would not be wise — so they went home quietly. It is also possible that the Marquis had considered using his very powerful jet as a primitive form of water cannon, if its noise alone hadn't been enough to solve the problem. The mystery of the Raglan water machine is still unsolved, but the remains of its mechanism may yet be found.

Raglan was also notable for its valiant part in the Civil War. Only three great royalist strongholds remained defiant after Charles I lost the Battle of Naseby in 1645. These were Pendennis in Cornwall, Raglan, and Harlech. Pendennis surrendered on August 16, 1646. Raglan capitulated reluctantly on August 19, and Harlech held out until March 1647. Henry, Earl of Worcester, had been a great supporter of the royalist cause, contributing funds estimated in excess of £1 million, and King Charles I had been a frequent visitor to Raglan.

The Welsh castles are among the finest, the grandest, and the most historical anywhere in the world. If their stones could only speak, they would tell their many admiring visitors of the courage and determination of the men and women who had lived, loved, and died within their time-defying walls.

The proud old castles of England lie to the east of these great Welsh fortresses, and they are the subject of the next chapter.

Ludlow Castle in Shropshire, England.

Chapter 8
English Castles

To UNDERSTAND THE castles, fortresses, citadels, and defensive structures of England, and to get their mysteries into context, it is important to see them against the historical background of the hostile, fiercely competitive groups who tended to settle their differences in battle rather than with diplomacy and negotiation. The earliest inhabitants seem to have been around some ten thousand years ago — perhaps earlier. From what archaeological evidence has been discovered so far, these indigenous people were travelling bands of hunter-gatherers. More advanced cultures arrived between 5000 BC and 4000 BC and started farming near Salisbury — thus separating themselves from the hunter-gatherers by establishing settlements and using simple agricultural technology.

Crops and settlements had to be defended. Fierce, well-armed hunter-gatherers would soon realize that conquering settlements with stored agricultural produce was a much easier way to live than pursuing fast, dangerous animals into forests containing predators that regarded Stone Age hunters as dietary input. From the hunter-gatherers' perspective, there were other good things to be found in the settlements besides food: the raiders would be keen to abduct females as well as victuals. Accordingly, the farmers' settlements had to be strategically placed and defended so effectively that the raiders would cease to think of them as soft targets.

The condition of prepared bodies in ancient burial mounds and tumuli, complete with ornaments and simple

artifacts of a type apparently considered useful in the hereafter, suggests that those who laid them to rest had a simple form of religion. In their minds, perhaps, magic, or the summoning of the aid of their tribal gods and ancestors, was just as important to defence as building physical ramparts and earthworks. England's mysterious old stone circles might have been astronomical or religious — or intended (like the Olmec stone heads, the statues ringing Easter Island, or the Peruvian Nasca lines) to be a psychic defence mechanism.

These Stone Age farmers from Europe brought a relatively advanced culture to England with them: they could make beakers, polish their stone tools, and domesticate animals instead of merely killing wild ones for their meat, bones, horns, and leather. Remains of their culture abound in Dorset, Sussex, and Wiltshire. They worked flint mines like the one at Grimes Graves near Brandon and Thetford in East Anglia; they created long barrows for their dead; and they built fortifications known to archaeologists as causeway camps, some of which have been covered over by later Iron Age peoples.

The famous fortifications at Winterborne Monkton, near Dorchester in Dorset, are known as Maiden Castle. It contained Neolithic remains, and in later years it was the site of a great battle between the indigenous British people and the Roman invaders. One British defender's body was found with the point of a Roman catapult bolt embedded in one of his vertebrae. Maiden Castle provides a classic example of these earliest fortifications and the way that they were used, and there are many more similar sites still visible. These include the Ivinghoe Beacon hill-fort in Buckinghamshire, Wandlebury hill-fort in Cambridgeshire, and Cam Euny in Madron, near Land's End in Cornwall. This last is an ancient village rather than a fortress, but it was sturdy and well-defended when its original people lived there — it also possesses a mysterious underground passage, known as a *fogou*.

The largest hill-fort in Derbyshire is on Mam Tor, between Eskdale and Castleton. It gave its ancient defenders a magnificent view of the countryside for many miles around. Attackers would have been seen long before they posed any serious threat to the defenders. Gloucestershire has the Crickley hill-fort near Coberley, and Kent has Bigbury Wood hill-fort at Harbledown near Canterbury. Specialist historians think that this was the site of one of Julius Caesar's battles against the British in 54 BC. The Wrekin hill-fort can be seen near Wellington in Shropshire, and Cissbury hill-fort is located at Findon, near Worthing in Sussex.

In about 1000 BC, Bronze Age Celtic peoples arrived from central Europe, bringing their languages with them. Around this time, the highly intelligent and culturally advanced Celtic Tectosage (literally, "the wise builders") was the dominant group in and around mysterious Rennes-le-Château. Another of these Iron Age forts is at Warham Camp in Norfolk, on the road between Wells and Holt.

Having arrived in AD 43, the Romans spread across England with relatively little trouble apart from Boadicea's Revolt, which occurred between AD 61 and 63. The Celtic Iceni of East Anglia had been a more or less happy and peaceful subject-kingdom of Rome, but when Queen Boadicea's husband, King Prasutagus, died, there were disputes about the succession.

Boadicea was publicly flogged by the Romans and her daughters were raped. Her loyal and devoted Iceni, infuriated by the way the women of their royal family had been treated, rose in a violent — and *initially* highly successful — revolt. Roman military discipline and experience, however, finally defeated the Iceni, and Roman superiority was re-established in England.

There are two major mysteries associated with Boadicea. It can logically be assumed that she died fighting when the Romans overcame her Iceni warriors, but historians and archaeologists are uncertain about precisely how, where, and when that final tragedy took place.

A mysterious Bronze Age round barrow can be found on Hampstead Heath in London, and folklore refers to it as Boadicea's or Boudica's Grave. The date is wrong, however, unless the brave Iceni queen was buried hurriedly by a few loyal survivors alongside some unknown Bronze Age chieftain in a burial mound that was already old when Boadicea fell. Legend suggests that a handful of her desperate loyal guard retrieved her body from that final battlefield and laid her to rest as best they could in this Bronze Age tomb. The method of burial would have been vitally important to them because the Iceni were a deeply religious and highly cultured people.

However, when Sir Hercules Read, the then keeper of the British Museum, excavated the site in 1894, he found that the top layers contained relatively modern rubbish. This does not entirely invalidate the historicity of the site, but it raises important questions. The Victorians were probably just as capable of fly-tipping as some unscrupulous and illegal garbage disposal operators are today. In yet another London variation of the mystery, Boadicea is buried below what is now platform 10 at King's Cross station.

Another account reaches a very different conclusion. This places her grave near the village of Mancetter, not far north of Coventry. In this version, Boadicea and her daughters poisoned themselves rather than fall into Roman hands once their great battle there was lost. Another legend places her controversial gravesite in Coggleshall in Essex.

The second Boadicea mystery is the location of the lost Iceni treasure. A great horde of ancient gold and silver items was discovered at Snettisham in Norfolk, England, and the beautifully crafted golden torcs there were very similar to those made and worn by the Iceni. It would have been just as important to the survivors to hide their treasure from the hated Romans as it would have been to give honourable burial to their gallant queen and her daughters.

Like the mystery of Dagobert's grave in or near Rennes-le-Château, the lost Iceni treasure may well have been buried with the dead monarch. Will they both be found one day below the earthworks of some ancient East Anglian fortress, or deep in an East Anglian forest like the one near Grimes Graves not far from Brandon and Thetford?

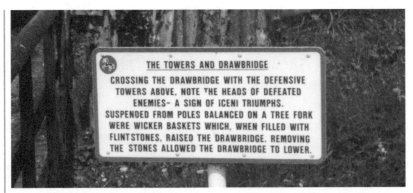

Iceni village reconstruction at Cockley Cley near Swaffham, Norfolk, U.K.

The Iceni severed their enemies' heads and placed them on spikes to deter other enemies.

This seventeenth-century drawing of Warrior-Queen Boadicea of the Iceni was photographed from the notice board outside the Iceni village reproduction at Cockley Cley in Norfolk, U.K.

Co-author Lionel beside the statue of Roman Emperor Hadrian and the remains of the Roman Wall in London.

At the start of the fifth century, Rome withdrew from England, and it is from this period that many historians believe the mysterious Arthurian legends can be dated. Was Arturo, or Arturus, actually a Romano-British warlord who preferred to stay and fight the invaders after the legions had withdrawn? There is undoubtedly a broad parallel between well-armed and well-organized Romano-British cavalry defending their territories against tides of European invaders, and the mythical, or *symbolic*, legends of Arthur's Knights of the Round Table. If it was, indeed, the twelfth-century Templars who disseminated the Arthurian stories as coded and enciphered versions of their own exploits, then some of those mysterious Templar secrets may well have dated back to Romano-British times. There are then *three* golden threads to the enigma: the historical, fifth-century Romano-British warlord, Arturo; the chivalrous and courtly Arthurian legends in the medieval format that Mallory and Geoffrey of Monmouth gave them; and, finally, the Templar codes and ciphers concealed in the symbolism of those Arthurian tales.

Cadbury Castle in Somerset has traditional Arthurian connections and was believed to have been the real Camelot. Reputable academic historians have expressed their belief that in the fifth or sixth century there was a Romano-British fortification there, which seems to have had a large garrison. It is also possible that it accommodated a community of well-to-do Romano-British citizens who were wealthy enough, and cultured enough, to import Mediterranean wine. These fifth- or sixth-century Romano-British occupants had apparently built their citadel over the foundations of a much earlier defence work at Cadbury, and other scientific investigations in 1967 revealed evidence of both Celtic and Saxon presences at Cadbury. The way that the strata lay made it highly likely that these Celts and Saxons had occupied and defended Cadbury *after* the Romans had left.

Other defensive sites associated with Arthurian traditions include mysterious Tintagel Castle in Cornwall, together with Glastonbury Tor. There is also believed to be a ground zodiac at Glastonbury, just as there is believed to be one at Rennes-le-Château. These may well relate to the theory of psychic, or magical, defences, along the same lines as the Olmec stone heads and the gigantic stone faces of Easter Island. Cultures that believed in paranormal powers may well have placed as much trust in spells as in stone walls and earthen ramparts.

This Arthurian era, and the centuries immediately following it, saw waves of Angles, Jutes, and Saxons moving into the power vacuum left by the Roman withdrawal circa AD 410. All of these groups found it necessary to contend with one another and with the earlier Celtic occupants of England. Between 600 and 700 the various newcomers more or less amalgamated into a series of Anglo-Saxon kingdoms.

Fearless and powerful Viking and Danish sea kings first raided, then landed, conquered, and settled in England, especially in East Anglia. Defensive positions and encampments were successively built and destroyed during this period. The Vikings and Danes were followed by William the Conqueror — whose Norman ancestors were themselves descended from old Viking stock. These Normans and their descendants were the great builders of English castles, and it was during the exigencies of the Civil War between Royalists and Parliamentarians in the seventeenth century that many of the medieval English castles were strengthened, refortified, garrisoned, and used again. From the Stone Age to the Civil War between Cromwell and Charles I, the English castles have been the milestones of history, and none more so than Berkeley Castle, which has been home to the noble Berkeley family since 1153 — an association between the site and its owners of nearly nine centuries.

The ancient Manor of Berkeley — midway between Gloucester and Bristol — goes all the way back to Anglo-Saxon times, long before a great castle occupied the site that looks down today over the Severn Estuary. It once belonged to Earl Godwin, father of King Harold, who lost the Battle of Hastings. Godwin also owned the mysterious, semi-legendary island called Lomea that became the treacherous and deadly Goodwin Sands when it was submerged by a gargantuan storm during the eleventh century. A beautiful silver chalice, carefully preserved in Berkeley Castle today, was once the property of Earl Godwin. The legend says that he unfailingly took his daily Mass from that precious chalice — except for one fateful day when he forgot. That was the day on which the devastating storm destroyed his fertile island of Lomea and turned it into the hazardous Goodwin Sands.

The Berkeley Castle keep, built on instructions from King Henry II in 1153, was one of the sturdy Marcher castles intended to provide a defence against the fearless and daring Welsh to the west of Berkeley. As a castle that saw a great deal of action in those dynamic days, it was equipped with such highly effective devices as tripping steps (causing an unwary enemy to stumble and fall at the defenders' mercy), murder holes, arrow slits for archers and crossbowmen, a portcullis, and huge doors that would defy battering rams and siege engine projectiles for long weeks — or even months. There were also vitally important flood-water defences. An attacker with enough time and skilled underground engineers and miners could bring down the sturdiest castle walls from below; the land around Berkeley could be flooded to prevent this.

The tragedy and irreparable loss of ancient libraries being raided and burnt down as the tides of war flow back and forth are all too well known throughout the world. One of the great mysteries of Berkeley is that it still contains and preserves incomparable archives dating back to the start of the twelfth century — the heyday of the Templars with their mysterious codes, symbols, and ciphers. There are twenty thousand items in the magnificent Berkeley archives, and more than a quarter of them relate to medieval times. Who knows what a knowledgeable expert, well versed in Templar codes and ciphers, might discover given enough time to sift through these priceless archives?

In addition to the mysteries in the archives, the Berkeley family has acquired and saved many priceless historical items — including Sir Francis Drake's famous sea-chest, the one that accompanied him on his round-the-world adventures aboard the *Golden Hind*.

Berkeley Castle.

What stories about the Oak Island Money Pit in Nova Scotia might that old cabin trunk tell? One of several viable theories about the Money Pit's origins is that it was created by the ingenious Francis Drake and his loyal seamen to conceal vast wealth that they had taken from the Spanish treasure galleons. Having already delivered huge amounts of captured South American treasure to the British Crown, it was speculated that Drake and his crew might have used the Oak Island excavations to conceal their own illicit "pension fund."

Sir Francis Drake's sea-chest preserved in Berkeley Castle.

The authors were involved with a similar sea-chest mystery at Peplow Hall in Shropshire. One ancestor of the titled family living in Peplow Hall was the famous Dr. William Harvey (1578–1657), who discovered the circulation of the blood. Another ancestor was Captain Harvey, who, like Drake, had been involved with raids on the Spanish coast in Elizabethan times. On one of these raids, Captain Harvey captured a massive iron treasure chest from a wealthy Spanish family, several of whom were killed in the accompanying skirmish. The dying owner cursed Harvey and the chest as he and his men went back to their ship. Memories of the curse lingered on in the Harvey family for nearly five centuries. Technically, authorities on antique chests described the Harvey box as an Augsburg chest, or an Armada chest. It was completely hand-forged from wrought iron and immensely strong and heavy. The locking mechanism had a keyhole in the centre of the lid, and bolts projected into each of the four sides when the lock was operated.

Experts always treat these Armada chests with caution and respect, as they are frequently booby-trapped in one of three ways: a swinging, spring-loaded blade that could slice through the unwary at waist height; a barbed spearhead that would thrust itself out at high speed and pierce an intruder's ribs at heart level; or a loaded gun (sometimes reduced to

an explosive charge) primed to go off when the lid was opened by anyone who did not know its sinister secrets.

Co-author Lionel was called in by a BBC Wales television producer
in two capacities: as a priest to lift, or neutralize, the legendary curse,
and as a professional TV performer famous for his willingness to take on
daredevil stunts. When expert locksmiths George and Val Oliphent had
skilfully defeated the intricate, antique lock, Lionel (suitably protected by
a carbon-fibre flak jacket) lifted the lid. Rather disappointingly, the
wonderful old chest wasn't booby-trapped — but it did contain some
valuable documents dating back to Elizabethan times.

Co-author Lionel with locksmiths George and Val
Oliphent and the mysterious "cursed" Armada chest
in Peplow Hall, Shropshire.

Berkeley also enjoys its share of literary mysteries: Shakespeare is connected to Berkeley just as he is to the strange Wogan Cavern below Pembroke Castle in Wales, which he almost certainly used as a model for one or more of the caves in his plays, like the Cave of Belarius in *Cymbeline.* The Berkeley-Shakespeare link is that he wrote *A Midsummer Night's Dream* as part of the celebrations for a Berkeley wedding. In 1596, Sir George Carey's daughter, Elizabeth, married Thomas, the son of Lord Berkeley. Elizabeth was the granddaughter of Lord Hunsdon, who was then Lord Chamberlain to Queen Elizabeth I. He was also the highly respected patron of the Lord Chamberlain's Men — Shakespeare's theatre company.

The greatest of the Berkeley mysteries, however, concerns the murder — or *supposed* murder — of the unfortunate King Edward II. His estranged queen, Isabella (known as the She-Wolf of France) was having a protracted affair with her lover, Roger Mortimer, and they launched a successful invasion from France in September of 1326 to depose Edward. With little or no support from the English public, and less from the barons, the King was soon captured. He was later taken as a prisoner to Berkeley Castle, where Sir Thomas Berkeley and Sir John Maltravers were responsible for keeping him secure. Rather mysteriously, Sir Thomas Berkeley was called away for reasons that some scholarly historians regard as suspicious. Whatever the truth behind Sir Thomas's absence was, his duties were apparently placed temporarily in the hands of Thomas Gurney and William Ogle.

It was imperative for the conspirators that the King should appear to have died of natural causes. According to the more graphic and gruesome descriptions of Edward II's horrendous murder, a red-hot iron was introduced into his bowels via a hollowed out cow's horn inserted into his anus for that purpose. The murderers, of course, wanted to avoid marking him *externally* in order to give the impression that he had died naturally. Although the details of the melodramatic accounts of Edward II's death differ, all agree that what were taken to be the dying King's final agonized screams could be heard far and wide over Berkeley. But *was* he brutally murdered? There is nothing more theatrical than a loud scream, or a series of loud screams, and the more blood-curdling the detailed accounts of Edward's hideous death, the more likely they would be believed.

Whose was the sinister skull in this room where Edward II was imprisoned at Berkeley Castle? It is reported that terrible, ghostly screams are still heard echoing here, and the spectral wraith of Edward II has allegedly been seen sitting behind this table.

There is, however, a strange twist to the supposed murder mystery. It was reported that long after he had ascended the throne, Edward III received a letter from Manuel Feschi, a Genoese priest, to the effect that his father, Edward II, had in fact *escaped* from Berkeley Castle disguised as a servant on an errand, and that he was still alive and living quietly and peacefully in Lombardy. The fateful screams, reported to have been heard all over the castle and Berkeley village, were, therefore, either theatrical in nature or emitted by some unfortunate who resembled Edward and had been brought to the castle by Ogle and Gurney to be brutally murdered and buried in Edward's place.

There is interesting evidence that the Bishop of Hereford supported the idea of murdering Edward. An ambiguous Latin message from him to Edward's warders read, "*Edwardum occidere nolite timere bonum est.*" It could have meant, "Do not kill Edward, for it is a good thing to be afraid." But it also could have meant, "Do not be afraid to kill Edward, for it is a good thing." Feeling, perhaps, that they had the Bishop's authority to murder Edward because of his real or imagined evil deeds, the warders did their best to aid and abet his "death from natural causes" by keeping him in a dungeon filled with decaying corpses.

It has to be remembered that Edward came to the throne of England in 1307 — the same year that the treacherous Philip le Bel (Philip IV of France) attempted unsuccessfully to wipe out the noble Templar Order on Friday, October 13. There are suggestions that Edward II had been in no hurry to comply with French and papal requests to deal harshly with the Templar Order in England. The most imaginative scenario connected with the mystery of Edward II's supposed death by torture in Berkeley is that there was a Templar plot to rescue him and get him away to Europe — on condition that he then took up the life of a religious recluse and kept right out of all dynastic entanglements and power politics.

An earlier historic moment in Berkeley Castle's long and eventful history was the meeting of the western barons in the great hall there in 1215, immediately prior to the reluctant signing of the Magna Carta by the infamous King John.

Berkeley Castle saw action again during the Civil War when it was a Royalist stronghold that finally surrendered to the Parliamentarians who besieged it. The defenders in the castle had been doing well enough, but the Parliamentarians captured the church and got a cannon up onto its roof; this brought the castle into vulnerable range. With that deadly threat hanging over them, the defenders inside the castle wisely decided to capitulate.

The graveyard around Berkeley Church contains the interesting tomb of the last court jester, Dicky Pearce, about whose death there is a sinister mystery — a long way removed from the traditional, colourful motley that was his jester's costume. He was giving a performance from the minstrels' gallery in Berkeley Castle when he either fell or was pushed. Pearce was buried on June 18, 1728, when Dean Swift of *Gulliver's Travels* fame was Lord Berkeley's chaplain and wrote the jester's epitaph, which was carved exactly as shown here:

HERE LIES THE EARL OF SUFFOLK'S FOOL.
MEN CALLD HIM DICKY PEARCE.
HIS FOLLY SERVD TO MAKE FOLKS LAUGH,
WHEN WIT AND MIRTH WERE SCARCE.
POOR DICK ALAS! IS DEAD AND GONE.
WHAT SIGNIFIES TO CRY?
DICKYS ENOUGH ARE STILL BEHIND
TO LAUGH AT BY AND BY.

BURIED XVIII JUNE MDCCXXVIII
AGED LXIII

The carving on the jester's tomb has deteriorated badly around the details of Dicky Pearce's age at death. The illegible figure in the photograph immediately after the X might have been a V rather than an I, so Dicky might have died at sixty-seven rather than sixty-three.

Dicky Pearce's epitaph written by Dean Swift.

The jester's tomb in Berkeley churchyard. Was Pearce murdered by a jealous husband?

Dean Swift, who composed the jester's epitaph, was notorious for at least two romantic affairs with girls whom he had met when he was their tutor, and Swift's cynical wit was often bitter. What does he mean exactly by *Dickys enough are still behind?* Is Swift suggesting that Pearce was as promiscuous as he was himself, and that the jester had left a brood of illegitimate children — young Dickys — behind? Or is he using *Dicky* in the old, colloquial sense of donkey, or ass, meaning a fool? Is Swift saying that the world need not cry over the death of Dicky Pearce, the court fool, as there are more than enough fools left behind in it? If the former theory regarding the jester's extramarital sex life reflects Swift's real intentions in the epitaph, then there might well have been several people who would have wanted to deal with Pearce.

The suspectedly amorous court jester was apparently on loan to Lord Berkeley from his friend the Earl of Suffolk. It seems reasonable to speculate that during his prolonged visit, Pearce would have paid attention to some of the lady members of the castle staff. It would not have been difficult for a jealous husband, or lover, who knew the Berkeley layout well, surreptitiously to trip, or push, the jester as he gave what was to be his final performance from the high minstrels' gallery.

Whether their jester was pushed or fell accidentally, the Berkeleys' exploits were by no means confined to England. In 1619, on December 4, a group of nearly forty English settlers arrived at Berkeley Plantation in the area that has become Charles City in Virginia, U.S.A. Captain John Woodleaf held a service of thanksgiving, and there is a reasonable case to be made that December 4 should be Thanksgiving Day. In any case it is yet another historical distinction for the Berkeleys. One of the earliest governors of Virginia — and the one who served longer than any other — was William Berkeley. Born in 1605 as the son of Sir Maurice and Elizabeth Killigrew Berkeley, he bought the governorship from Sir Francis Wyatt in 1641.

Throughout British history, the Berkeleys were always warriors of courage and distinction who served at Agincourt, Crecy, Poitiers, Flodden, and Culloden.

The great castle at Ludlow was built by Roger de Lacy in 1086 and was part of the chain of thirty-two Marcher castles defending the border between England and Wales. Roger made the mistake of rebelling against King William Rufus and was lucky to escape into exile with his life. The King's own very mysterious and suspicious death while hunting in the New Forest may well be traceable to Roger or an associate acting on his behalf. After exiling Roger, Rufus granted Ludlow to Roger's brother. When he died it became crown property. After Henry I came to the throne, Ludlow went to one of his supporters named Fitzjohn — who was killed in a battle with the Welsh in 1136. During the protracted civil war between Stephen and Matilda, Gervase de Paganel, who was on Matilda's side, took Ludlow in her name. One of the few good and heroic actions attributed to the otherwise undistinguished King Stephen was that during the siege he personally saved the life of the young Prince Henry of Scotland when the boy was almost dragged off his horse by a grappling hook thrown from one of the Ludlow towers.

Hugh de Lacy had possession of the castle for a time, until the very unpleasant King John took it from him, but it was eventually restored to Hugh's brother, Walter. Because of the castle's proximity to the turbulent Welsh border, it was heavily garrisoned for many years. In 1311, Ludlow was in the possession of the notorious Roger Mortimer, lover of Queen Isabella and instigator of the probable murder of Edward II at Berkeley.

During the Wars of the Roses, Ludlow belonged to Richard, Duke of York, and the River Teme was the site of the decisive battle of Ludford Bridge. Henry VI and his men decided to attack the Lancastrians early in the morning while they were still half asleep. Sir Andrew Trollope, however, suddenly changed sides. He and his war-hardened veterans left quietly during the night and joined Henry VI. Richard realized that he had no chance against them, left Ludlow, and fled to Ireland. The Lancastrians then held Ludlow until the Battle of Northampton in 1460.

The two tragic young princes who finally met their mysterious deaths in the Tower of London lived at Ludlow from 1472 until 1483.

Like Pembroke with its great Wogan Cavern, which inspired Shakespeare's *Cymbeline*, containing scenes enacted in the Cave of Belarius, and Berkeley, which was associated with *A Midsummer Night's Dream* in 1596, Ludlow has its important literary associations, too. Milton's *Comus* was first performed in Ludlow Castle for John Egerton, then Earl of Bridgewater. The performance was to celebrate his installation as Lord President of Wales on September 29, 1634. His two sons and their sister, Alice, took part in the performance. Samuel Butler (1612–1680) actually wrote his famous *Hudibras* in the room over the castle gateway.

During one twelfth-century episode in the checkered history of Ludlow, Josse de Dinan had charge of it, while the owner with the better claim, Walter de Lacy, was ousted. Not surprisingly, Walter made a determined bid to reclaim what he regarded as rightfully his. Josse watched with considerable anxiety as Walter and his determined followers drew ever closer. What were Josse's choices? He could stay safely behind Ludlow's thick walls and wait for Walter to give up and go away, or he could ride out boldly and take on his men. The disadvantage in staying put was that Walter's men might decide to burn down the village and the crops in the surrounding fields. Taking his courage in both hands, Josse decided that riding out to settle the matter in battle was better than waiting to see what Walter might do.

History often rides on the character and prowess of one brave individual: on this occasion that individual was a teenaged pageboy named Fulk who was in Josse's service but considered too young to fight. Although Josse needed every man he could muster, it says much for his sense of humanity and fair play that he left the lad in the relative safety of the keep with Josse's wife, daughter Hawise, and step-daughter.

As Fulk and the ladies watched in horror, Josse was separated from the rest of his men by Walter de Lacy, Arnold de Lisle, and three other knights who were allied to de Lacy. Fulk had the highest regard for Josse, who had clearly treated the boy well and earned his loyalty and respect. The young page felt that this was one of those extreme emergencies when it was appropriate to disobey his master's well-intentioned orders. Fulk grabbed an axe and helmet and rushed out to defend Josse. Perhaps it was the element of surprise; perhaps it was the teenager's rush of adrenaline; perhaps his boyish looks camouflaged the strength and ferocity of a young warrior champion in waiting — but for whatever reason, Fulk was as effective as David had been against Goliath of Gath. His battle-axe killed two of de Lacy's knights before they realized what was happening. De Lisle and de Lacy prudently surrendered to this incredible boy-soldier. Fulk triumphantly led them, as prisoners, back into the castle.

That night's celebrations were understandably memorable: Fulk was rewarded by being betrothed to Josse's daughter, Hawise.

There was, sadly, a lethal fly in the ointment at Ludlow during the weeks that de Lisle and de Lacy were prisoners in the castle. That fly was a girl named Marion de la Bruére, who was tragically destined to become one of the most regularly reported ghosts of Ludlow Castle. Arnold de Lisle talked better than he fought. He was an unscrupulous charmer with the lack of integrity of Philip le Bel and the guile and cunning of Machiavelli. He inveigled the naive, innocent, and unsuspecting Marion into bed with him on the promise that he would marry her as soon as he could get away from Ludlow. She secretly collected sheets, which were knotted into a rope, down which both Arnold and Walter made their escape under cover of darkness.

Arrangements were made to celebrate the marriage of Hawise and Fulk, so, seizing her opportunity, Marion pretended to be ill and stayed behind at the castle with only a small garrison to take care of her. Having made a truce with de Lacy, Josse felt that things were now settled and safe enough for the castle — and Marion — to be left. Arnold and Walter, however, were totally untrustworthy. They communicated with the lovelorn girl, asking her the height of her window and how many guards were still stationed in Ludlow Castle. Trustingly, Marion measured the height precisely with a silken thread and sent it to Arnold — who promptly had a leather ladder of the right size constructed. As they had arranged, Marion lowered a strong cord and pulled up the ladder for her lover. While she entertained him enthusiastically in the adjoining bedroom, de Lacy's men crept silently up the ladder, infiltrated the castle, murdered the gatekeepers, and flung wide the gates to admit hundreds of men who had been waiting in concealment. They massacred the garrison, set Ludlow village on fire, slaughtered helpless civilians, and generally created mayhem.

As she listened to the screams of the dying, Marion realized how badly Arnold had deceived her. Leaping in fury from the bed where they had been making love only moments before, Marion seized his sword and killed her treacherous betrayer. Then, overwhelmed with guilt and remorse at the suffering her stupidity and naivety had brought to the good and loyal guards who had been her defenders, she hurled herself from the tower window and died on the jagged rocks below.

In sharp contrast to Arnold de Lisle's heartless betrayal of Marion at Ludlow, the ghostly lovers of Goodrich Castle were totally loyal to each other and died bravely together rather than be separated. During the Civil War of the seventeenth century, a young Royalist officer, Charles Clifford, had accommodations in Goodrich. He and his fearless lady love, Alice Birch, set off together on horseback to ford the dangerous River Wye. Despite their courage and tenacity, the waters overwhelmed their horses, and the brave young lovers died together in the swollen river. Several reports have been made of paranormal sightings in which their ghosts were seen struggling not only in the water but in the castle as well.

Goodrich Castle stands high on a hill overlooking the powerful River Wye where Charles and Alice died so bravely together. The keep

Goodrich Castle in Herefordshire, haunted by the ghosts of Charles and Alice.

was built on the orders of King Stephen during the twelfth century to protect the ford where the ancient Roman road between Gloucester and Monmouth crosses the Wye. Sandstone cliffs protect Goodrich Castle on two sides, and a moat carved out of the solid rock protects the rest. During the thirteenth and fourteenth centuries the castle was enlarged and developed, but despite these improvements it was successfully besieged in 1326. Although it had held out stubbornly for several months for Charles I, it was eventually overrun by Parliamentarians in 1646. One of their most formidable weapons was a huge mortar known as "Roaring Meg," which was able to fire a 13.25-inch shot.

Another mysterious legend attached to Goodrich Castle concerns an Irish chieftain who was imprisoned there in what was once called Macbeth's Tower. In some versions of the legend, he made a wild attempt to escape, and now he features among the hauntings attributed to the Goodrich site.

As well as its tragic ghosts of the young lovers, Goodrich is also famous for its literary connections. The incomparable nature poet,

One of the great towers of Goodrich Castle in Herefordshire.

William Wordsworth (1770–1850), visited Goodrich in 1798. While there, he met a small girl who told him about her family and her two siblings, a brother and a sister, who lay in Goodrich churchyard. Her insistence that they were still an essential part of her unbroken family inspired Wordsworth to write his deeply moving poem "We are Seven."

When co-author Lionel worked as chief training executive for the Phoenix Timber Group in Essex in the 1970s, they expanded their range of timber and sheet materials to include an extruded plastic cladding material manufactured in Holland and known in the building trade as Wavin X. As part of the promotional work for Wavin X, Phoenix employed an ex–Fleet Street photographer to take pictures of the product to show to interested customers. This photographer, Sid, told Lionel that as a young photojournalist just after the Second World War, he had been given a commission to take the publicity pictures for an official government publication intended to raise British morale after the war and to counteract the hardships of rationing and general shortages. The main point of this production was to emphasize how well Britain had survived the war and what famous buildings and landmarks had come through the blitz unscathed. Over a pint in an Essex pub one lunchtime, Sid related how he had been issued a special high-level pass from Downing Street when Churchill himself was prime minister. Sid said that this pass entitled him to go almost anywhere and photograph practically anything that would enrich the planned government publication.

As one of his calls, he duly turned up at the Tower of London and showed his top level pass to the senior officer on duty that day, who asked, "Does this include access to the lower dungeons?" As any good journalist would have done, Sid — who had not even heard of their existence until that moment — answered, "Yes, of course." He was then duly escorted to an area that is not open to the public. His guide led him through a series of what Sid described as deep, dark, forbidding dungeons, labyrinthine passageways, and descending stairways, where he glimpsed hoards of antique weapons and even the mouldering skeletons of long dead prisoners in chains.

It was a very strange story, one that may well have been exaggerated in Sid's mind during the quarter-century that had elapsed since his adventure took place, but there was also a curious ring of truth about it. The Tower of London has been there for a long, long time, and one set of buildings after another has been raised over much older structures. Surface features can be destroyed and lost all too easily, but mysteries below ground level can — and do — survive. If Sid's account was accurate, what weird enigmas yet lurk beneath the Tower of London?

The ancient Tower of London, steeped in the mysteries of many centuries. What riddles lie beneath it?

The Romans had defended their early settlement at what they then called Londinium Augusta with sturdy stone walls, and, where their old south and east walls met, William the Conqueror's Normans built their first fortifications on the site of the present Tower of London. Almost certainly, there were ancient Stone Age, Bronze Age, and Iron Age settlements and defences here long before the Romans arrived. Its true age is one of the Tower of London's strangest mysteries.

The great White Tower was William's work and is thought to be based on the design of an earlier tower in Rouen in Normandy. This White Tower in London does not have regular sides, and its corners are not right angles. Its enduring walls are five metres thick at ground level.

Over the centuries since William built it, London's Tower on its eighteen-acre site has served as a palace, a fortress, a prison, an arsenal, a mint, and a zoo. It enshrouds many curious mysteries, and one of the strangest took place in October of 1817, when Edward Lenthal Swifte was the official keeper of the crown jewels, which in his day were housed in the Martin Tower. Edward was having his evening meal in the sitting room near the jewels, along with his wife, his young son, and his sister-in-law. It was a cold, dark night and all the doors and windows were not only closed but also secured with stout shutters. Suddenly, Mrs. Swifte shouted in alarm. She had seen a weird glass tube, about as thick as a human arm. It was floating in mid-air and looked as though it was filled with a curious white and blue liquid, or thin gel, which moved continuously. The whole tube, or transparent cylinder — or whatever it was — glided along the line of the Swiftes' table and showed a clear reflection of itself in a mirror. It reached Mrs. Swifte, who cried in terror as it touched her: "It's seized me!" Edward instantly leapt to her defence and struck at it with his chair, but it vanished as he did so.

Swifte's son and sister-in-law, however, saw nothing. What could the weird cylindrical phenomenon have been? Theories have suggested ghosts, apparitions, spectral visitations, time travellers, and strange visitors from other probability tracks or unknown dimensions. One most unusual and ingenious theory, which may well have some mileage in it, suggests that the appearance of the inexplicable light cylinder was part of an attempt to steal the crown jewels. The glowing cylinder may have been some sort of quasi-chemical attempt to render the thief *invisible*, so that he, or she, could approach the priceless jewels unobserved. According to this theory, the experiment was only partially successful, however, because Swifte and his wife were able to see the cylinder, while his son and sister-in-law were not.

The mystery of the Swiftes and the cylinder remains unsolved to this day. There was, however, a tragic happening shortly afterwards that may, or may not, have had some connection with the riddle of the blue and white tube. A sentry guarding the jewel chamber in the Martin Tower reported seeing a curious, unearthly mist, or vapour, making its way under the door. As he watched, horrified, this mist condensed into the unmistakable outline of a huge, ferocious-looking bear. (It has to be remembered that the Tower at one time housed a collection of exotic wild animals.) The sentry did his best to do his duty, and struck at the apparition with his bayonet — and then collapsed unconscious. He died two days later as a result of the trauma.

Another tragic and sinister unsolved mystery connected with the Tower of London concerns the mysterious disappearances of Edward V (1470–1483) and his younger brother, Richard, Duke of York (1473–1483). These two boys were the sons of Edward IV and Elizabeth Woodville. Upon their father's death on April 9, 1483, twelve-year-old Edward inherited the throne, but their uncle, Richard III, soon had them imprisoned in the Tower of London. On June 25 the boys were formally decreed to be illegitimate by Parliament in the act *Titulus Regius*. In law, a marriage at that time could be declared invalid if there had been a pre-contract of marriage with another partner. It was argued that a pre-contract between Lady Eleanor Talbot and King Edward IV had invalidated his marriage to Elizabeth Woodville. If Parliament was satisfied that the pre-contract between Edward and Eleanor existed, then his marriage to Elizabeth was bigamous and their two sons, Edward and Richard, were illegitimate.

After a short time in the Tower of London, young Edward and Richard were never seen again. *Or were they?* Is there any absolute proof that Perkin Warbeck was an impostor? The traditional view is that Warbeck was a Fleming who had been born in Tournai circa 1473–4. Warbeck turned up in Burgundy in 1490 and declared himself to be Richard, Duke of York, the younger of the two princes allegedly murdered in the Tower of London in 1483 — and the rightful king of England. He tried unsuccessfully to find support in Ireland, and then had more luck in France, where Charles VIII accepted him as genuine. Margaret of Burgundy, the widow of Duke Charles the Bold, was the sister of Edward IV — and *she* claimed to recognize Warbeck as her nephew, Richard, Duke of York. After a few more unsuccessful attempts to claim the English throne, Warbeck (or Richard?) was captured, imprisoned in the Tower of London, and hanged at Tyburn on November 23, 1499. Another angle on the Warbeck mystery is that Perkin bore a strong resemblance to Edward IV. Could he possibly have been one of Edward's illegitimate sons?

It seems logical to assume that both Richard and his elder brother, Edward, were murdered for dynastic and political reasons, but the riddle of *who* was responsible for their deaths is not an easy one to solve. In alphabetical order, the four prime suspects are the Duke of Buckingham, King Henry VII, John Howard (later the first Duke of Norfolk), and Richard III, who had the worst reputation — and was much maligned in history — but who had little or nothing to gain by the boys' deaths.

The Duke of Buckingham, who seems to have been Richard's hatchetman, always appeared very obliging as far as Richard was concerned. When — rather surprisingly — he rebelled against Richard and was promptly executed in October of 1483, it could have been because he had acted outside his remit and taken it upon himself to murder the boys in case they could be viewed as rivals to Richard. If Richard was nowhere as evil as Shakespeare — and popular history — painted him, he might have been genuinely fond of the boys and furious about their unnecessary murder. It might also have seemed practical to Richard to dispose of Buckingham swiftly before he could say anything out of place. Another practical reason for Richard's prompt termination of Buckingham was that the Duke claimed descent from previous kings, and might himself have tried to replace his former master. In some respects, Buckingham had a stronger claim than Henry Tudor, who became Henry VII.

The next suspect, of course, must be Henry VII himself. His ruthlessness and efficiency are in no doubt, and after achieving the throne, he lost no time in getting rid of rival claimants. He wisely reinforced his claim to the throne by marrying in 1486 Elizabeth of York, the eldest sister of the dead boys. Her right to the throne, however, depended upon her brothers having predeceased her. Henry wouldn't have had the power or opportunity to dispose of the young princes until *after* he came to the throne in 1485. But was the wily Buckingham playing both ends against the middle and working for Henry Tudor *as well as* Richard III? In times when treachery and betrayal stalked a very troubled Britain, that was perfectly possible. A curious piece of trivia connected with Henry VII and his queen, Elizabeth of York, is that playing cards as we know them today were introduced into England during his reign, and the portrait of the traditional queen on the court cards is hers.

John Howard, who went on to become the Duke of Norfolk, had a claim to the estates of the Mowbrays, who had been dukes of Norfolk. It was Howard who was in charge of the Tower of London when the boys vanished, but he seems to have acquired those crucial responsibilities in a rather irregular manner. He plainly had the opportunity to dispose of the youngsters, but did he have a motive? Under the quaint dynastic marriage and inheritance laws of the fifteenth century, Richard, the very young Duke of York, was entitled to the Mowbray dukedom of Norfolk because his child-bride Anne (who had predeceased him) had been the daughter of the last Mowbray duke. Therefore, if Howard was to succeed to the Norfolk dukedom, Richard of York had to be removed from the scene.

The final suspect, Richard III, was not threatened by any claim the boys might have had because of the *Titulus Regius*. Had the boys been alive when Richard was linked to their deaths by the widespread rumour and scandal of 1483 and 1484, he need only have produced them in public and all suspicions against him would have evaporated. His inability to produce them seems to point to his guilt, or at least to his implication in the plot to have them assassinated.

By a curious coincidence, it was Walt Tyrrell who allegedly shot William Rufus "accidentally" while hunting in the New Forest in 1100, and another Tyrrell — this one Sir James — allegedly confessed to murdering the two young princes in 1483. However, as Sir James's confession was obtained under torture in 1502, its validity is questionable, especially as he was unable to say where the bodies were buried. It is true that James was a loyal follower of Richard III and might well have killed the boys if Richard had ordered him to, but it must be remembered that the Tudors were in power when Sir James's confession was wrung from him.

In 1674, when reconstruction and repairs were being carried out at the Plantagenet Royal Lodgings at the Tower, during the reign of Charles II, an outer stairway was demolished and the workmen unearthed a wooden chest three metres down. It contained two small skeletons, which seemed to be those of children. The larger of the two skeletons lay on its back, with the smaller one lying face down on top of it. Having initially thrown the bones on to a rubbish heap, the builders continued with their work. The remains, however, were retrieved and placed in a marble urn; then, on Charles II's direct orders, they were interred in Westminster Abbey. The studious Elias Ashmole (1617–1692), founder of the Ashmolean Museum in Oxford, was a keen Royalist, and Charles II rewarded him with the post of Windsor Herald. Ashmole was a keen student of archaeology and other antiquities, and it seems that some of the bones thought to belong to the murdered princes found their way into the Ashmolean collection. If they did, their current whereabouts remains a mystery.

In 1933, the bones in the marble urn were examined again, using the best scientific methods available at the time. It was decided that they belonged to two children whose ages were estimated at ten and twelve years, but there were insufficient remains to indicate those children's genders. The investigation was also hindered by the presence of animal bones among the human remains. One theory put forward at the time of the investigation in 1933 was that robbers had taken some of the human relics and replaced them with animal bones, but the motive seems obscure, unless it was some form of primitive magical belief.

Co-author Lionel with two of the Tower ravens.

One of the most famous legends and mysteries attached to the Tower of London is the riddle of the ravens. The legend is basically that as long as there are ravens on the site, the Tower will stand unconquered and invincible. A relatively recent version of it goes back to the reign of

Charles II (1660–1685), but people have been fascinated by ravens for millennia, and the great age of raven mythology provides intriguing pointers to the origins of this particular Tower legend.

Crows, rooks, and ravens are linked to the awesome Celtic goddess of war, known as the Morrighan. She was queen of the battlefield and assumed the form of a raven so that she could fly over the ranks of the desperately struggling, straining warriors and call them to her. After the slaughter had ended and night fell, the field would be left until morning so that the Morrighan could collect her "acorns" — the heads of the dead soldiers whom she had selected! Her ravens had two purposes: to announce the approach of death and afterwards to feed on the dead.

One grim, practical reason for keeping ravens at the Tower when there were frequent executions was to clean up any small pieces of victims that remained near the block after the executioner's work was done and the head and body had been removed.

The great Irish hero Chuchulain had an unpleasant encounter with the Morrighan, who was able to transform herself into other forms as well as a battlefield raven. Although she attacked him first in her raven form, she changed swiftly into a wolf and then a great red cow. Chuchulain dealt effectively with all her metamorphoses. She was not a good loser, however, and threatened to destroy him in battle. He met her again later when she was washing a dead man's armour in a shallow ford — and she announced that it was his! Sure enough, the mighty Chuchulain fell in his next battle, and the triumphant Morrighan duly settled on his corpse in her carrion crow form.

Rooks, crows, and ravens also feature in Arthurian myths and legends, with their probable links with secret Templar codes, ciphers, and symbols. In one story, Arthur and Owain are playing chess watched by three hundred ravens. When a quarrel leads to fighting, the birds attack the warring knights. To a medieval chess player, the castle, known as the *rook*, may have been associated with these birds of the battlefield, although experts on chess history date the name back to the Persian word *rukh*, meaning chariot.

There are conflicting versions of what became of Bran's head (as detailed in Chapter Seven) and whether it is buried in Harlech in Wales or in the Tower of London. The London version of the legend maintains that the Tower ravens are Bran's sacred birds and that their real purpose is to guard his head. Ravens are also associated with the Vikings and the Valkyries, who flew the dead heroes from the battlefield to Valhalla. Daring sea rovers like the Vikings sent out ravens to search for land — a tradition that predates them by several millennia. According to Genesis 8: 7, Noah used the same method. In the ancient Norse mythology, Odin's ravens, Huginn and Muninn, served him rather like Internet search engines, flying around everywhere to gather news for him.

In his showbiz role as a TV presenter, co-author Lionel was at the Tower of London filming an episode for the widely acclaimed international series *Bloody Towers*, also known as *Castles of Horror*, which he presented for the Discovery Channel. The story being recorded concerned an innocent young victim from an age of religious hatred and intolerance who was being led up the steps of Traitors' Gate beside the River Thames to face torture and death for her faith. Her name was Anne Askew, and she was a twenty-five-year-old Protestant girl with a Catholic husband whom she had tried unsuccessfully to divorce. She was burned at the stake on July 16, 1546.

Film and TV companies needing the unique features of the Tower of London pay by the hour to use that superb setting, and it was important for the production budget for us to finish exactly on time, or preferably a few minutes before, so that an extra hour's costs were not incurred.

Lionel and the crew were running very close to their finishing time of 9:00 a.m. (The Tower authorities like visiting film teams to finish before the day's tourists start to look around.) Lionel memorized his lengthy, moving, and solemn piece about Anne, the brave girl who had suffered and died because of the unfortunate religious bigotry of her era.

The director had planned the piece to be spoken as Lionel walked up the steps of Traitors' Gate. Certain words and phrases had to be broadly synchronized with the pace of the ascent. It wasn't an easy shot, but the whole team knew it had to be done in one take if we were to avoid paying for another hour's rental. The scene began in shallow water at the edge of the Thames where the river just overlapped the lowest of the Traitors' Gate steps. Lionel was accordingly fitted out with BBC wardrobe department rubber boots for the scene. Both he and the director estimated the depth at no more than thirty centimetres: probably rather shallower than that. *How wrong can you be?*

Lionel stepped confidently into the water to begin the slow, dignified ascent — and found he was in way over his boot tops! Every step thereafter was accompanied by the squelch of a boot full of Thames water. Nevertheless, the scene was done satisfactorily — and inside the vital time deadline. Just as the scene finished, one of the Tower's security team ran up to Lionel, looking very concerned.

"Have you just been in that water?" he asked anxiously. Both Lionel's boots were overflowing with evidence at this juncture. The security officer then explained that one of his colleagues had suffered severe skin damage to his legs caused by the water in that area because very powerful chemicals were used just there to keep the water clear of algae and weeds. Kind-hearted, generous, and practical, he gave Lionel the key to his flat and told him to go and shower his legs thoroughly. He also lent Lionel his gardening trousers for the rest of the day's shoot! Perhaps brave little Anne Askew was acting as Lionel's guardian angel that morning in return for having the story of her faith and courage transmitted to millions of viewers worldwide.

Anne Askew was only one of countless men and women to suffer in the Tower. Another famous victim was Henry VIII's former Lord Chancellor, Sir Thomas More. Once again it was the tragic nonsense of disagreement over religious trivia that brought More down. King Henry wanted a divorce from Catherine of Aragon so that he would be free to marry Anne Boleyn, and in those days a divorce or annulment required the pope's permission — which was not forthcoming. Henry, nothing if not radical and decisive, promptly proclaimed himself Head of the Church in England in place of the pope — whose permission, therefore, was no longer required. Sir Thomas was a devout and scrupulous Catholic who was unhappy about the royal divorce — and even more unhappy about recognizing Henry VIII as Head of the Anglican Church. Disagreeing with Henry was never healthy: More found himself in the Tower with death not far away. He was beheaded on July 6, 1535, after declaring with his final words that he was "the King's good servant — but God's first."

Henry's tragic Queen Anne Boleyn was yet another victim. She was tried in the Great Hall of the Tower of London, along with her brother George, on Monday, May 15, 1536. He was executed two days later. Anne died on Tower Green, her head severed by one swift, sure blow from an expert swordsman brought over from France especially for the occasion. Her head and body were placed in a chest, which was then buried under the floor of the chapel of St. Peter ad Vincula, next to Tower Green. During Victorian renovations of that chapel — three centuries and more after Anne's execution — her remains were identified, and the place where she lies is now marked.

One of the most intriguing unsolved mysteries associated with the Tower of London concerns a remarkable adventurer, Colonel Thomas Blood (1618–1680). Born in County Clare in Ireland, Thomas was the son of an ironmaster and landowner. He served as an officer in Cromwell's army during the Civil War, and this seems to be where the Blood mystery really began. He appears to have worked as a double agent, spying for both the Royalists *and* the Parliamentarians. After the Restoration brought Charles II to the throne, Blood lost his lands in Ireland: that was a mystery within a mystery.

In 1671, Blood, disguised as a clergyman, made friends with Talbot Edwards, the custodian of the crown jewels. His pretext was that he hoped to arrange a marriage between his nephew (who didn't exist) and Talbot's daughter. On his frequent visits to the Tower in connection with these marriage plans, Blood and his gang learned all there was to learn about the security arrangements for the crown jewels. The plan was executed on May 9. Blood asked the trusting Edwards to show his friends the crown jewels. As soon as they were within reach, Edwards was tied up and gagged, and the Blood gang made their escape with the royal treasure. Talbot broke free and raised an urgent alarm, whereupon Blood and his henchmen were captured. The daring colonel found himself imprisoned in the Tower with what seemed like inevitable execution not far away.

The affair then took a very strange turn indeed. Blood would speak to no one but the King himself, and Charles readily agreed to meet him. Following that secret meeting — and whatever information passed between them — Blood was released from the Tower on July 18, his confiscated Irish estates were given back to him, and Charles granted him a lavish pension of £500 a year.

Charles's surprising generosity seems to indicate that was something very secret that put the newly restored King deeply into Blood's debt. What might that strange enigma have been? Was it something that made Charles II grateful to Blood? Or was the complicated Irish adventurer blackmailing him? The first supposition suggests that Blood had saved Charles's life during the years when he was a fugitive from Cromwell's Puritans — perhaps at risk of his own, because he was then acting as a double agent. The second hypothesis is that Blood knew something about Charles that would have made the newly restored monarchy totter precariously if it had ever become public knowledge.

Unless the mysterious colonel had concealed the evidence for whatever he might have been holding over Charles in such a way that Blood's death would have led to its being made public, the simplest way to cope with a blackmailer would have been to remove him permanently. There was no shortage of loyal and efficient servants who would gladly have done that for the King — Blood was not the most popular of men. If that rules out the blackmail theory, what had Blood done for Charles that made the King so permanently and generously grateful? Had Blood deliberately led the Parliamentary hounds away from the royal fox at some crucial moment during Cromwell's supremacy? The details remain shrouded in mystery — but there's little doubt that some very powerful, secret bond united Charles and Blood.

Are there any other theories to explain the Blood mystery? It has been suggested that Blood took the crown jewels purely as a demonstration of what he could do. The message to Charles was this: "If I don't get my lands back, plus a royal pension, I'll do worse than this!" Another hypothesis is that Blood had been employed by Charles to take the jewels, sell them secretly on the Continent, and give Charles the proceeds for his own private use independent of any Parliamentary scrutiny.

Such was the respect for Blood's powers of deception that after he had died on August 24, 1680, his body was exhumed and examined carefully to make sure that it really *was* the infamous colonel inside the coffin that bore his nameplate!

If Blood's association with the Tower had been what might be described from some angles as a happy and exciting one, Lady Jane Grey's story is one of unrelieved tragedy. It was her misfortune to be born into the royal succession and to be the helpless, innocent pawn of avaricious, power-mad schemers. The worst offender was her father, Henry Grey, Duke of Suffolk. Against her will, Henry forced her to marry Guildford Dudley, whose father, John Dudley, Duke of Northumberland, intended to rule through him, after he had put the hapless Jane on the throne. His plans failed abysmally, and the quiet, gentle teenager found herself in the Tower awaiting execution. The saddest part of her death was that after being blindfolded, Jane couldn't find the block at which she was to die, and asked pathetically, "Where is it? What shall I do?"

Co-author Lionel at the site on Tower Green where the executions took place.

It was reported in 1957 that a sentry on duty at the Tower heard a noise from the Bell Tower and saw the ghost of Lady Jane Grey on the battlements. Over the centuries, many similar apparitions have been reported from the Tower of London. These include Thomas Becket, the assassinated Archbishop of Canterbury, whose ghost was said to have demolished walls "as if they had been destroyed by an earthquake," and Catherine Howard, executed by Henry VIII, who glides along the walls at night — and even her uncaring husband allegedly appeared and terrified a sentry in 1890. Anne Boleyn's ghost also forms part of this frequently reported spectral parade, which also includes Sir Thomas More and the chivalrous Walter Raleigh.

Another pitiful apparition reported from the Tower is that of the elderly Margaret Plantagenet, Countess of Salisbury, who was hacked to death by her clumsily inefficient executioner in 1539. It seems that the Countess had tried to escape by running from the block instead of kneeling there passively and waiting for death. The appalling haunting reputedly re-enacts her pathetic flight around Tower Green with the executioner in hot pursuit and raining inaccurate and inadequate blows in her direction.

The numerous grisly hauntings reported from the Tower of London are in marked contrast to the solitary haunting of Castle Rising in Norfolk. Built in 1140 by William d'Albini, Castle Rising has done duty as a hunting lodge, a prison, and a royal residence. This William d'Albini had married Adeliza de Louvain, the widow of King Henry I. She was a teenager when the Henry married her following the death of his first wife, Matilda, daughter of Malcolm III of Scotland. William d'Albini, created Earl of Arundel by King Stephen, constructed Castle Rising to celebrate his marriage to the former queen consort, who was also known by her anglicized name, Alice.

Historians have generally supposed that King Henry had married the attractive teenager in order to produce a male heir, but his fifteen-year marriage to Adeliza was childless. Ironically, after Henry's death, she and Arundel became the parents of at least seven children, from whom were descended the two most tragic of Henry VIII's wives: Anne Boleyn and Catherine Howard, *who both haunt the Tower of London.*

William was justifiably known as Stronghand because of his powerful physique, and in particular because of his encounter with a lion that had been deliberately launched against him by a furiously jealous French princess. He had politely and diplomatically turned down her advances because he preferred Adeliza. Like Samson of Old Testament fame, William killed the lion with his bare hands.

There are two weird and mysterious stone carvings over the sturdy gateway of Castle Rising. One theory is that the figure on the left represents the unattractive French princess who set the beast on William, while the strange image on the right is the lion itself that he killed.

These grotesque and enigmatic stone figures look down from over the gateway at Castle Rising. What do they represent? What does their weird symbolism reveal? Are they the angry French princess and the lion?

Another of Castle Rising's claims to historical fame came during the years that it incarcerated Queen Isabella, the "She-Wolf of France," who was implicated in the murder of her husband, Edward II. According to legend — and many reports from local witnesses over the years — the ghost of the imprisoned Queen could be heard cackling with maniacal laughter that alternated with dismal wailing and howling.

The mystery of Isabella's so-called imprisonment, however, is somewhat complicated by accounts of her having enjoyed an annual royal revenue of £3,000. This was at a time when a skilled workman earned only four or five pence a day. Not only did Isabella travel the country and stay wherever she chose, but her son, Edward III, frequently came to visit her at Castle Rising during the hunting season.

Another mystery connected with Castle Rising dates from the time of Kett's Rebellion in 1549. This was basically a protest against the Enclosure Acts, which had badly affected the poor, depriving them of much of what had been their common grazing land. The main focus of the rebellion, led by Wymondham brothers Robert and William Kett, was on Norwich, which the rebels captured and held for several weeks. There were, however, further insurgents in the Castle Rising area, where things did not go well for them. Pursued by superior forces, they fled towards the town of Watton, battling their way through the village of Holme Hale on the way. Witnesses in Holme Hale have reportedly heard the sounds of ghostly fighting and galloping horses in the village, as the battle between the rebels, led by Kett supporter John Walker, and his pursuers, led by Sir Edmund Knyvett, is spectrally re-enacted there.

Co-author Lionel researched the story of Kett's Rebellion for one of his many TV shows and wrote a folk ballad to go with the program:

'Twas in the sunshine of July in 1549,
Men wandered into Wymondham to pray at Becket's shrine.
They tore down all the fences around the common land.
With Robert and with William Kett, they swore to make their
    stand.
Beneath a mighty oak tree, on the road to Hetherset,
They listened to the stirring words of gallant Robert Kett.
He marched them close to Norwich wall; they camped on
    Mousehold Down.
King's Herald came to warn them — but the Ketts attacked
    the town.
Their cannon roared and thundered as they battered down
    the wall.
The rebels stormed the city — and by night they'd won it all...

The story ended in tragedy, however, as did so many peasants' uprisings in medieval times. Skilful, ruthless mercenaries were called in, and the Ketts' inexperienced farm workers had no real chance against them. Hundreds were killed in the one-sided battle; many more were savagely executed by being hung, drawn, and quartered. Both Ketts were hanged — one in their hometown of Wymondham, the other from the wall of Norwich castle.

There is a strange synchronicity in the way that castles and literature often go together. Just as Shakespeare had connections with the Wogan Cavern under Pembroke Castle, and Wordsworth had links with Goodrich, so Samuel Pepys, the famous seventeenth-century diarist, was associated with Castle Rising. In his day it was one of the boroughs that sent members of Parliament to Westminster — and the literary Pepys was its MP. Another of Castle Rising's political distinctions was that it was part of the constituency from which Sir Robert Walpole rose to become prime minister in 1721.

Okehampton Castle, Devon, England.

Turning next to Okehampton Castle on the northern edge of Dartmoor in Devon, the literary connection between castles and writers continues. This time it is the poet Sidney Godolphin who is associated with the fortifications at Okehampton. His best-known verse is "The

Passions of Dido for Aeneas." Born in 1610, Godolphin was a friend of
Ben Johnson and Thomas Hobbes. The young poet was a stalwart
Royalist and rode valiantly in the Okehampton area with his commanding officer, Sir Ralph Hopton. In 1643, while still only thirty-three
years old, Godolphin died bravely in action there. He is remembered in
a romantic poem by Clinton Scollard, the American poet, writer, and
editor (1860–1932), which pays a warm tribute to Godolphin's courage,
determination, and idealism.

> THEY rode from the camp at morn
> With clash of sword and spur.
> The birds were loud in the thorn,
> The sky was an azure blur.
> A gallant show they made
> That warm noontide of the year,
> Led on by a dashing blade,
> By the poet-cavalier.
>
> They laughed through the leafy lanes,
> The long lanes of Dartmoor;
> And they sang their soldier strains,
> Pledged "death" to the Roundhead boor;
> Then they came at the middle day
> To a hamlet quaint and brown
> Where the hated troopers lay,
> And they cheered for the King and crown.
>
> They fought in the fervid heat,
> Fought fearlessly and well,
> But low at the foeman's feet
> Their valorous leader fell.
> Full on his fair young face
> The blinding sun beat down;
> In the morn of his manly grace
> He died for the King and crown.

Much of Okehampton Castle is now in ruins.

Baldwin FitzGerald built the first castle to occupy this strategic site at Okehampton. William the Conqueror had appointed him sheriff of Devonshire after the success of the Norman invasion, and Baldwin proved himself ruthlessly efficient as he put down several dangerous rebellions in southwest England. In the fourteenth century, residential additions and extensions were made, and the castle became a dwelling place rather than a fortification.

The Marquis of Exeter, who was then in charge, was accused of plotting against Henry VIII — whom it was extremely dangerous to offend. Exeter paid with his life, and Okehampton was dramatically reduced by the King's men in 1538. In spite of the damage inflicted on the castle during that attack, Okehampton was still able to take part in the Civil War.

The great mysteries surrounding Okehampton are supernatural ones. The ghosts include the "Wicked" Lady Mary Howard, who was accused of murdering her four husbands and at least two of her children. The legend is that she rides every night in a spectral coach between Okehampton and Tavistock. The coach itself is constructed from the bones of her victims, and one husband's skull is located on each of the coach's four corners. A skeletal hound with one glowing red eye lopes alongside the coach. The legend details her laborious punishment: she has to pick a single blade of grass from around the castle each night. When the last of the grass has gone, her protracted punishment will cease. As it seems to grow rather faster than Lady Howard can pluck it, the phantom coach is likely to run for a few years yet!

Dover Castle was mentioned very briefly in Chapter One because of its profoundly deep, bombproof tunnels and strange subterranean chambers. Many of these were created during the Napoleonic Wars (1800–15), but some may be much older than Bonaparte's threat, and others may be much more recent, relating to an age that understands the power of nuclear bombs all too clearly. The tunnels that Lieutenant Burgoyne was responsible for when he was inspector general of fortifications during the Napoleonic Wars were equipped with a cunning system of doors that could be operated by remote control — and were deliberately designed to incarcerate any invaders foolish enough to venture down them.

One of the mysteries of Dover Castle is the *real* nature and age of the secret labyrinths that lie beneath it. There was an Iron Age fortification there long ago — and even that may not have been the first on the site. The Romans made the best of the site, and they also built the Pharos (or lighthouse) there. It still stands next to the church of St. Mary in Castro. There was certainly a fortress on the site in Anglo-Saxon times, and the prudent Norman conqueror had the wisdom to extend and increase its ramparts. Under Norman patronage no fewer than twenty-seven towers were added to the outer wall, and fourteen square, sturdy watchtowers were added to the inner wall. In the late twelfth century, Maurice the Engineer, the equal of the famous Master James of St. George, was employed by Henry II to make Dover Castle a masterpiece.

Early in the thirteenth century, Hubert de Burgh successfully held Dover Castle against Louis, the French dauphin. The attackers blew out the northern gate with an enormous explosive charge, but Hubert was more than equal to the challenge. Working like fury to stop the French from gaining entry, he and his men blocked the breach with stalwart timber barricades. Hubert's superb and spirited defence provided the vital time that enabled English forces to be raised to defeat Louis. After the English army was victorious, it was Hubert who led the naval force that defeated Louis's ships decisively in August 1217.

The ghosts of Anne of Cleves and the headless drummer boy have both been reported as haunting mysterious Dover Castle.

Dover Castle was also a great source of comfort and reassurance for Henry VIII. After the end of his marriage to Catherine of Aragon, and the excommunication that ensued, Henry was getting nervous because France and Spain had settled their differences and were lined up against him in 1538. Consequently, he visited Dover Castle in 1539 to check the defences. A great many locked strongboxes were sent to the castle at this time: some contained state papers, while others held simple provisions, but the contents of yet others remained a mystery to all except Henry VIII and a very small, privileged inner group of his confidants. What mysterious secrets were so vitally important to the ruthless and bloodthirsty Henry VIII that they had to go into the secure depths of Dover Castle when the King thought that England was in danger? The ghost of Anne of Cleves, to whom Henry was married for only a few short months in 1540, is reported to have been seen looking wistfully out of a window of Dover Castle.

Among Dover Castle's many other mysteries is the phantom of the headless drummer boy, said to have been seen walking the battlements on several occasions during the past two centuries.

Another mystery — this time a military one — occurred during the Civil War, when Dover was strongly garrisoned by Royalist forces. Somehow, against all the odds, a Parliamentary hero by the name of Drake — with only a dozen men to support him — inveigled his way into the castle and took it from the much larger Royalist garrison. The mystery of quite how he managed it has never really been fully explained to the satisfaction of historians. Drake very soon added over one hundred more Parliamentarian soldiers to his original tiny contingent, and Dover was effectively Cromwell's. It was a military feat that ranks alongside what Odysseus did with his wooden horse at Troy and what the Constable of Cardiff did to the bishops' troops guarding the gate at Caerphilly.

Prefabrication is by no means an invention of our modern industrial technology. William the Conqueror prefabricated wooden castles — or at least many of their "ready-to-assemble" components — and brought them over to England with him in 1066. So confident was he of victory that he intended to erect them on the sites that he was about to

Co-author Patricia examining the ruins of Hastings Castle.

capture in order to hold his newly acquired territories safe and secure from Anglo-Saxon counterattack. Sure enough, having won the Battle of Hastings, William rapidly erected two of these prefabricated wooden castles above traditional earthen mottes at Pevensey and Hastings.

Co-author Lionel researching the mysteries of Hastings Castle.

Less than four years after his coronation on Christmas Day, 1066, William gave orders for the prefab at Hastings to be replaced by a permanent stone structure. As things turned out, it wasn't a good idea. In 1287, barely two hundred years after it was built — which isn't long in the life of a castle — Hastings' sandstone cliffs surrendered to the fury of a great storm and collapsed, taking much of the castle with them. With most of its defences under the sea, Hastings was attacked by the French in 1339 and again in 1377.

What the sea didn't destroy, Henry VIII did, when his henchmen took everything of value they could find at Hastings. Most significantly, they took the castle's protective lead. After Henry's marauders had done their worst, the Pelhams bought the agricultural land; as time passed, the unwanted ruins almost vanished among the undergrowth until the early nineteenth century.

In 1824, however, while Robert Banks Jenkinson, the Earl of Liverpool, was prime minister during the reign of William IV (who as prince regent had run things while his father, George III, was mentally ill), the overgrown Hastings ruins were rediscovered and excavated. The sixth Earl of Chichester, Thomas Pelham, was responsible for the work, during which a mysterious vault was found containing coffins and the remarkably well preserved remains of their occupants.

This was also the time when wealthy nineteenth-century families were beginning to discover the delights of seaside holidays, and south coast resorts like Hastings were drawing large numbers of lucrative tourists. Parts of the ruin were restored and rebuilt as an additional tourist attraction.

East of the castle is a plot of land referred to rather strangely as "The Ladies' Parlour" because it was the site of medieval tournaments and jousting matches. There would always have been at least one distinguished noble lady present to encourage the competitors and preside over their tournament. Witnesses have reported a spectral lady in a shimmering white gown in the area — especially when the moon was full.

Another of the Hastings mysteries is its connection with the martyred Archbishop of Canterbury, Thomas Becket. Just as witnesses have reported the phantom lady in the jousting area, so others report having seen the ghost of Thomas Becket in various parts of the castle ruins. What connection was there? Among his many church offices before rising to the rank of archbishop of Canterbury, Becket was dean of Hastings. It is as reasonable, therefore, to hear that his ghost has been reported from there as from the great cathedral where he was martyred.

Bodiam Castle beside the River Rother in East Sussex.

Mighty Bodiam Castle was originally a Saxon hall prior to 1066, and then it became a modest little manor house belonging to Elizabeth Wardieu's family. In 1385, she married the bold, resolute, and adventurous Sir Edward Dalyngrigge, who had made his fortune in France as a follower of Robert Knolles. This had come about because under the terms of the Treaty of Bretigny, which the English King Edward III had signed in 1360, England retained control of Calais and Aquitaine, together with some other French territory. In return for these areas, Edward gave up his claim to the throne of France itself. In the ensuing confusion over who owned what, freelance British soldiers known as *routiers* acted like land-based pirates and pillaged France wherever and whenever they could. Robert Knolles was one of the main leaders and co-ordinators of these mercenaries, and Edward Dalyngrigge was one of his ablest and most enthusiastic lieutenants. These routiers looted and stole wherever they went, and many of them — including Dalyngrigge — became very wealthy.

These mercenary raids were by no means one-way affairs: the French felt a justifiable need to come over to England to pay back men like Dalyngrigge in their own blood-stained coinage. Consequently, Sir Edward, who knew only too well what could happen when such raids were

Co-author Lionel investigating Bodiam Castle.

successful, decided that a sturdy and reliable castle would be a prudent investment. In 1385, Dalyngrigge received a licence from the King that permitted him "to fortify his house." As it turned out, he did rather more than that. What had been a simple manor house became part of a huge castle complex, which could have withstood any attack, had the French raiders ever got that far. Dalyngrigge reached the height of his fame and power when he was appointed governor of the City of London and keeper of the Tower. It didn't last long, however, as he died in that same year.

Originally occupied by the second Earl of Thanet, John Hufton (a Royalist), during the seventeenth-century Cromwellian Civil War, Bodiam Castle didn't seem to get actively involved in the conflict, nor did it then suffer any external damage. In 1644, Hufton sold Bodiam to Nathaniel Powel, who was, rather surprisingly, a Parliamentarian. After a time, the castle was no longer inhabited, and it began to decay gently into an overgrown ruin rather as Hastings Castle had done. Sir Godfrey Webster, who owned the decaying remains of Bodiam in 1828, was on the verge of dismantling it when Jack Fuller, a wealthy and very popular local MP and squire, came to its rescue. He had also come to the rescue of the unemployed labourers in the area after the Napoleonic Wars had ended in 1815. One of his projects to provide work and wages for them was to build a wall six kilometres long around his Rose Hill estate: much of it still stands today. Sir Francis Dashwood of the notorious Hellfire Club at West Wycombe was even wilder than Jack Fuller — and just as kind to the unemployed labourers in his area. Francis paid for miles of road to be built, just to provide work for them and food for their hungry families.

Deservedly popular because of all the help that he gave to the poor, kind-hearted and generous Mad Jack Fuller paid £3,000 for the castle and the land around it. This saved Bodiam for posterity. The colourful squire had a few thoughts about his own posterity as well. In 1811 he built a huge stone pyramid in Brightling Churchyard and had a verse from Thomas Gray's "Elegy Written in a Country Churchyard" engraved on it:

> The boast of heraldry, the pomp of pow'r
> And all that beauty, all that wealth e'er gave
> Await alike th' inevitable hour:
> The paths of glory lead but to the grave.

Fortunately for all the poor and needy whom Jack helped, he didn't occupy his pyramid until 1834 — and that's when the mysterious legends began. Jack, it was said, had been buried inside his pyramid sitting in his favourite chair with a roast chicken and glass of wine on the table in front of him. These stories of the bluff, death-defying squire — who could have been a model for the squire in Stevenson's famous *Treasure Island* — circulated in the area, and were widely believed until 1982, when repairs and renovation work on the tomb revealed that the good and great Mad Jack Fuller was buried under it in the conventional way.

Rochester on the River Medway in Kent began its military life as a Roman camp on the all-important road from London to Dover. After the Romans left, the Saxons fortified it. The present Rochester Castle is therefore the third fortification to occupy the site. Gundolf, who was bishop of Rochester at the end of the eleventh century, was an extremely competent builder and an expert in massive stone structures. His skill and influence could clearly be seen in Rochester Cathedral and at the Tower of London. From 1127 onwards, Rochester was under the control of the archbishop of Canterbury, and it was then that the vast square keep was constructed from a tough and durable material known as Kentish ragstone. In the local dialect, *rag* meant hard, or difficult to work with, which implied that it would be ideal for building fortifications. Technically, this Kentish ragstone is limey sandstone, a sedimentary rock that was laid down over many thousands of years over the seabed where the modern town of Maidstone now stands. The stones that now comprise part of the towering keep were formed 120 million years ago in the Early Cretaceous era — when dinosaurs walked the Earth.

Bishop Gundolf wasn't the first building expert to value the qualities of Kentish ragstone: the Romans were quarrying it and building with it a thousand years before Gundolf used it so effectively.

The enormous square keep — about forty metres high — is built of this Kentish ragstone, and during the early thirteenth century it proved its worth when King John besieged the keep. The political situation was that King John and his rebellious barons were at each other's throats, and both sides were waiting for troops to arrive from France. This meant that whoever defended Rochester held a key point on the road to London. The barons sent a detachment to take and hold Rochester

The vast keep of Rochester Castle, undermined by King John during his wars against the barons.

Castle only two days before John got there. He had in the meantime gone to the coast to collect some European mercenaries whom he had hired — only to find that at least half of them had drowned. If John had believed in omens he would have been discouraged by the floating corpses of his hoped-for reinforcements. He was nevertheless determined to take back Rochester Castle at whatever cost, and threw all his resources into the attack.

Despite the losses his men had suffered at sea, John was able to command a group of Flemish mercenaries, who were somewhat surprised at the King's determination to lay siege to the castle with so few men. John was contemptuous and dismissive of the defenders. He is reported to have said of the barons, "They are not to be made much of or feared. We could fight them safely with far fewer men than we've got here!" Thus encouraged, his troops cut their way confidently through a small party of the barons' guards, who were trying to defend the bridge, and then went on to establish themselves in Rochester, where both men and horses were soon quartered in the cathedral.

John then set up a lethal line of trebuchets and catapults that hurled missile after missile against the thick Kentish ragstone, which proved impervious to even the heaviest shots. John had to find another way in. This time he resorted to mining. Down below the southern corner of the enormous, towering keep, John's miners worked purposefully. As they cut their way below the gigantic stone fortress, they propped up their tunnel with timbers — but these were timbers with a sinister difference. John had sent for forty fat pigs, which were duly slaughtered and rendered down. The pork fat was smeared thickly over the miners' timber support props. When they judged that they were far enough in to collapse that corner of the huge keep, the miners withdrew to safety and set fire to the fat-smeared timbers under the castle. They had calculated rightly: the undermined south corner of Rochester Castle fell with a ruinous crash. The fight was over. John and his mercenaries were inside.

He was surprisingly lenient with the rebel barons — not because he was good-natured and forgiving, but for shrewd, political reasons. A king in the thirteenth century depended on popular support and goodwill: hanging a group of powerful lords was not the way to win the affection of their equally powerful relatives and friends or of their loyal followers. Much as he would have loved to execute the lot, John held back from vengeance. Historically, it was of relatively little significance, as he died the following year (1216) — almost certainly as a consequence of eating too much overly rich food.

John's use of miners to get into Rochester, and the miners' use of pig fat to ensure that the timber props burnt away and caused the wall above to collapse, are reminiscent of the mystery of Greek fire — one of the deadliest weapons known throughout the Middle Ages. Was it only pig fat that made the props burn so fiercely underground? Was something more inflammable mixed with it? The secret of Greek fire was guarded so carefully because of its terrifying potency that within a few years of its discovery it was lost — and, as far as is known, it has never been rediscovered. It seems to have been invented by a brilliant Syrian engineer named Callinicus (spellings of his name vary) who lived in the seventh century. He worked for Byzantium, and the weapon was also referred to as Roman fire, because Byzantium was still thought of as the vestigial traces of the old Eastern Roman Empire. The Byzantine navy apparently discharged Greek fire at enemy ships via long metal tubes — forerunners of the flame-throwers of modern warfare.

There are records of the destruction of a huge Muslim fleet with the loss of thousands of lives in AD 678 when the Byzantines used Greek fire against them. It was, apparently, used again in 717 when the great Caliph Suleiman attacked Constantinople itself. Just as before, the Byzantine navy used Greek fire and destroyed many of the Caliph's ships and soldiers. Suleiman's attack failed.

Throughout the Middle Ages, with their characteristic castle warfare, Greek fire, or a weaker version that was closely akin to it, was used on arrows and crossbow bolts. It was also thrown at the enemy in hand-held glass containers like the ancestors of the Molotov cocktails that knocked out so many German tanks in the Second World War. Greek fire was hurled over castle ramparts in vast quantities from trebuchets and catapults. It may also have been poured down deadly murder holes on to the attackers below.

Lord Walter of Cureil, who fought on the Seventh Crusade, described an attack by Muslim forces using Greek fire as "the greatest peril that we have ever yet been in."

The speed and efficiency with which John's miners burnt through the timber props below the great keep of Rochester Castle gives cause to wonder whether pig fat was one of the secret ingredients of Greek fire — although Muslim war chemists would have had the strongest religious reasons for avoiding it.

The mysterious ruin of Chartley Castle in Staffordshire, where expert dowsers came to the end of a ley line.

The mystery of Chartley Castle in Staffordshire is a strange one indeed and concerns the fascinating work of two members of the British Society of Dowsers, who reported their studies at one of the society's congress meetings. These researchers were working on EE (Earth Energy) lines that seemed to form an enormous decagon covering many parts of North Wales and the West Midlands. Some of the places involved in their research were Malvern, Bransford, and Wichenford — but their most surprising discovery came at the ruins of Chartley Castle. That was the place where the EE line that they were working along simply stopped dead. It went to the Chartley Castle ruin and vanished. Researchers into anomalous and paranormal phenomena have many interesting theories about the nature of the ley lines that cut across so many interesting ancient sites. Some hypotheses suggest that where such EE lines begin and end there are unusually active sources of this strange, unknown energy. This raises the tantalizing question of whether the medieval castle at Chartley is built over the site of something far older and stranger.

Mysterious Clifford's Tower in York, where Roger de Clifford was said to have been hanged in chains for opposing Edward II.

Clifford's Tower is all that remains of one of the two fortifications that William the Conqueror built at York in the closing decades of the eleventh century. The second was at Baile Hill on the far side of the River Ouse. Both were traditional Norman motte-and-bailey designs and were originally timber constructions, rebuilt in stone afterwards.

The Jews of York were severely persecuted during the Middle Ages. They had established a Jewish community in the city in 1170 and had made valuable contributions to the social and business life of the city. Jewish financial expertise had enabled many businesses to thrive in York and had accordingly provided extra employment and its accompanying increased prosperity for the city. Religious bigotry and prejudice, however, led to irrational anti-Semitism, and many of the Jews were forced to take refuge in Clifford's Tower. The chief troublemaker was an odious character named Richard Malebys, who was deeply in debt to the Jewish financiers who had helped him in the past. There is something of a parallel situation here to the way that the treacherous and ungrateful Philip le Bel (Philip IV of France) attacked the Templars in 1307, because he was deeply in debt to their noble order and didn't want to repay what he owed them.

The mob's anger against the Jewish defenders of Clifford's Tower was made worse by an imbecilic monk, a religious fanatic who paraded ostentatiously in front of the tower every morning, celebrating Mass and preaching crude anti-Semitism. Almost certainly by accident rather than design, he was killed by a falling stone, and the mob went wild. Seeing that their situation was now hopeless, many of the Jewish defenders committed suicide rather than fall into the hands Malebys's vengeful followers. The few who surrendered and begged for mercy were promptly massacred. When the attackers searched the tower and failed to find the records of their debts to the Jewish financiers, they ransacked the cathedral instead, found the documents there, and destroyed them.

Do the restless spirits of those massacred defenders lurk in the shadows at the foot of Clifford's Tower, and does the unhappy spirit of Roger de Clifford glide among them?

These, then, are a selection of episodes from England's strangest and most mysterious castles: all are different, yet all have remarkable common denominators. Many of these ancient fortifications are the melodramatic stages on which human greed, vengeance, ambition, and treachery have acted out the most memorable scenes from English history. If some psychic investigators' theories of strong emotions being "recorded" in stone have any basis in scientific fact, then these mysterious old English castles are a veritable archive of such recordings.

Mysterious Edinburgh Castle in Scotland, site of many reported paranormal activities.

Chapter 9
Irish and Scottish Castles

ONE OF THE friendliest and best-loved castle mysteries in Ireland is the famous Blarney Stone in Blarney Castle. Blarney village itself is only eight kilometres northwest of the city of Cork. A stone castle was built there at the start of the thirteenth century and stands on the site of what was once a tenth-century hunting lodge. The present structure, however, was the work of the shrewdly wise Dermot McCarthy, royal ruler of Munster and lord of Blarney in the fifteenth century. The powerful and decisive English Queen Elizabeth I was almost invariably able to get her own way in negotiations, but she met her match when she tried to negotiate with Dermot. Whenever the Queen's emissaries, ambassadors, and diplomatic representatives visited Dermot with Elizabeth's demands, he was able to sidetrack them with his brilliantly persuasive speeches, while making sure that his distinguished visitors had no shortage of wine, women, dancing, and song while they were in Blarney. Dermot's many admirers maintained that if his enemies had ever tried to hang him, he could have talked the noose off his neck. Eventually, the furious and frustrated Elizabeth stamped her foot and shouted, "What he says he does not mean, and what he means he will not say! It's the usual Blarney!"

Dermot's gift of charming and persuasive speech was supposed to have come from kissing the magical Blarney Stone in his castle. Robert the Bruce gave the stone to Dermot's ancestor, Cormac McCarthy, in 1314, in gratitude for Cormac's help at the fateful Battle of Bannockburn.

NINE

There is evidence that a group of surviving Templars (whom the hospitable Scots had sheltered and befriended after the Templar disaster of 1307) had also played a significant part in Bruce's victory there. Did their secret, esoteric knowledge from the Middle East have an *extra* input into the famous stone? The Blarney Stone was believed to have strange supernatural powers and was thought to be part of the original Stone of Scone over which the kings of Scotland were crowned.

Blarney Castle belonged to the McCarthys until 1646, when Cromwell's brutal cannon proved too much for the ancient stone. King Charles II restored it to them at the Restoration, but unfortunately they lost it again after the Battle of the Boyne in 1690. Sir James Jefferyes, who was then the governor of Cork, bought it at the start of the eighteenth century, and it subsequently passed into the care of its trustees.

Another of the ancient paranormal mysteries attached to Blarney is the area known as the Rock Close. This is a very mysterious ancient Druid site with ponderous rocks that could have been brought there for strange ritualistic purposes. There is also a dolmen — a type of megalithic tomb composed of uprights that support a broad, flat stone cover. Who once lay beneath it? There is also what looks very much like a sacrificial altar and an area associated with traditional Irish witchcraft.

As evidenced by Hastings, Pembroke, and Dover, castles are often closely associated with caverns, dungeons, and labyrinths, and one of the most spectacular of these is the mysterious cavern that runs through the gaunt rock to the land at Dunluce Castle on the rugged, rocky coast of Antrim. Archaeologists specializing in the Antrim area generally agree that fearless and intrepid seamen crossed from Scotland as long ago as 5000 BC. In the primitive craft available to them, it must have been an awesome voyage, but they left their flint implements all over the areas that they first explored and then settled. The Irish put up a fortress here in early times, and the Normans (who had a keen eye for a good defensive site) built one of theirs at Dunluce too. According to half-remembered Irish legends, this part of Ulster was the haunt of fearsome giants and ogres, wailing banshees presaging doom and disaster to the fearless, fighting MacDonnells who ruled it, and the pale, sad ghosts of dead warriors.

A Norman overlord, John de Courcy, who lived during the reign of Henry II of England, had established himself as ruler of the territory between Fair Head and Carlingford Lough. He needed to protect the route to Belfast Lough, and the answer to his problems was Carrickfergus Castle, which he put up in 1180. It may well be the earliest of the magnificent stone castles in Ireland. John de Courcy might have heard of other, more sinister dangers than Irish freedom fighters, rebels, insurgents, and outlaws when he felt the need to guard the land near the lough. Did he believe that strange things dwelt below the water?

Yet another of the mysteriously persistent links between castles and literature can be found in the connection between William Butler Yeats and Thoor Ballyle (also spelled Ballylee) near Coole Park, close to Gort in County Galway. Until he restored it in 1917, it had been a bleak and derelict Norman tower. Yeats transformed it into a beautiful and atmospheric summer home for himself and his young bride-to-be, Georgie Hyde-Lee. Like Yeats himself, Georgie was deeply interested in the paranormal, and found while they were on honeymoon that she had a psychic gift for automatic writing. Their long and happy marriage produced two children, Anne and William.

The brilliant Yeats of *Celtic Twilight* fame, who in 1923 won a Nobel Prize for Literature, wrote from a vast reservoir of mystical knowledge. He was deeply sensitive and perceptive, and was convinced that strange, esoteric *living things* were hidden in many of the Irish lakes. He wrote, "there are of a certainty mightier creatures, and the lakes hide what neither line nor net can take."

Irish myths and legends are full of accounts of such creatures, and it is well within the bounds of reason to assume that more than one Irish lakeside castle was built as protection, not only against human enemies, but also against the nameless perils that were thought to dwell in the depths. Reports of the dreaded horse-eels of Connemara keep knowledgeable local residents away from the water's edge after dark. Similar beasts referred to as *wurrums* have been reported from Kerry, and other dangerous water beasts known as *peistes* are said to make the Shannon a dangerous river. County Mayo's lakes were thought to be the habitat of ferocious aquatic creatures known as the *dobhar-chu.*

The age-old question remains: if strange monsters do, in fact, exist in Ireland's deep, dark lakes and rivers, why haven't their carcasses come to light for scientific examination? When a lake has a high peat content, it's normally low on oxygen. Lack of oxygen slows down the work of the decayer microbes. The remains sink and remain near the bed of the lake, where other predators will quietly devour them, leaving no evidence for a cryptozoological post-mortem. However, there were convincing reports from Connemara in the late nineteenth century from the area between Derrylea Lough and Crolan Lough. It seems that there had been so prolonged a drought that what had once been waterways large enough to accommodate wild, weird water creatures had dried up almost to nothing. According to the local accounts, at least one of the creatures that the locals termed *horse-eels* became jammed in a culvert and died there.

A far friendlier and more human spectre — or perhaps even a group of spectres, or time-travellers — is associated with Ballygally Castle on the Antrim coast road, not far from Larne and only thirty kilometres from Belfast. The castle is reputedly haunted by the ghost of a lady named Nixon, who lived there three centuries ago. Another variation refers to the lady as Isobel Shaw. She is an audible rather than a visible psychic presence, and witnesses have reported hearing the rustle of her silk dress. She also has a sense of humour and seems to enjoy knocking on bedroom doors in the middle of the night. She is experienced most often in a particular room in one of the turrets. Another ghost (accompanied by several of his colleagues) played a similarly harmless joke on two guests who were staying in Ballygally over Christmas. The guests were advised that there was soon to be a fancy dress party, organized by the staff, and that they would be very welcome to attend and join in the fun. In due time, a waiter arrived, resplendent in historical costume, and conducted the two guests down to the ballroom — where they had a very enjoyable evening at the costume party. Over breakfast they thanked the manager for arranging the event and told her how much they'd enjoyed it. There was a stunned silence. Then the manager said, "There wasn't an event last night. The party's tomorrow." Is it remotely possible that the guests had been looking forward to the party so much that they had both experienced very similar dreams about attending it, and had then mistaken those dreams as a real event? Is it possible that there had been a time slip, and they had participated in a convivial social evening that had actually taken place two or three centuries earlier? Had the time slip worked the other way and projected them a few hours into the future? Or were the mysterious Wheels of If at work in Ballygally Castle, spinning the guests out onto another probability track, one along which the date of the fancy dress party had been brought forward a day?

Kilkea Castle in County Kildare was built in 1180 and claims the title of being the oldest castle in Ireland that has been continuously inhabited. It was constructed by Sir Walter de Riddlesford, a kinsman of the king.

One of the strangest mysteries associated with Kilkea is the carving that is sometimes referred to as the "Evil Eye Stone." This carving is probably akin to the sheela-na-gigs that are found all over Britain but are most plentiful in Ireland. The style of carving seems to place them in the eleventh to thirteenth centuries — once again, the Templar period — and the sheelas may well have some connection with the codes and symbols of the noble order. Did medieval Templars bring back some strange knowledge from the Middle East (especially Egypt) that was enciphered and symbolized in these weird images? A sheela is often referred to as "The Hag of the Castle" and is frequently carved to represent a grotesquely ugly old woman in a blatantly exhibitionistic sexual pose. There is no certainty about their real meaning or origin. One hypothesis suggests that they are simply meant to represent evil and to act like psychic lightning conductors by attracting other evil away from the house and its occupants.

The unusual stone at Kilkea, however, is far stranger than a mere sheela. It seems to have been placed horizontally at some period in the past, although it was almost certainly vertical originally. There is a dog-like creature biting the rump of one of the other figures. Another character has a human body with a wolflike head, and a female figure is sitting on its knee facing it.

It might be suggested that the animal-headed *thing* twenty feet up the wall at Kilkea Castle is an Egyptian god. Anubis, the jackal-headed god, took care of the dead and supervised the mummification process. If this figure at Kilkea is meant to be Anubis, then the dog can also be explained. Dogs were sometimes used to guard ancient Egyptian cemeteries and so were associated with Anubis and his grim work.

Additionally, in the ancient legends, Egyptian goddesses — including Isis, Nephthys, Meskhenet, and Heqet — were said to have mingled with ordinary human beings by dressing up as travelling actresses, dancers, and entertainers: these itinerant performances had strong erotic overtones. Does that help to explain the sheelas — especially as they were carved at a time when Templars were bringing back stories about the Egyptian gods and goddesses?

Another thought about the Evil Eye Stone at Kilkea is that it might illustrate some medieval myth or legend about attacks by sexually predacious werewolves in Kildare.

Strange as it is, the Evil Eye Stone has a rival mystery: a monkey is carved on one of the Kilkea chimney brackets. The mystery relates to the thirteenth-century rescue of the infant John Fitzthomas Fitzgerald, later to become the earl of Kildare. Part of Woodstock Castle near Athy caught fire, and in the ensuing panic, the infant John was left behind. When the family and servants realized that he had been overlooked, they raced back to his room — which the fire had gutted. It seemed impossible that the tiny child could have survived. As the heartbroken family made their way slowly out of the ruins, they heard the Woodstock pet monkey chattering excitedly from an undamaged room on the far side of the castle — the monkey was holding the unharmed infant John safely in its strong, protective arms.

Co-author Lionel, as an infant in 1936, in the motherly arms of a protective chimpanzee.

That story is of particular personal interest to the authors; on a visit to a children's zoo in 1936, co-author Lionel was picked up gently and lovingly by a female chimpanzee that had recently lost its own baby. Lionel's mother — despite her surprise and anxiety — had the presence of mind to take a picture. The family joke has, of course, always been that if Lionel had been left there, he might have become another Tarzan!

We move now from the jackal-headed Egyptian god Anubis (or the medieval Irish werewolf) carved on the Evil Eye Stone of Kilkea to another mysterious hound: the wolfhound of Antrim Castle.

These events date back to 1613, when Sir Hugh Clotworthy brought his young bride, Marian, to live in Antrim, not far from Lough Neagh, the biggest expanse of fresh water in Ireland: fifteen kilometres wide and thirty kilometres long. Five of Northern Ireland's six counties have borders on the lough: Antrim, Armagh, Derry, Down, and Tyrone. The legend of the lough's creation concerns the mythical giant Finn McCool (Fionn mac Cumhail). Angered by another giant in Scotland, Finn scooped up a great handful of earth to throw at his rival. He missed, and the huge handful of earth landed in the Irish Sea and became the Isle of Man. Such are the local legends attached to the area.

One day, as Marian was walking through the forest that bordered Lough Neagh, a ravenous wolf raced towards her. She fainted and collapsed, believing that her last moments had come. But rescue was at hand. A brave Irish wolfhound — big enough and strong enough to offer the wolf a fair match — bounded to Marian's rescue. When she recovered from her faint, the wolf was dead, and her rescuer was quite severely wounded. Marian led him gently home with her, where her servants tended his wounds and fed him.

One stormy night, several years later — after Antrim Castle had been built — the baying of the great wolfhound woke up everyone inside. Climbing up to the battlements to see if they could see the dog, Marian and Sir Hugh spotted raiders creeping towards their castle to launch a surprise attack. With its sturdy men-at-arms now awake and ready to repel the attackers, the castle was no longer a soft target. The raiders — having lost the essential element of surprise — wisely decided to withdraw. Once again the great hound had saved Marian.

The grateful Sir Hugh commissioned a statue of the giant wolfhound, which stood for years on the castle roof: the legend arose that as long as it watched over them from there, no harm would befall the castle or its residents. Centuries later, in 1922, the statue was removed to be cleaned and renovated. In its absence, the castle burnt down. The statue, however, survives, and can be seen in the grounds of Antrim Forum.

During the tragic fire of 1922, a young servant girl was trapped by the flames. On seeing her at a high window, screaming for help, a gallant rescuer risked his own life to save her. He got her out alive, but she died later of her burns and massive smoke inhalation. Her ghost has been seen on many occasions gliding around in the castle and its grounds.

Some of the strangest mysteries have tantalizingly scant records attached to them, yet they are the ones that most repay close inspection and diligent pursuit. Such is the case with the legend of McMahon Castle in County Clare. Legend has it that inside the derelict shell of what was once the castle is a sealed room containing a horror so indescribably sinister that no one has dared enter the chamber since the 1920s. It is related that an exorcist went into the sealed room to challenge the nameless horror that lurked there. According to the traditional version, he died of shock during the night, and his body was discovered next day with a look of indelible terror frozen across the dead face. Since then, no one has dared venture into the Room of Horror. (No one in authority connected with the ruined castle and its mysterious sealed room has yet invited co-author Lionel to conduct an exorcism there. He'd accept the challenge like a shot, if invited!)

Skyrne Castle in County Meath stands between Gnoc Ghuil (the hill of tears and sorrow) and the ancient Hill of Tara. Many battles were fought across this region, and consequently great numbers of skeletons have been found in the district. The castle dates back to the 1100s when it was erected on the orders of Adam de Feipo, a Norman knight. Over the centuries, the castle has acquired its full contingent of ghosts, including the shrieking wraith of poor Lilith Palmerston, who was raped and murdered there by Phelim Sellers; a solitary cloaked figure who takes his equally spectral hound for long walks in the dark; and a wandering nun who resembles the nun in the sightings reported from Borley Rectory in Suffolk.

Leap Castle is situated in County Offaly, near the site of an ancient Celtic hill-fort at Aghancon. The district has been inhabited for many thousands of years. The later Leap Castle is remembered most for the mysterious death of an O'Carroll priest at the hands of his own brother. Rivalry for who should become the head of the family erupted upon the death of the O'Carroll chieftain in 1532. The priest was celebrating Mass when his brother burst into the family chapel and ran him through with his sword. The fatally wounded priest slumped, dying, over the altar.

Leap also contained an oubliette in which the remains of hundreds of human skeletons were found. This dismal dungeon lay below a small room with a drop-floor. Those who were destined for death in the oubliette were ushered into this little waiting room, and the mechanism was operated. There were sharp spikes in the floor below, but those who didn't actually land on their points died slowly of thirst and starvation surrounded by the rotting corpses of the dead and the feeble moans of the dying. When a party of workmen was engaged in cleaning and refurbishing the area over a century ago, they found enough bones in the gruesome oubliette to fill three carts. Significantly, they also discovered a watch that had been made as recently as 1840. That raised the grim question of whether the oubliette murder chamber had been used as recently as Victorian times.

In 1909 Mildred Darby wrote of her experiences at Leap in a journal dealing with the paranormal; she said that she had been physically touched by a *thing*, part-human and part-ovine, which gave off an appalling stench of decay and corruption — like the odour of a decomposing corpse. It placed a hand on her shoulder — an unforgettable experience for her.

So horrible were the many ghost stories and reported sightings associated with Leap that knowledgeable local people gave it a wide berth at night. Many reported, however, that strange lights were seen in the upper windows long after the castle had been gutted by fire in the 1920s and more or less abandoned.

Courageous new owners have been restoring Leap for the last fifteen years or so, despite occasional attention from whatever haunts the tragedy-steeped old building.

Slane is mysterious and intriguing both for its castle and its very ancient monastery. The enigmatic mound on the Hill of Slane might simply have been a Norman motte on which a wooden bailey could have stood in the twelfth century, but it is more likely to have been constructed originally as the burial mound for Sláine, King of the Fir Bolg, on which the Norman castle was a later addition.

The monastery is far older than the Norman castle built by Richard Fleming in the twelfth century and is deeply involved with the Rennes-le-Château mystery. According to Mézeray's *Histoire de France*, compiled in 1685, King Dagobert II (who is central to the saga of Bérenger Saunière's treasure) was sent as an infant to the good monks of Slane, who cared for the boy and saw to it that he was educated to the level where he would be able to take up his kingship in south-western France in due course. While in Ireland, young Prince Dagobert met and married a beautiful Celtic, or Saxon, princess named Mechtilde. History is very blurred about the events after Dagobert II's own death, but it seems highly probable that the strong and spirited Mechtilde escaped with their infant son after Dagobert was murdered. If so, she might well have brought the boy back to Ireland, where she had met and married his father. Did the wise and loyal monks of Slane care for the young widow and her son as they had once cared for Dagobert II?

Just as the inspired Marquis of Bute refurbished and restored Castle Coch in Wales, so three equally inspired men rebuilt and refurbished the great castle of Slane. They were James Gandon, James Wyatt, and Francis Johnston. The work on Slane Castle began in 1785.

Elizabeth, wife of the Marquis of Slane in the early nineteenth century, was famous for being a very attractive courtesan who was the last mistress of King George IV. She was at that time referred to by jealous rivals at court as the Vice Queen. The King doted on her, and, as well as the many precious gifts of jewels and money, he gave her his walking cane, which had great sentimental value for her later on. Long after George's death, she became a familiar figure in the district, hobbling along to Slane Church leaning heavily on that very special cane. She lived to the grand old age of ninety-two, and there are even suggestions that her ghost has been seen gliding along between the castle and the church using the cane that meant so much to her in the closing years of a long, happy, and adventurous life.

If the great stones of Edinburgh Castle could speak, they would recount stories of the castle's role as a prison and an execution site — like the Tower of London — as a palace, as a treasury as secure as Fort Knox in the U.S.A., as a royal residence, and, in times of emergency, as a well-defended fortress. The castle stands on an outcrop of igneous rock some 150 metres high.

The oldest part of the castle as it stands today is the minute St. Margaret's Chapel, built for the wife of King Malcolm III of Scotland during the eleventh century. Malcolm III was the eldest son of Duncan I and was a formidable warrior king in the proud old Scots tradition. His first wife, Ingibjorg, was the widow of the ruler of Orkney, one of the noble Mors, or Sinclairs, whose later descendants befriended the Templars during the fourteenth century and were associated with the codes, symbols, and other mysteries of Roslyn Chapel, not far from Edinburgh itself. Malcolm greatly revered his second wife, Margaret, who was the great-niece of the pious King Edward the Confessor of England. Although Malcolm was an awesome warrior, he could not read. Nevertheless, he had beautiful jewelled bindings made for Margaret's holy books, and, largely out of deference to her, ordained that the court language should be changed to Saxon. Malcolm and his beloved Margaret certainly had a very close personal bond. When news of his and his eldest son's deaths in battle at Alnwick, in Northumberland, on November 13, 1093, reached Margaret in Edinburgh Castle, *she died of grief.* Her love and piety were duly recognized in 1250 when she was canonized by Pope Innocent IV. Her feast day as Saint Margaret of Scotland is celebrated on June 10.

Edinburgh Castle was coveted by both sides during the long and hard-fought wars between England and Scotland. In 1291 Edward I laid siege to it, and, strong though it was, it fell within eight days. The English held it for nearly a quarter of a century, but in 1313 the Earl of Moray stormed it in a surprise attack and reclaimed it for Scotland. Robert the Bruce (1274–1329) destroyed the castle, except for St. Margaret's Chapel, but the decimated ruins soon became an English stronghold once more.

Just as Troy and Caerphilly fell to trickery, so did Edinburgh. In 1341, William Douglas and his companions disguised themselves as traders, wedged their cartloads of goods between the gates to prevent them from closing, and captured the castle. King David II of Scotland (1324–1371), son of Robert the Bruce, had been imprisoned in England. When he regained his freedom, he returned to Scotland and established his administrative centre in Edinburgh Castle.

With all this history, it's hardly surprising that Edinburgh has a reputation at the forefront of the haunted cities of Europe, and Edinburgh Castle is the scene of many of the city's frequently reported hauntings and other paranormal phenomena. These include a phantom piper, a headless drummer, the ghosts of French captives, the spectres of American prisoners from the War of Independence, and a ghostly dog that glides around the castle and its immediate environs.

In an age of scientific investigation into the paranormal, with organizations such as ASSAP (the Association for the Scientific Study of Anomalous Phenomena, of which the authors are president and first lady), it is interesting to report on the meticulously conducted investigations that leading psychologist Dr. Richard Wiseman of Hertfordshire University carried out there. Taking very great care that none of the 240 international participants had any previous knowledge of haunted sites in and around Edinburgh Castle, Dr. Wiseman and his team of experts used all the latest high-tech scientific instruments, including digital cameras, thermal imagers, geomagnetic sensors, and temperature probes. By the time the big experiment was concluded, nearly 50 percent of the participants had reported inexplicable phenomena, such as changes in temperature, glimpses of spectral forms, and strange sensations of being observed and touched by something invisible. As an extra precaution several areas with no history of anomalous phenomena were deliberately visited — but, significantly, it was from the traditionally "haunted" sites that many of the strange phenomena were reported.

Another mystery of Edinburgh Castle is that, like Dover Castle, Pembroke, and Hastings, there are strange underground locations there. In the case of Edinburgh Castle, there are tunnels allegedly connecting the castle to the Royal Mile and Holyrood.

Holyrood itself is connected to Saint Margaret and King Malcolm III by the legend of the miracle that was said to have saved the life of their son, King David I. In 1128 David was hunting when his horse was startled by the sudden appearance of a stag, and David was thrown to the ground. He was in grave danger from the stag's antlers and reached up to grasp them. As he did so, according to the legendary account of the episode, they changed into a crucifix, and his life was saved. There are deeply religious devotees of Saint Margaret who would put forward the idea that it was David's holy mother who had been keeping watch over him and acting as his guardian angel that day in the forest. Whatever saved his life, David vowed to build a suitable abbey for holy men devoted to the cross — hence Holyrood.

Holyrood Palace is also associated with the tragic Mary, Queen of Scots, whose secretary, friend, and confidant, Rizzio, was murdered there on orders from her then husband, Lord Darnley. Does Rizzio's mournful spectre still glide through the room where he met his death?

Whether the tunnels actually get as far as Holyrood Palace is a matter of speculation, but the story of the Tunnel Piper is a persistent one. According to this tradition, when the tunnels were first discovered centuries ago, no one knew where they began or ended. A fearless highland piper volunteered to go down them and play his pipes as he walked so that those above him could follow the brave sound and trace the route that the strange tunnels took. For several hundred metres all went well, and the stirring sound of the pipes was clearly heard by those above. Then the music suddenly stopped. The fearless piper was never heard again. Dauntless volunteers raced down the tunnels to rescue him — *but he was never found.* The piper had simply vanished into the labyrinth. Although the gallant piper was never seen again in earthly form, his ghost has been reported from several different locations, including the battlements of Edinburgh Castle.

Tales of fearless musicians who vanished into mysterious tunnels are not restricted to Scotland. Fiddler's Hill is close to the village of Binham in Norfolk, the authors' home county in England. The hill was once a Bronze Age tomb, dating back about four thousand years. An associated Binham legend referred to the wraith of a mysterious black monk, who glided around near the entrance to the secret tunnel that supposedly connected Binham's Benedictine priory with the priory at Little Walsingham. The itinerant fiddler and his dog turned up in the village and offered to explore the secret tunnel on behalf of the villagers. A friendly crowd of well-wishers turned up to see them safely on their way, and, just as the piper had done in Edinburgh, the fiddler promised to play as he walked through the tunnel so that his villager friends on the surface could trace his progress. All went well, and they heard his music playing boldly as far as Fiddler's Hill. Then, like the piper's music on the way to Holyrood, the sound of the fiddle suddenly stopped. No one dared go down into the tunnel to see what had befallen the brave fiddler. Three days later his terrified and bedraggled little dog emerged alone. That night a violent storm did considerable damage — including blocking and concealing the entrance to the Binham tunnel.

Binham Priory in Norfolk, which is associated with Fiddler's Hill and the mysterious secret tunnels.

There are similar tales told in the village of Blakeney, which is no great distance from Binham. Blakeney was a major seaport in earlier centuries, and a network of secret tunnels would have benefited local smugglers. The village sign at Blakeney actually shows a fiddler and his dog, and the Blakeney version of the story says that he volunteered to explore an old tunnel, the entrance to which had been uncovered in the fourteenth-century Blakeney Guildhall. Local tradition maintains that this tunnel was over eleven kilometres long and connected with the village of Baconsthorpe.

There are records that in 1924 a workman unearthed the top of a barrel-roofed tunnel while digging on Mariners Hill in Blakeney, and as recently as February 4, 1976, there was an article in the *Eastern Daily Press* referring to tunnels being found in the precincts of the White Horse Hotel. Could the Blakeney and Binham stories be a conflation of the same episode? There is evidence that when a road-widening scheme cut into the earth in the area, two human skeletons and the skeleton of a small dog were found. Now, if there were two fiddlers, each of whom had a dog, and if one dog managed to struggle back, then two men and one dog did *not* emerge from the fatal tunnels — any more than the dauntless piper emerged from the Edinburgh labyrinth. Were the skeletons found by the road wideners in 1933 those of the Blakeney fiddler, the Binham fiddler, and one of their dogs?

Linlithgow Castle in Scotland. Near here the King ignored a warning that cost him his life.

The strangest mystery associated with Linlithgow Castle concerns the weird apparition of an old man who warned King James IV of Scotland (1473–1513) not to march south to attack the English forces led by Henry VIII — the brother-in-law to James's wife, Queen Margaret. James foolishly ignored the ghostly old man's advice and launched his army against a stronger English force. Scotland lost the battle, and forty-year-old James was killed just as the spectre had predicted. Not realizing that she was already a widow, Queen Margaret Tudor waited anxiously for his return. Shortly afterwards, however, she married the Earl of Douglas — whom James IV had always regarded as his worst enemy! A mournful female ghost has been reported more than once haunting the chamber in Linlithgow known as Queen Margaret's Bower — the room where she waited in vain for James to return. Is it the spectral Queen Margaret, still waiting for her King to return? Or is that sad female ghost really the spectre of tragic Mary, Queen of Scots, who was born in Linlithgow Castle in 1542 and beheaded in 1587?

Mary, Queen of Scots, was crowned in the chapel in Stirling Castle in 1533, and the ghost of a beautiful woman wearing a dazzling pink silk gown, suitable for just such an occasion, has frequently been reported from the castle. But is it really the unhappy Queen Mary? Another account suggests that it is the melancholy ghost of a woman searching loyally for her husband's body after he had died trying unsuccessfully to defend the castle against Edward I, who captured Stirling in 1304. Besides the beautiful Pink Lady, there is a spectral Grey Lady associated with Stirling. It is suggested that this Grey Lady is the apparition of a brave and loyal servant girl working for Mary, a maid who risked her own life saving the Queen when the curtains around Mary's bed caught fire — ignited by a misplaced candle flame, perhaps, or a fire-filled warming pan that was handled incorrectly. In any case, whoever this Grey Lady of Stirling was in life, she is associated with narrowly averted disasters — and the legends about her appearances maintain that she only visits Stirling to warn the occupants that serious trouble of some sort is on its way to the castle.

The ghost of the Green Lady is so well documented from Crathes Castle that even Queen Victoria was said to have witnessed the apparition during the nineteenth century. The magnificent castle is barely eight

Co-author Lionel researching Stirling Castle in Scotland where the ghost of Mary, Queen of Scots, has been frequently reported.

kilometres from Banchory in Aberdeenshire, and the land on which it stands has belonged to the Burnett Family since the early fourteenth century. One of the unique treasures it contains is the jewel-encrusted ivory hunting horn given to the Burnetts by Robert the Bruce in 1323.

One version of the story of the Green Lady's tragedy is that she was murdered by the evil and domineering old Countess Agnes, who had ambitious plans for her son to marry into high society — instead of marrying Bertha, whom he loved. The foul old woman poisoned the girl, and then died of shock when her victim's ghost appeared and accused her of the crime.

Another version of the Green Lady's origins is that she was a young girl in the laird's protection who became pregnant by a servant — whom the laird promptly and conveniently dismissed. The young mother and her baby disappeared, and the assumption was that she had followed her dismissed lover — until the ghost of a girl holding a baby was seen crossing the floor of the haunted room. Eventually, workmen carrying out renovations and repairs uncovered the skeletons of a young woman and a baby under the floor.

Perhaps there are *two* separate tragic ghosts in Crathes Castle: the poisoned Bertha and the murdered mother and babe.

Castle Urquhart stands proudly on the north shore of Loch Ness like some implacable stone custodian of whatever strange life forms hide in the dark waters — well over two hundred metres deep. Urquhart looks down from a strong rocky promontory that would commend itself to any medieval military architect. Master James of St. George would have loved to build here. Graves from 2000 BC or even earlier are within a stone's

Co-authors Lionel and Patricia on the bridge near Urquhart Castle.

throw of the castle at Corrimony, and those who now lie in those graves may well have fought on the same rock on which the ruins of Castle Urquhart stand today. There was probably an Iron Age fort here in ancient times, and Pictish remains have also been discovered by archaeologists. The present ruins, however, go back to the thirteenth century.

The medieval history of Urquhart starts with King Alexander II (1198–1249), who was faced with rebellion from the citizens of Moray, a fertile territory at the northeast end of Loch Ness. Their rebellion started in 1298, and it took Alexander the best part of two years to reassert his control over the district. The triumphant King put his son-in-law, Alan Durward, in charge of Urquhart, and from what records remain, it seems likely that it was Alan who built the earliest parts of Castle Urquhart during the middle years of the thirteenth century. Durward died in 1275 and was replaced by John Comyn, one of Edward I's men. John Balliol (1249–1315) was king of Scotland from 1292 to 1296 and then abdicated after a series of dispiriting military defeats. Scotland became what was euphemistically referred to as an "English Dependency" until 1306. These were turbulent times that saw the great Scots heroes Wallace and Bruce in the thick of many battles — and Urquhart Castle experienced its fair share of the action during this period.

Andrew Moray led a surprise attack on Urquhart under cover of darkness in 1297, but failed to take it. A subsequent onslaught led by Alexander Forbes was successful — and Urquhart was again in Scots hands. This phase lasted until 1303, when the indomitable Edward I of England (1239–1307) recaptured the castle, but it was destined to be a short-lived triumph for Edward Longshanks. Under his direction, Alexander Comyn of Badenoch commanded the Urquhart garrison — a force that was destroyed by all-conquering Robert the Bruce, who thereupon became king of Scotland and reigned from 1306 to 1329.

There was almost continuous action at Urquhart during the fourteenth century, when the powerful McDonalds and the Crown captured, lost, and then recaptured the castle in turn — like frenetic checkerboard players snapping up each other's pieces. When the McDonalds' power waned, Urquhart Castle was held by the Grants, who were allies of the Gordons. The McDonalds then returned with a vengeance, and the bloodshed started all over again. In the relatively peaceful seventeenth century — although it was far from quiet — the Grants more or less gave the castle to the local citizens, who used some of its vast stone resources to build their houses and barns. In 1688, when James II of England (who was also James VII of Scotland) fell from power to be replaced by his daughter, Mary, and her husband, William III of Orange, a group of James's supporters attacked Urquhart. They were soon dealt with, however, by the highly efficient Captain Grant and his three hundred dauntless highlanders. The castle was more or less abandoned in 1692, and then, in the early eighteenth century, much of it was damaged profoundly by a terrifying storm.

The great mystery adjacent to Urquhart Castle is the ancient riddle of the Loch Ness monster, and there are some researchers who would suggest that the earliest fortifications on the site were intended as a defence against the unknown denizens of the loch as well as marauding human warriors.

There are widely and persistently reported Loch Ness phenomena. A report from the year 565 records how Saint Columba, while travelling up to Inverness on a missionary journey to the Picts, rescued a man in danger on Loch Ness. The original account reports that "a strange beast rose from the water."

The geological history of Loch Ness suggests that it was at one time connected to the North Sea, and this would support the argument that members of the plesiosaur group are reasonably strong claimants for being the Loch Ness monster — if there is one at all.

To add more detail to the 565 account, it was said that Columba and his followers already knew that a local swimmer had been fatally mauled by *something* big and dangerous in the loch. (Good reason again for the existence of a fortification at Urquhart to provide safe refuge.) Despite this earlier fatal attack, one of Columba's followers had valiantly started swimming out into the loch to retrieve a drifting boat. Suddenly, a huge creature reared up out of the water and made towards the terrified swimmer. Some early accounts, which give the monster its Gaelic name, Niseag, describe it as resembling an enormous frog. This would link it with the vodyanoi of Finland.

Columba himself ran fearlessly into the water to save his companion, shouting sternly to the monster: "Go no farther! Touch not thou that man." Columba was a powerful man in mind and body, as well as a good and courageous one. Whether it was the saint's forceful voice or some paranormal power of holiness surrounding him, the monster decided that on this occasion it had met more than its match and that discretion was definitely the better part of valour: it retreated ignominiously. Could the creature even have been a thought-form like the Tibetan *tulpa*, which retreated when attacked by a powerful mind like Columba's?

Loch Ness is about thirty-five kilometres long: a spacious enough home for the largest aquatic monster. Duncan McDonald, a diver, was working there in 1880 (albeit with the rather primitive equipment then available). As he carried out his salvage operations on a wrecked ship in the loch, he claimed that he had seen the monster swimming past him. In his report he paid particular note to the monster's eyes, saying that they were small, grey, and baleful. They gave him the impression that annoying or interfering with Nessie would not be prudent.

Fifty-odd years after Duncan McDonald's encounter, George Spicer and his wife were driving along the south bank of Loch Ness when they saw a strange creature *on land* — actually emerging from the bracken beside the road. The Spicers said that it appeared to have a long, undulating neck resembling an elephant's trunk. The head was disproportionately small, but big enough for the monster to hold an animal in its mouth. As the Spicers watched, the thing lumbered down the bank and into the loch, where it vanished below the water with a loud splash. In a later interview with a journalist, George said that it had made him think of an enormous snail with a long neck and small head. The knowledge that the monster could leave the water and move around on land would have provided a further motive for building a strongly fortified refuge at Urquhart in the distant past.

During the 1930s, excitement over reports of Nessie reached fever pitch. Among hundreds of reported sightings at that time was one from an AA motorcycle patrolman. His description of the monster coincided closely with what George Spicer had reported. Hugh Gray, an engineer, actually managed to get a photograph of it — but although it was agreed by scientific experts that the picture had not been tampered with, it was not sufficiently clear and distinct for the creature to be zoologically identified.

Alexander Campbell, a journalist, described his sighting in the summer of 1934. His cottage was situated beside the loch, and, as he left home one morning, he saw the creature rear up out of the water, looking remarkably like a prehistoric monster. He confirmed the descriptions of the long, serpentine neck given by other witnesses, and added that he had seen a flat tail as well. Alexander said that where the neck and body joined there was a hump. He watched it sunbathing for some moments until the sound of a boat on the Caledonian Canal apparently unnerved it. Its sudden dive into deeper water produced a miniature tidal wave.

Saint Columba was by no means the only holy man to see the monster. Some fourteen centuries after Columba rescued the intrepid swimmer, Brother Richard Horan, a monk from St. Benedict's Abbey at Fort Augustus, also saw the creature. Richard said that it was in clear view for almost half an hour. Horan added that the head and neck were silvery grey and thrust out of the water at an angle of about forty-five degrees. Just as a boat had disturbed the monster when Alexander Campbell saw it, so Brother Horan's view of it ended when a motorboat went past. At the sound of the engine, the monster sank back into the impenetrable darkness of the loch.

The gaunt ruins of Urquhart Castle still guard the shores of Loch Ness.

There have been so many reliable and sensibly reported sightings over so many years that it is not easy to dismiss Nessie as a figment of the imagination, an optical illusion, or a shrewd publicity stunt. Was the awesome presence of a mysterious creature in Loch Ness the real motive for building Urquhart Castle?

From the mysteries of the romantic castles of Ireland and Scotland, we voyage next across to the Continent where two grimly mysterious castles relate to the classic horrors of Bram Stoker's Dracula and Mary Shelley's Frankenstein's monster: yet more connections linking castles with literature.

Konigstein Castle near Dresden. Did it once harbour an alchemical mystery?

Chapter 10
Castles of Germany and Beyond

FRANKENSTEIN CASTLE IS situated in Nieder Beerbach, which is very close to the city of Darmstadt in Germany. For many centuries Darmstadt was home to the royal family of Hesse Darmstadt, and a thirty-metre-high statue of Ludwig X of that famous dynasty still stands in the city. The area is also famous for quarrying high-quality stone, and the name *Frankenstein* originally meant "the stone of the Franks."

Castle Frankenstein dates from 1252 — possibly earlier — and was owned by the von Frankenstein family until the middle of the seventeenth century. It served as a combination of military prison and military hospital until the mid eighteenth century, when it was more or less abandoned.

Just as Arthur's Knights of the Round Table went adventuring and rescuing those in need, so the equally noble and courageous knights of von Frankenstein rode out chivalrously to help people in distress. One of the knights — most appropriately named George — set out to save a beautiful maiden (known as "Rose of the Valley") from the clutches of a dragon. After a colossal struggle, the valiant George slew the beast and saved the girl, but the spikes in its immensely powerful tail had pierced his armour during the fight and inflicted fatal wounds. He lived only long enough to see Rose of the Valley freed and restored to the loving arms of her grateful family.

Mary Wollstonecraft Shelley immortalized the castle in her novel *Frankenstein, or the Modern Prometheus* (1818). She was born in Somers Town, London, an area south of

Camden Town, close to the British Library and the present King's Cross and St. Pancras stations. Her mother died eleven days after the future author was born, and from the age of three, Mary was raised by her stepmother, Mary Jane Clairmont. Their relationship tended to be less than harmonious, and her daughter, Jane Claire Clairmont, became involved with Mary and Percy Shelley in a ménage à trois. Through Jane Claire and her mother, however, Mary Shelley heard about Castle Frankenstein and its most famous eccentric inhabitant: Johann Conrad Dippel. Mary visited Castle Frankenstein in 1816 and wrote her immortal classic a few months later.

Some of the stories about Dippel seem to be highly exaggerated, but in essence he appears to have been an eccentric proto-scientist and mystic whose lifespan crossed over from the late seventeenth century to the early part of the eighteenth. Records of births and deaths tended to be less than reliable then, but there are legends that by using the weird potions and electrical therapies that he allegedly pioneered, Dippel was able to extend his lifespan to almost 150 years. His name in these legends is also associated with building human beings from parts of corpses, and — in the wildest of the stories — actually bringing them to life. These Dippel legends seem to have been the foundation on which Mary Shelley built the character of Victor Frankenstein, the man who created the monster.

Sharing pride of place with Frankenstein, Dracula heads the list of best-known fictional horror characters. Just as the legends surrounding the historical Dippel provided a basis for Mary Shelley's novel, so the real-life Vlad III, also called Vlad Dracula, Vlad Tepes, and Vlad the Impaler, a fifteenth-century prince of Wallachia, provided the basis for Bram Stoker's best-known work. Castles are associated with Vlad just as they are with Frankenstein, so once again the literary link exists. There were actually three castles associated with Vlad the Impaler: Poenari, Arges, and Bran. Stoker placed his castle in the sinister Borgo Pass. The best candidate for Castle Dracula is Arges Castle. The walls were very thick, able to cope with Turkish cannon fire. There was also a secret staircase leading to a subterranean passage that saved Vlad's life on at least one occasion.

Bran Castle also claims to be associated with Vlad. It was originally built by the Teutonic Knights in the second decade of the thirteenth century, when it was known as Castle Dietrichstein. By the end of the century it was in Saxon hands, and later it was used by Vlad as a convenient springboard for his military adventures in Transylvania.

The creators of outstanding and enduring fiction — like Mary Shelley and Bram Stoker — are often the product of traumatic lives. Bram Stoker (1847–1912) was such a sickly child that he seemed unlikely to survive. For the first seven years of his life, he needed help even to get to his feet, but things changed dramatically for the better as he reached adulthood. By the time he was a student at Trinity College, he was an outstanding athlete. He read mathematics successfully and rose to be president of the Philosophical Society and the Historical Society. Yet another castle-and-literature connection was that Bram worked as a civil servant at Dublin Castle between 1870 and 1877. He wrote *Dracula* well over a century ago in 1897 — and it still sells well today.

Stoker was Oscar Wilde's rival for the love of the exquisitely beautiful Florence Balcombe, who finally chose Stoker over Wilde. They married in 1878 and moved to London, where Bram had a new job as business manager of the Lyceum Theatre. Their only son, Noel, was born in 1879.

A major influence in Stoker's life was his lasting friendship and deep devotion to his employer, the great Victorian actor Henry Irving. Bram went everywhere with Irving, overworking to an extent that probably contributed to his death. He was, in fact, so close to Irving that when the actor died suddenly in 1906, Stoker was so overcome with grief that he had a stroke. He survived his hero by only six years, dying in the same year that the *Titanic* went down.

Where did the historical parallel for Stoker's Dracula originate?

The Hungarian King Sigismund became Holy Roman Emperor in the early fifteenth century and founded a secret society known as the Order of the Dragon. Their sacred symbol was a dragon hanging from a cross, and it is possible that some of his Dragon Knights were descended from those Templars who had escaped the bloody mayhem launched against their noble order by Philip le Bel in 1307. Service for the Holy Roman Emperor would certainly have appealed to them. Vlad II (father of Dracula) was admitted to the Dragon Order in 1431 as a reward for his great courage in the wars against the Turks. He was so proud of his membership that he always wore the order's emblem and had it incorporated into his Wallachian coinage.

In Romanian, *drac* means "devil" — but it can also mean "dragon" — and their definite article "the" is simply the addition of *ul* as a suffix. *Dracul*, therefore, meant "the dragon." Just as *ap*, *mac*, and *bar* mean "the son of" in Welsh, Scottish, and Hebrew respectively, so does the Romanian suffix *ulea* or *ula*. Vlad Tepes, King Vlad III of Wallachia, was Vlad Dracula — "the Son of the Dragon" — or, to his many opponents, victims, and enemies — *"the Son of the Devil."* There is a certain grim irony in the part of the legend that says a vampire can be destroyed by hammering a wooden stake through its heart: the man who gave Stoker's monster its name destroyed his agonized victims with wooden stakes. It was as if Stoker saw a kind of poetic justice there.

The background to Vlad III and his castles is a world in which what is now southern Romania was the Kingdom of Wallachia in the chronically war-torn Balkans. Just as the Kingdom of Israel had been sandwiched between the Assyrio-Babylonian powers on one side and Egypt on the other for many years, so fifteenth-century Wallachia was caught between the two great powers of Hungary and Turkey. Hungary was busily strapping itself into the armour that Byzantium had dropped and was already taking over as leader of Christendom, even before Mohammed the Conqueror knocked out Constantinople in 1453. During these crucial years, Wallachia was walking a precarious diplomatic tightrope to appease one or other of the two much greater powers on each side of it. Although hated for his loathsome cruelties, Vlad III made a reasonable success of this delicate balancing act.

Accession to the kingship of Wallachia was almost as complicated as becoming leader of a major political party in one of today's Western democracies — and marginally more hazardous: the boyars — the wealthy Wallachian nobility — elected one of the royal family as king. The $64,000 question was *who got nominated?* Vlad II and his son both unhesitatingly resorted to assassination when they deemed it necessary in order to achieve their goals. (Machiavelli would have admired them as much as he admired the Borgias.)

Sigismund of Hungary made the future Vlad II governor of Transylvania in 1431 — the same year that the future Vlad III was born. In 1436, from his convenient power base in Transylvania, Vlad senior fought and killed Alexandru I, the then king of Wallachia, so becoming Vlad II.

The political, military, and diplomatic balancing act now began to go badly wrong for Vlad II. He backed the wrong horse when the Turks attacked Transylvania — and lost to the might of the Hungarians under John Hunyadi. Vlad and his family fled from Wallachia but were restored to the kingship in 1443 with a lot of Muslim help.

Very prudently, the Sultan had about as much trust in Vlad II's loyalty as he would have had in a leaking ship that had just caught fire. Vlad now had to send young Wallachians to join the Turkish Army — and two of his sons (the future Vlad III and his brother Radu) were also sent to Turkey as hostages.

Huge trouble flared between John Hunyadi and Vlad II, when Hunyadi demanded Vlad's support at the Battle of Varna. The Turks won an overwhelming victory there, but Hunyadi escaped — and that was Vlad II's downfall. He was assassinated along with his eldest son, Mircea, who suffered an appalling death when boyars opposed to the Vlads buried him alive. Predictably, Vlad III later took his savage revenge on them.

As soon as Vlad II was killed, the Turks released Vlad III as their candidate for the throne of Wallachia. The political weathervane continued spinning from Hungarian alliances to Turkish ones, but the outcome was that Vlad III of Wallachia finally established himself by killing a rival named Vladislav II. His reign of fear lasted from 1456 until 1462. No wonder that, in those unpredictable Turko-Hungarian Balkan wars, Vlad was very glad indeed of three sturdy castles. The one by the Arges River was built with the slave labour of his prisoners, most of whom died of exhaustion during the process.

Despite his insane cruelties, Vlad had a curiously strict moral code. He would mutilate and impale any woman accused of promiscuity or adultery: one such victim was skinned alive in the main square at Tirgoviste. He was equally savage with businessmen and traders accused of cheating their customers — they too were impaled.

In 1462 the Turks attacked his castle of Arges, but Vlad escaped through secret underground passages, leaving his wife to commit suicide by leaping from the battlements rather than fall into Turkish hands. Vlad appealed to the Hungarian king for help — and was promptly arrested and imprisoned. Amazingly, knowing his history and untrustworthiness, the Hungarians changed their minds about him, and Vlad married a member of the royal family who bore him two sons.

The complications grow more convoluted still: Vlad's brother Radu was now on the throne of Wallachia and pursuing pro-Turkish policies. Maybe the Hungarians thought that Vlad would be a viable counter-candidate?

By 1476, Radu was dead, and Vlad attacked Wallachia with help from Bathory and his Transylvanian forces. They won an easy victory, and Vlad was once more king of Wallachia — but, happily, not for long. Bathory and his Transylvanians went home, leaving Vlad vulnerable to a Turkish attack — which was not long in coming. Vlad was killed in battle near Bucharest in December of 1476. The sultan had his head sent to Constantinople to be displayed there as proof that the unspeakably evil Impaler was dead. According to legend — nothing is certain concerning the disposal of the rest of Vlad's body — his mortal remains are said to lie in a tomb at Snagov, a beautiful forest and lake resort with picturesque islands. Other accounts refer to a body being examined in Snagov Monastery in 1935. It was dressed in expensive, ornate robes — but headless. Was it Vlad?

A very different mystery is attached to Konigstein Castle near Dresden, one that centres on a man who was a prisoner there in the eighteenth century. His name was Johann Frederick Böttger, and as a teenager, he started to learn as much as there was then to be learnt about the apothecary's profession and simple pharmacy. Like many other ambitious and imaginative young men of his age, Böttger became more interested in alchemy than in the pharmaceutical side of chemistry. He rolled out pills and mixed medical potions, but his heart was in making gold out of base metals and finding that other alchemical dream: the elixir of life. The apothecary to whom he was apprenticed warned him on several occasions about the dangers of alchemy.

As gold was known to be soluble in mercury, numerous alchemists over the centuries used mercury in their experiments — with predictable results as far as their health was concerned. There were also dark superstitions linking alchemy with demons and with other enigmatic evil forces. In an age when European science was very much in its infancy, many people found it all too easy to confuse primitive proto-chemistry with magic. If people suspected that an early experimental scientist was trying to devise a perpetual motion engine, create life, prolong life, resurrect the dead, or turn base metals into gold, there would be a greater than even probability that an angry mob would storm his laboratory.

There were also several notorious confidence tricksters around who were ready and willing to persuade the gullible that this or that wizard had the necessary secret formulas and techniques, and that a relatively small investment now would ensure future longevity — and an infinite supply of gold with which to enjoy it. Several such fraudulent alchemists, it was said, ended on gibbets, ironically festooned with strands of golden thread.

Unfortunately for Böttger, he dazzled some credulous friends by performing a conjuring trick that made it appear that he *had* made gold from lead.

Augustus the Strong, who forced Böttger to try to make gold in Konigstein Castle.

The story reached no less a grandee than Augustus the Strong (1670–1733), so named for his legendary sexual prowess, his abundant illegitimate offspring, and his bearlike physical strength. He was officially Augustus, King of Poland and Elector of Saxony. His unsuccessful and expensive wars against Sweden crippled the Polish economy, and the chance to make gold alchemically must have been a big temptation to Augustus. Not in a thousand years would he have fallen victim to one of the fraudulent alchemists had one of them been stupid enough to knock at Konigstein's awesome gates. But the Böttger story was altogether different. This was no cheap trickster trying to sell his non-existent secrets. According to what Augustus had heard, the man could actually *do* it. With his avaricious brain in overdrive, Augustus had Böttger apprehended and brought up to the dungeons at Konigstein. It would never do, thought Augustus, for one of Saxony's many jealous enemies to get hold of this amazing young alchemist and spirit him away to some foreign shore to make gold for them. His constant wars had taught Augustus all too plainly that money bought mercenaries, and the more mercenaries and up-to-date weapons a man could buy, the greater were his chances of victory and territorial conquest.

The nineteen-year-old would-be alchemist heard Augustus's unequivocal ultimatum with abject terror: "Make gold for me here and now in Konigstein — or die."

The incarcerated Johann Frederick Böttger was given a laboratory within his prison quarters, the best scientific equipment that was available at the time, servants to help him as and when he said that he required help — and more than enough motivation. Augustus had a sinister way of saying "You disappoint me" that would have turned a stronger heart than Böttger's into flaccid jelly.

Powerful and ursine man that he was, Augustus had a great love of delicate and beautiful things: he loved pottery work and delicate Chinese porcelain. He and Böttger came to another arrangement: if the young alchemist couldn't make gold, could he make porcelain instead? The exact ingredients and the processing were closely guarded oriental secrets. Böttger knew that if he could once rediscover them, his life was saved. It took years, but at last he succeeded: the porcelain he finally produced was even better than the most beautiful material that could be imported from China.

At the age of only thirty-seven, the hapless alchemist died. He had written over the door of his laboratory: "God created a potter out of a gold maker."

The beautiful, scenic, wooded area known as Taunus stretches eighty kilometres from Hesse through the Rhineland-Palatinate, and includes

Konigstein Castle. It is here in Taunus that the strange mystery of the Siren Lorelei is to be found. According to Homer, the wily Odysseus ordered his crew to block their own ears, and then tie him to the mast as they sailed past the Greek sirens, so that Odysseus could hear the indescribable beauty of their magical songs without succumbing to them. The Siren Lorelei is associated with the Lorelei rock (German spelling *Loreley*) on the banks of the River Rhine near Sankt Goarshausen. Various versions of the tragic legend of Lorelei suggest that she was a heartbroken, abandoned girl who flung herself into the Rhine after her lover had seduced and then deserted her. One aspect of the mystery of the Lorelei Rock is that it has a peculiar echo, which might have contributed to the myth of a super-natural singer luring sailors to their deaths.

One tower of sinister Wewelsburg Castle, where witches were tortured in the seventeenth century and Nazis planned to rule the world in the twentieth century.

Wewelsburg Castle was built in the early seventeenth century as a residence for the bishops of Paderborn, who took an unhealthy delight in arresting innocent women on charges of witchcraft and torturing them in the castle dungeons here, as already outlined in Chapter Two. When immeasurable pain finally wrung a confession of witchcraft from the innocent victims, they were executed.

When Heinrich Himmler, one of the prominent Nazi leaders (who had been a chicken farmer before Hitler raised him to power), was in charge of Wewelsburg, he used slave labour to reconstruct the castle in a weird, symbolic style. There were traces of these designs almost everywhere in the castle. Thousands of the slave labourers died as a direct result of Nazi cruelty and inhumanity.

The Nazis looted and stole from those they considered their enemies, and filled Wewelsburg with a collection of priceless medieval treasures and antiques. When the Americans liberated it at the end of the war, one British officer who had accompanied them reported finding rare paintings, carpets, Gobelin tapestries of the kind that had once delighted Louis XIV, the Sun King, and what looked like the contents of a looted museum.

When co-author Lionel was filming there, both he and the TV crew felt that there was a subtly negative atmosphere in the castle — as though the cumulative sufferings of the falsely accused witches and the desperately deprived and dying slave labourers had somehow soaked its way indelibly into the fabric of Wewelsburg.

Colditz Castle, a high-security prison from which escape was almost impossible — yet several daring escapes did take place.

Although there was no escape from Wewelsburg, there were certainly some famous escapes from Colditz, which, like Konigstein, had once been the property of Augustus the Strong.

Colditz Castle was originally built in 1014, but by the fifteenth century it had become a popular hunting lodge used by the rulers of Saxony, technically known as Electors because they had the privilege of voting for the Holy Roman Emperor — rather as cardinals have the privilege of voting for the pope. In the last decade of the seventeenth century, Augustus the Strong expanded and developed the former hunting lodge until it had an estimated seven hundred rooms. One of the stories associated with Augustus's sexual prowess was that he had sired an illegitimate child for every day of the year, and that he was now expanding Colditz so that each of them could have his, or her, own bedroom. The rooms in excess of 365 were an indication of his future plans in that area.

Things changed dramatically for Saxony over the following century, and Colditz Castle became a last refuge for the poor and destitute. In the early nineteenth century it was used as a mental hospital until the First World War, when it was adapted to incarcerate prisoners of war.

The rise of Hitler and the Nazis in the 1930s gave Colditz another change of use. They used it as a brutal labour camp for political prisoners and others whom their perverted social philosophy regarded as "undesirables."

It was rumoured that the amazingly fertile Augustus the Strong could have filled Colditz's seven hundred rooms with his illegitimate offspring.

When the Second World War began, Colditz Castle was transformed into a *sonderlager,* a very special prison indeed. It was numbered *Oflag IV C* and became the highest of high-security prisons for captured American, British, French, and Polish officers who had already escaped at least once from almost everywhere else.

The escape plans that were hatched by the ingenious Second World War prisoners in Colditz were many and varied. An officer of the French Chasseur Alpin regiment asked his wife to smuggle various items of women's clothing into Colditz. He also acquired a long blonde wig. With practice, he could evade the German sentries' eyes for a few seconds in the exercise yard and transform himself into the guise of a tall, attractive woman. This was working well until "she" attracted too much admiring attention from the prisoners who didn't realize that it was their colleague, French Lieutenant Boulay. "She" was duly caught, inspected carefully, and put back inside the prison.

Co-author Lionel in the cell once occupied by heroic Major Pat Reid in Colditz Castle.

Other great escapers included British war hero Airey Middleton Sheffield Neave (1916–1979). His first escape attempt from Colditz in August 1941 failed when the security forces realized that his German uniform was not a real one. His second attempt succeeded in January 1942, and he made it all the way home to Britain. Airey Neave was the first British officer to succeed in getting all the way back from Colditz, and he later worked for British Intelligence.

Another outstanding hero was Major Pat Reid (1910–1990), who escaped in October 1942, after being leader of the escape committee in Colditz. While filming in Colditz Castle, co-author Lionel was able to visit the cell where Pat Reid had been held and to try wriggling through one of the tiny escape tunnels the Colditz heroes had used. As a two-hundred-pound weight trainer with a forty-eight-inch chest, he didn't get very far into the tunnel!

From the gruesome horrors of Frankenstein and Dracula and the "alchemy" at Konigstein to the amazing courage and ingenuity of Pat Reid and Airey Neave, the fascinating castles of Germany have amazing stories to tell, but we move on now to other European castles with equally strange histories.

The magnificent Aljaferia in Saragossa.

Chapter 11
Castles of Portugal and Spain

THERE ARE TWO mysteries close to the ruins at Cabo
Espichel, near the Portuguese city of Sesimbra, less than
thirty kilometres south of the history-soaked castles in the
Lisbon area of Portugal. The first concerns ancient
dinosaur tracks from millions of years ago, long before any
human foot marked the soft earth there. Where did those
vast saurian creatures go? The Cabo Espichel tracks clearly
indicate that they were little short of a herd. Were some of
the dinosaurs social animals? What disaster — biological,
evolutionary, or cataclysmic — perhaps a huge asteroid
colliding with the Earth — led to their extinction?

The second concerns the good monks of Cabo
Espichel, who constructed and manned a lighthouse there
in the fifteenth century. Using medieval flaming torches,
the only lights available to them at the time, these heroic
and pious men climbed to the top of their lighthouse in all
weather — particularly when storms and high winds
increased the danger to shipping. It has been said that the
spirits of these deeply spiritual but intensely practical men
still stand guard over the area — and perhaps they do.

When co-author Lionel was filming at Cabo Espichel,
one scene required him to ride a big Harley Davidson Deuce
around the ruins. To make the scene exciting and spectacular,
he was opening the throttle speedway style and raising
showers of dust and gravel. Even at that speed, he spotted a
large red and white notice board that appeared to carry a
hazard warning of some type, and which he passed on every

circuit. Having completed the shot to his director's satisfaction, Lionel walked across to see that the board said, "Extreme hazard — unfenced cliff edge." He looked down and saw that his 110-kilometres-per-hour circuits had taken him within a few metres of a sheer thirty-metre drop down to the jagged, sea-girt rocks below — from which the good monks of Cabo Espichel had saved the lives of countless seamen centuries before. Lionel's inclined to think that they still protect visitors to Cabo Espichel.

Saint Jorge of Lisbon.

Thirty kilometres north of Cabo Espichel stands the mysterious and historic city of Lisbon, which was once known as Olisipo. Like Rome, Lisbon is built on seven hills. St. George's Castle, known as Castelo de Sao Jorge, is an awesome fortress that dominates the city. In pre-Roman times another ancient fortification stood on this eminently defensible site, and the Romans built over that older structure when they occupied Lisbon in the third century BC. The Moors conquered it early in the eighth century and held it until 1147.

In that year, Pope Eugene III called for a Crusade, and suggested that as it was more or less en route to the Holy Land, the Crusaders might as well stop off at Lisbon and drive the Muslims out of there as well. Eugene got a surprisingly good response: a band of brave English volunteers sailed from Dartmouth; German heroes set out from Cologne; and fearless Flemings — who enjoyed a fight more than anything else, especially if the rewards looked promising — were also well to the fore. There was no shortage of inducements. Alfonso, King of Portugal, promised the spoils of war to every soldier who helped him take Lisbon. The point was also made that Lisbon was in desperate need of law and order. One contemporary chronicler described twelfth-century Lisbon as "a breeding ground for every kind of lust and impurity." As the crusading armies disembarked ready to attack the city — and especially the all-important Castle of St. Jorge — they saw a very strange sign in the sky: *the Miracle of the Clouds.*

The great Castle of St. George in Lisbon — stormed by the Crusaders in 1147.

French Crusaders observed that clouds blowing in from the north — from their own beloved France — looked as though they were fighting against the clouds hovering over Lisbon. In the twelfth century that was an omen no one could ignore — especially with a battle pending. To the watching Crusaders, the victory of the French clouds above them was a sure portent of their own victory on the ground.

They stormed into the city, but the great Castle of St. Jorge proved almost impregnable, and the heroic Moorish defenders fought as hard as the Christian attackers.

A turning point came when a party of hyper-tough British East Anglians — widely acknowledged to be among the very hardest fighting men available anywhere — built a siege tower and took everything the desperate Moorish defenders could throw at them for two days and nights as they dragged it remorselessly closer and closer to the walls of St. Jorge. When it was barely a metre away, and the Norfolk and Suffolk men were about to lower their attack-bridge and swarm over the walls to slaughter the Moors, the defenders took one look at them and prudently decided that it would be suicide not to surrender. The mighty Castle of St. Jorge had finally fallen.

Co-author Lionel (also a Norfolkman) researching the mysterious Castle of St. Jorge (St. George) in Lisbon.

Co-author Lionel examining the mysterious Lisbon griffoul associated with the Rennes-le-Château mysteries.

Some secret signs and symbols are ubiquitous. One essential key to the unsolved mystery of the priest's treasure at Rennes-le-Château near Carcassonne in southwestern France is the strange statue of the griffouls on their ancient fountain at Couiza Montazels. They turn up again in Lisbon. What can they really mean? We go into these intriguing griffoul theories in greater depth and detail in *Mysteries and Secrets of the Templars: The Story Behind the Da Vinci Code*, published by Dundurn Press in spring 2005.

King Manuel of Portugal had tried to convert the Jewish community in Portugal to Christianity: one of the many tragic, bigoted religious errors that led to so much suffering death at that time. Those Jews who consented to Manuel's ideas were suspected by the long-established, traditional Christians of being only "camouflaged" Jews and not "real" members of the church. Things reached a devastating climax in 1506, when members of both groups — "New Christians" and "Old Christians" — were attending a service at a Dominican church. One of the side chapels there, the Jesus Chapel, contained a crucifix that was reported to be radiating miraculous light. The traditional Christians took this as a special sign of divine favour, but at least one of the Jewish New Christians was more skeptical. When he questioned their miracle, the traditional Christians exploded in fury. The massacre that followed caused the deaths of about two thousand Jewish New Christians.

There were some outstanding Jewish scholars and mystics living in Lisbon at the time of the massacre, many of whom had a deep knowledge of the secrets of the Kabbalah (spellings vary). Two ancient, enigmatic books, known as *Sepher Yetzirah* (the Creation Documents) and *Zohar* (the Documents of Enlightenment), form the foundation of this secret kabbalistic wisdom. The former is attributed to the Patriarch Abraham and tells how the universe was created; the latter explains how the first five books of the Hebrew and Christian bibles are really codes and ciphers for deep and powerful magical mysteries. Taken together, the *Sepher Yetzirah* and the *Zohar* claim to provide magical means of controlling the secret powers of the universe.

Among those who died in the Lisbon massacre of 1506 — within sight of the Castle of St. Jorge — was a mysterious Jewish scholar, also named Abraham, like the Patriarch. Just as Dan Brown's world famous *Da Vinci Code* is an intriguing blend of fact and fiction, so is *The Last Kabbalist of Lisbon* by Richard Zimler. In Zimler's award-winning volume, a hero named Berekiah Zarco tries to find the killer who murdered his wise old uncle, Abraham the Kabbalist. According to Zimler's fascinating introduction, there was a *real* Berekiah Zarco, whose *real* wise old uncle Abraham was killed during the 1506 tragedies in Lisbon. What secrets died with that erudite old scholar? Was he murdered by those who wanted the amazing, *real* mystical and magical secrets in his priceless books?

The "lost" medieval kingdom of Septimania, which had once occupied part of southwestern France, had very strong Jewish components, and its scholarship and wisdom would have undoubtedly reached the Jewish academics of Lisbon during the centuries before the horrors of 1506.

There was no shortage of Jewish learning in Spain. As a typical example of this remarkable Hebrew scholarship, an archivist was looking through some fourteenth-century works stored in the lovely old cathedral of Tarazona in northern Spain, when he came across a medieval Hebrew manuscript hidden inside the cover of one of these old tomes. It turned out to be a document from a synagogue that had served Tarazona's Jewish community prior to their expulsion from Spain in 1492.

Another aspect of the secret, mystical knowledge at the heart of the Kabbalah, which was at its deepest and most mysterious among the learned Jews of Spain and the Languedoc of France, seems to have been developed in parallel with Greek mysticism as it was known and practised during the earliest centuries of the Christian era. This esoteric teaching was centred on making mysterious *journeys* by projecting the astral body through what its adepts believed to be seven Spheres of Being, or zones of enhanced astral consciousness. In the Jewish version of this deep mysticism, the expert astral traveller could make his way up to the very presence of God, who then appeared as he had done in the chariot vision seen by the ecstatic prophet Ezekiel (Ezekiel 1:26): "And above the firmament that was over their heads was the likeness of a throne, as the appearance of a sapphire stone: and upon the likeness of the throne was the likeness as the appearance of a man above upon it."

In addition to these teachings about ecstatic, mystical journeys through the Seven Astral Spheres, or the Ten Sefirot (mysterious realms or planes), the secrets of the Kabbalah, and the legends derived from them, also refer to the creation of golems. These are figures made from earth or clay and brought to life by inserting into their mouths a slip of paper, or parchment, on which was written the secret name of God. According to legend, the creature can be returned to its original form-lessness by removing the parchment. Although it was the famous Rabbi Löw of Prague who was credited with actually creating and using a golem in the sixteenth century, the Kabbalah and its associated golem legends would have been well known to the learned leading members of the Spanish Jewish communities prior to 1492.

There could be coded, symbolic references to the creation of a being out of "unperfect formlessness" — a significant aspect of the golem legends — in Psalm 139, verses 15 and 16: "My substance was not hid from thee, when I was made in secret, and curiously wrought in the lowest parts of the earth. Thine eyes did see my substance, yet being unperfect; and in thy book all my members were written, which in continuance were fashioned, when as yet there was none of them."

The golem was supposedly the obedient slave of its creator, but as with Frankenstein's creature, and with various anecdotes about the Tibetan tulpa, or thought-forms, golems tended to develop independent thoughts and wishes that were frequently negative and destructive. It then became necessary for their creators to destroy them.

Strange old Belmonte Castle in Spain, where Don Quixote charged at a windmill in Cervantes' immortal classic.

Belmonte Castle was built in the fifteenth century. It is basically hexagonal and is flanked with twin circuits of round towers. The castle — together with the many windmills that were once a feature of the local landscape — is associated with the misadventures of the hapless Don Quixote in Cervantes' immortal classic. In this way it continues the strong nexus between castles and literature, which we have encountered throughout our research; Belmonte is also associated with the outstanding Spanish poet Luis de Leon, who was actually born in the fortified village adjacent to the imposing castle. De Leon was a remarkable, mystic poet, as well as a very effective biblical scholar — which caused him to cross the path of the Inquisition more than once. He was an academic at Salamanca, where he held the chair of theology, and much preferred the old Hebrew texts to the Vulgate — an attitude that further infuriated the Inquisitors. De Leon was steeped in Hebrew mysteries and was almost certainly engrossed in kabbalistic studies of the kind associated with Berekiah Zarco of Lisbon and his mysterious murdered uncle. De Leon's interest in kabbalism would not have endeared him to the Inquisition. A genuine man of mystery, de Leon displayed his true character most clearly in his strangely beautiful, exciting, and challenging poems.

Another of Belmonte's strange mysteries, however, is to be sought in its connection with the tragic Empress Eugenie, widow of the French Emperor Napoleon III. The daughter of a Spanish aristocrat, she visited Paris when her future husband, Louis Napoleon, achieved the presidency of France's Second Republic in 1848. She married him in January 1853, when he became Emperor Napoleon III, and their son, Napoleon-Eugene-Louis Bonaparte, was born in 1856. After the Battle of Sedan in 1870, Napoleon III and his family were exiled to the U.K., and he died — a disappointed and broken man — in 1873. Barely six years later, Eugenie lost her only son. The young Prince Imperial, as he was known, had had ambitions to become a successful soldier and eventually to rule his beloved France as Emperor Napoleon IV. He longed to join the British Army and had learnt soldiering at a British military academy, but as he was not a British national, it was impossible for him to join the British Army. Nevertheless, he was able to visit South Africa — purely as an observer — during the Anglo-Zulu War of 1879. He was a member of a small party of cartographers, mapping a district that was supposedly safe from Zulus. It wasn't. The geographers were ambushed by a vastly superior Zulu force — and fled. The Prince's pommel broke, and he was unable to get away in time. Greatly to his credit — against such odds and against such doughty opponents — the Prince Imperial turned to fight. Inevitably, he was killed there, but he died as a warrior. His body was eventually brought back to England and now lies near his father's in a huge granite sarcophagus in St. Michael's Abbey in Chislehurst. Eugenie's grief was incalculable.

Understandably, the tragic empress often returned to her beloved Spain and was frequently seen at Belmonte Castle. It has been said that her tragic, grieving spectre still broods and wanders there — contemplating what might have been. Yet, despite her heartbreaking double bereavement, Eugenie remained strong in mind, body, and spirit — and lived to the grand old age of ninety-four.

Mysterious wall carvings in Belmonte Castle: a fish, a phoenix rising from the ashes, and a winged dragon. What do they all mean?

The second ruler of the illustrious Banu Houd Dynasty, Abu Jafar Ahmad, built the palatial Aljaferia fortress in Saragossa in the eleventh century. It is, in fact, named after him in the *jafer* part of its title, which is derived from Jafar. Early in the twelfth century, however, the formidable warrior king Alfonso I of Aragon conquered Saragossa, made it his capital, and used the Aljaferia as his headquarters.

The superb building is designed overall as a trapezium, a geometrical figure having four sides, only two of which are parallel — and these parallel sides have different lengths. The area of a trapezium is calculated by finding the mean of these sides and then multiplying by the vertical distance between them. In the case of the Aljaferia, the sides are very close in length, so that although it is a genuine trapezoid, it is almost square with sides of approximately eighty metres. Its four outer walls are protected by a series of circular towers. The art and architecture of the Aljaferia are among the most impressive and beautiful anywhere in the world with its multiplicity of interlaced arches and its axially symmetrical interior structures — but its sinister mystery lies below ground level.

Just as in the other Spanish cities, the Jewish community of Saragossa was cruelly persecuted and expelled during the fifteenth century, but Saragossa was cursed with a particularly foul and avaricious inquisitor by the name of Pedro de Arbues. As in the other Spanish cities, the persecutors had singled out the distrusted *conversos* — the former Jews who had become "New Christians" when compelled to do so. Pedro sniffed them out and bore down on them like some bloodhound from hell in human form. As the law stood, if a converso could be convicted his property went to the king and the inquisitors — which was quite an incentive for a man like Pedro.

Knowing how thoroughly he was hated, Pedro took precautions: he wore the medieval equivalent of a flak jacket and a steel helmet wherever he went. He also carried a short lance. Despite his spear and armour, three assassins caught up with him while he was worshipping in the cathedral. The first stabbed him through the neck, the second disabled one of his arms when he tried to fight back, and the third drove a sword through his entrails. The hated Pedro de Arbues was dead. Instead of deterring the Inquisition, however, Pedro's richly deserved assassination only made things worse for the conversos and the Inquisition's other victims.

The conspirators behind Pedro's assassination included Juan de Esperandeu, Juan de la Badia, Mateo Ram, and Tristanico Leonis. The first to be apprehended was Vidau Druango, who "confessed" following the usual torture and implicated the others. His hands were amputated and nailed to a door. He was subsequently beheaded and cut into quarters. The others were similarly tortured, mutilated, and executed.

Reports of several supernatural mysteries accompanied Pedro's death. The great bell of Villela rang of its own volition, and the dried blood on the cathedral floor became liquid again. When the conspirators tried to escape, they were stricken with paralysis at the border and were captured easily.

Just as was the case in Wewelsburg, the agony of hundreds of innocent, falsely accused victims seems to have etched its way into the stone of the Aljaferia dungeons where they suffered and died. Some of those who fell into the cruel, avaricious hands of tormentors like Arbues and, later, Torquemada, were said to have been thrown into the deepest part of a bottomless dungeon below the Aljaferia where their remains still lie.

There was certainly a strange, sad feeling percolating through this grim passageway that led down into unknown depths.

This bricked-up tunnel once led to the torture dungeons below the Aljaferia, where victims of the Inquisition often died in indescribable agony.

Co-author Lionel exploring the reputedly haunted dungeons below the Aljaferia in Saragossa.

Originally called Lusitania, what is now the historically rich treasure of ancient Merida was formerly known as Augusta Emerita. The Augusta part of its title was in honour of the Roman Emperor Augustus; the Emerita part referred to the many retired Roman legionaries who had settled there. It was after the Moorish conquest that the name changed yet again to Merida. The Roman soldiers who retired within the city's fortifications lived a life of luxury even by Roman standards. The theatre and amphitheatre are huge. The entertainment included chariot racing, naval battles in the flooded arena, bathing, and all of the other attractions that wealthy Romans enjoyed in Herculaneum, Pompeii, and Rome itself. The most intriguing mystery of Merida, however, is the strange Temple of Mithra, the Mithraeum or Casa de Mitreo, situated close to the Merida bull ring. That in itself is historically significant because important sections of the secret worship of Mithras were concerned with the ritual killing of a sacred bull.

Of all the religious mysteries of the ancient world, Mithraism is one of the strangest. In many Mithraic centres of worship, like the one in Merida, there are representations of a giant-sized human figure. Frequently, it is depicted with the head of a lion — but its anthropoid body is entwined within the coils of an unusually long snake. Various experts in Mithraism have suggested that it is meant to be the Persian Anro-Mainyus, also called Ahriman, the god of evil, tantamount to Lucifer or Satan — but rather more powerful because of the dualistic nature of some branches of those old Persian religious theories.

In traditional Islam, Judaism, and Christianity, the evil entity is greatly inferior to the infinitely powerful and absolutely benign God who created and sustains the universe. Ahriman, on the other hand, is seen as the equally matched opponent of Ahura-Mazda, also called Ormuzd, the beneficent Persian god. It was, therefore, not entirely unknown for worshippers of Mithra during Roman times to pray to Ahriman, or make sacrifices to him, believing that *placating* the evil god might help to avert disasters that he had otherwise intended. The huge, snake-entwined, lion-headed figures frequently associated with Mithraic sites were, therefore, thought to be representations of Ahriman.

There are equally interesting theories postulating that the strange figure associated with Mithraism when it was so popular among Roman soldiers was, in fact, Aion — the god of time — who was known as Zervan to the ancient Persians. According to Zarathustra, Zervan was a benign god, and a loyal servant of Ahura-Mazda. Is it, then, Aion, the time god, rather than Ahriman, whom the Mithra worshippers venerated via the lion-headed, snake-wrapped figure associated with their shrines?

Some carvings of Mithra show him carrying a huge rock on his back — like the giant Atlas carrying the Earth. Mithra also wears a star-lined cloak, and in other depictions he seems to be emerging from a cosmic egg. In other carvings he looks as if he is being born out of the rock. The bull motif is associated with the idea that Ahura-Mazda sent a sacred bull into the Cave of Mithras with instructions that it was to be slaughtered so that from its body and blood all the flora and fauna of Earth could grow. There is also an idea in Mithraism that their god could control the twelve signs of the zodiac, so that Taurus the bull, the sign of early summer, was in the power of Mithras, and hence he made young animals and new plants from the body of the bull.

There seem to have been seven distinct ranks among the worshippers: *corax*, the raven; *nymphus*, the bride; *miles*, the soldier; *leo*, the lion; *perses*, the Persian; *heliodromus*, messenger of the sun; and *pater*, the father. Of these, pater was the highest, and corax was for the new initiates.

Whatever the real mysteries of Mithraism might have been, it was the Roman legionaries who carried them all around the Empire — including the fascinating old Roman city of Merida, where traces of the Mithraeum still remain.

The mysterious Castle of Maqueda, which was once a Moorish fortress. In the district around Maqueda there were medieval reports of visions of the Virgin Mary.

What was then the imposing Moorish fortress of Maqueda featured prominently in the battles between the powerful Almohad Caliph Abu Yusuf Yacqub and the Christian kings of Castile and Leon in the late twelfth century. In medieval times the castle was incorporated into the city walls as part of the defences of the city of Maqueda. The stalwart and effective Moorish remains formed the basis of the current impressive castle, which was largely rebuilt in the fifteenth century, and then improved and extended by Don Gutiérrez de Cardenas. The castle of Maqueda is rectangular, with four strong, circular towers commanding the open ground on the slopes below it. Its walls are twelve feet thick, and its curious merlons (architectural features associated with battlements) make it rather unusual.

Castle Maqueda has looked down for centuries over an area where various scholarly works dealing with reports of mysterious apparitions of the Virgin Mary in medieval Spain have been centred. These reports have included messages about the need for penitence, together with healing miracles. Is there something special and sacred in the area surrounding Maqueda?

The Iberian Peninsula is rich in both ancient castles and intriguing mysteries. Do the shades of the good monks and their lighthouse still protect travellers who pass Cabo Espichel — by land as well as by sea? Did the awesome castle of St. Jorge of Lisbon once look down on learned, medieval kabbalists so advanced in their strange, secret arts that they could create and then destroy a golem — as their counterparts were said to have done in Prague? Why is the enigmatic griffoul carved there in Lisbon — just as he is carved near Rennes-le-Château in France? Who or *what* can that strange water creature really be? What does he symbolize? Could he be meant to represent the legendary Quinotaur who allegedly sired the race of Merovingian kings? And what of the riddles posed by the carvings inside Belmonte: the phoenix, the winged dragon, and the rest? Do the pathetic remains of some of the Inquisition's victims still moulder in the "bottomless pits" below the beautiful and stately Aljaferia? What are the real secrets behind Mithraism, and how many of them are hidden in the ancient Mithraeum in Merida?

From these strange Iberian mysteries, we proceed to the riddles surrounding the romantic old castles of France.

The ornate and beautiful Blois Castle.

Chapter 12
Mysterious French Castles

THERE ARE SEVERAL intriguing mysteries associated with Blois and Blois Castle. The rather dull and unpopular Henri II of France (1519–1559) married the brilliant, ambitious, and dangerously Machiavellian Catherine de Medici (1519–1589). In the room in Blois Castle known as her "cabinet," Catherine concealed secret potions, ointments, lotions, and other strange products of the herbalist and apothecary arts. Her detractors said that these were poisons of various kinds, and that she used them to dispose of her opponents. Some, at least, were probably harmless cosmetics with which Catherine retained her youthful looks despite the passing years. Whatever they really were, Catherine concealed them very carefully behind the wall panels in her "cabinet" — and there were almost 240 such panels.

In an age when superstition and an obsession with foretelling the future were widespread, Catherine called on the services of Nostradamus. In response to her request for a prophecy, he foretold that her husband Henri II would die on the field of honour, that she would mourn him for seven years, and then live on into old age and govern her kingdom well.

One of Nostradamus's famous quatrains also seemed to refer to the death of the King:

> *Le Lion jeune le vieux surmontera,*
> *En champ bellique par singulier duelle*

Dans cage d'or les yeaux lui crevera
Deux classes une, puis mouris, mort cruelle.

This rather unusual early French translates broadly to:

The young lion will overcome the old one,
In single combat, on a military field,
Inside a golden cage his eyes will be pierced,
Two wounds shall result from one blow, and afterwards he
will die a painful death.

The events of June 28, 1559, bore a remarkable similarity to this prophecy. Henri, then aged forty, insisted that Montgomery, a young Scot who was captain of the king's guard, should enter the lists against him. The day was almost over, and the light was fading. Montgomery was very reluctant to take part, in case he accidentally injured the King. At their third clash, Montgomery's worst fears were realized: his lance splintered. Part of it penetrated Henri's golden visor and destroyed the King's eyes; another fragment went into his throat. He died of his wounds ten days later. Catherine went into seven years of official mourning and never remarried. She served as regent of France from 1560 until 1563.

Blois also seems to have strange connections with the highly controversial Priory of Sion, which features prominently in the Rennes-le-Château mystery; it was visited by the enigmatic Francis Bacon when he was in France with Sir Amias Paulet in 1577, and it is also associated with the amazing nineteenth-century stage magician and pioneering electrical scientist Robert-Houdin.

The Priory of Sion connection concerns that segment of the Rennes treasure mystery that investigates the theory that the priory is a genuinely ancient secret organization, and that it was inextricably intertwined with the Knights Templar in the eleventh, twelfth, and thirteenth centuries. If that hypothesis has any basis in fact — and the most that experienced Rennes investigators can say is "not proven" — then rumour and legend point to Blois as a secret meeting place for members of the priory.

Some supporters of the various Priory of Sion theories maintain that there was a link between the priory and the dashing, charismatic Duc de Guise. He *might* have been one of its grand masters, although his name doesn't appear on the usual lists. He was, however, closely associated with Louis, Duke of Nevers, who *is* listed as a grand master of the priory.

In essence, this Blois-and-priory mystery was connected to the French religious wars of the late sixteenth century. The Duc d'Anjou died in 1584, and that made Henri of Navarre the heir presumptive to the French throne. This raised religious fears of a Protestant king, and Pope Sixtus V excommunicated both Navarre and his cousin as heretics.

The Duc de Guise claimed that he could trace his ancestry back to no less a major historical figure than Charlemagne — and perhaps he could — but there were very imaginative genealogists around in those days who would, for a price, trace any wealthy man's ancestry back to Pharaoh Rameses, Romulus, Julius Caesar, or Noah. Whatever his distant antecedents, the Duc de Guise could genuinely claim a heroic father and grandfather, and he himself was more than capable on the battlefield. Accordingly, he became head of the Catholic League and fought successfully against Navarre and his imported mercenaries.

The Catholic League's successes in Paris led to the Duc coming within a hair's breadth of taking the French throne, but what King Henri III lacked in military skill he made up for with Machiavellian guile. The league had insisted on a major meeting of the Estates General in Blois, which the triumphant Duc de Guise naturally attended.

It was becoming obvious that King Henri might be asked to abdicate in favour of de Guise, and on Christmas Eve, 1588, the Duc accepted Henri's invitation to meet with him to discuss things in the King's private apartments at Blois. The honest and unsuspecting Duc went there alone. Henri had forty or fifty men at arms waiting for his guest. De Guise put up a remarkably good fight, but the odds were impossible. As though performing some strange ritual of political exorcism, Henri had him cut to pieces, burnt, and finally scattered to the four winds.

The league's response to the treacherous King Henri was swift and effective. Their anti-royalist propaganda roused the people against Henri, and it was declared that regicide was morally acceptable considering what manner of man the King was. In the event, a fanatical monk named

Jacques Clément actually did the deed with a knife. Was Jacques secretly a priory member avenging one of his beloved leaders, the murdered Duc de Guise?

Francis Bacon's link with the Blois mystery is also tied in with the riddle of the Priory of Sion and its mysterious grand masters. Bacon lived from 1561 until 1626, which makes him a contemporary of the mysterious Elizabethan magician Dr. John Dee (1527–1608). Dee may, or may not, have been formally listed as a master of the priory, but Robert Fludd, his successor as a "royal magician" certainly was. Born in 1574, Fludd was also a contemporary of Bacon — and tutor to another, younger Duc de Guise.

Although Francis was officially said to be the son of Sir Nicholas and Lady Anne Bacon, there was a rumour — based on the notorious Biliteral Cipher found by Mrs. Gallup among Bacon's writings — that he was actually the son of Queen Elizabeth herself. As well as hinting at Francis Bacon's royal parentage, the mysterious Biliteral Cipher also suggests that he was the real author of the plays attributed to Shakespeare.

There were two possibilities concerning the mystery of his suspected natural father: the prime suspect was Lord Robert Dudley, Earl of Leicester, who was also suspected of murdering his wife, Amy Robsart. The other, more romantic theory, names the dashing young Sir Francis Drake, who was born around 1540. That would have made him twenty and Elizabeth twenty-seven when Francis Bacon was conceived. Lady Bacon was at that time Elizabeth's chief lady-in-waiting, and the suggestion is that she and Sir Nicholas offered to take the baby secretly, pretend it was Anne's, and rear him as their own. Whatever his true parentage, Francis Bacon grew up to be highly intelligent, resourceful, and secretive. His visit to Blois with Sir Amias Paulet in 1577 was a significant event in his life — especially if it was his introduction to the mysterious Priory of Sion, who were thought to meet regularly at Blois.

The Biliteral Cipher raises significant questions about Bacon, but there are also curious watermark codes with their occasional use of castle symbols. These odd watermarks appear in various documents, books, letters, and other works by Amias Paulet, Bacon himself, Philip Sidney (1554–1586), and their contemporaries — and Philip Sidney was also an associate of the mysterious Dr. John Dee. Another curious link with the

Rennes mystery and the Priory of Sion was the recurrence of the symbol of the Arcadian shepherds in the Rennes enigma — and one of Sidney's best-known works was a long pastoral romance entitled *Arcadia*.

Some of the strange symbols used on watermark codes, including those on documents issued by Amias Paulet, who visited Blois with Francis Bacon in 1577.

Another mystery of Blois features the remarkable Jean-Eugene Robert-Houdin. He was not only a highly skilled conjuror and prestidigitation artist but also an outstanding engineer, technician, and craftsman. He toured many high-class theatres and other expensive venues throughout the 1840s and 1850s, whereas most of his conjuror predecessors had performed at fairs and street markets.

Combining pioneering electrical science with his illusionist's abilities, one of Robert-Houdin's most effective tricks was the little wooden box that could not be lifted. He was one of the first to understand how an electromagnet could assist a conjuror, and the innocent-looking little wooden box had a steel plate concealed between the wooden panels of its base. He would either lift it himself or invite a member of the audience to do so. Then he would perform various mystical hand movements and say that the box was now massively heavy and impossible to lift. His concealed assistant then switched on the powerful electromagnet hidden under the stage, just below the box. Needless to say, the box wouldn't budge. At the end of the volunteer's most strenuous efforts, Robert-Houdin made other passes and gestures at the box and announced that it was now of normal weight again. His hidden assistant switched off the power, and the box came up as easily as ever.

Outside of his stage entertainments, Houdin was sent to Algeria by the French government. At the time, various Algerian showmen were eating broken glass and apparently healing wounds magically. They were then persuading Algerian nationalists to rise up against the occupying French military forces. Houdin used his electromagnet trick, claiming that his enchantment could make a strong Algerian so weak that he couldn't lift a simple wooden box. The wily Blois conjuror then rigged not only his faithful electromagnet but also a handle that would give the lifter an electric shock. The powerful Algerian was so surprised by the current — and the weight of the magnetized box — that he ran from the stage.

But Robert-Houdin's greatest claim to fame is the range of ingenious automata that he created. Some of these robot-like figures could write, others could play musical instruments, and one swung on a trapeze like a circus acrobat. Houdin's legacy of high-performance automata can still be seen in Blois today. Realistic "monsters" — that can perform much as his nineteenth-century automata did — can still be seen moving impressively in the windows of Blois.

Mysterious moving mechanical monsters in the windows of Blois.

Chinon Castle stands on a great spur of rock that dominates the Vienne Valley. Thibault le Tricheur, Count of Blois, built the first Chinon fortress in the tenth century. Henry II of England, the Plantagenet King, built the Plantagenet Empire, which included Anjou, Normandy, Aquitaine, and England, and made Chinon its headquarters when he moved there in the eleventh century and strengthened the fortifications. He died there in 1189, as did his Crusader son, Richard the Lionheart, in 1199.

Chinon Castle, where Joan of Arc met Charles VII.

The strange interior of Chinon Castle, associated with the mystery of Joan of Arc.

As though that was not enough to ensure Chinon's place in history, it was at Chinon in 1429 that Joan of Arc immediately identified Charles VII of France despite his disguise. Her meteoric rise to fame and glory, and her cruel betrayal and subsequent descent into tragic martyrdom, are unique in military annals. One of the greatest mysteries attached to Joan was her refusal of the sword that Charles VII offered her for the battle. As is well known, Joan was led by enigmatic "voices," and on this occasion they apparently told her that she was to retrieve an ancient blade concealed behind the altar of Saint Catherine of Fierbois. A successful search was made, and the mysterious old sword was recovered.

After Joan's betrayal and imprisonment, the despicable ingratitude of those she had helped and the treacherous malice of her captors ended with her execution at the end of May in 1431. She was just nineteen years old when she died in the flames — *or did she?*

In 1436, a mysterious armoured figure was reported from the little town of Metz. An unknown knight was performing feats of skill, riding backwards and forwards at great speed and plucking wooden stakes out of the ground as expertly as a Cossack chieftain. Joan of Arc's brothers,

Jehan and Pierre, had heard strange rumours that someone was claiming to be their dead sister. They had come grimly, intending to challenge this sacrilegious impostor to a fight to the death to preserve Joan's honour. They approached the armoured rider, whose visor was down, and whose shield and armour showed no identification. Jehan asked, "Who are you?" The visor was raised. Pierre and his Jehan saw the face of their beloved sister, whom they thought had been martyred five years previously.

It was not only at Metz that Jeanne la Pucelle, as Joan of Arc was known to so many of her adoring followers, appeared. She visited Arlon in Luxembourg and was warmly welcomed by Elizabeth de Gorlitz, the ruler of the duchy. There is also an interesting record among the accounts of Orleans for August 9, 1436, giving details of payments made to a courier *who had brought letters from Joan.*

Even more surprisingly, it was later recorded that Joan met and married Robert des Armoises, thus becoming Dame Jeanne des Armoises. Following their wedding, another intriguing accountancy record appeared. On July 18, 1439, a wine merchant named Jaquet Leprestre was paid for wine supplied to Dame Jeanne des Armoises and her attendants. It seems that this same wine merchant had supplied Joan of Arc with wine in 1429: just a coincidence, or had she deliberately gone back to the same merchant who was able to supply a particular variety of wine that she enjoyed and that was significant for her?

In 1457 there are records that she was seen again in Anjou — but those are the last that have been traced. Was it really Joan? If so, what became of her after that?

Clearly and rationally, if the girl who turned up in Metz giving a brilliant display of military riding was really Joan of Arc, then someone else was burnt at the stake at the end of May in 1431. The real Joan would never have allowed a brave substitute to die in her place, but there is another possibility: the substitute was already dead. Joan was a charismatic inspiration to many of her devoted followers. They would have done anything for her. Physically overpowering or heavily bribing the guards would not have been impossible for them. In the fifteenth century, death visited too many people too soon. It would not have been difficult for Joan's rescuers to obtain the body of a young pauper girl who had succumbed to illness or malnutrition. It was also within the bounds of probability that a young female prisoner in an adjacent cell might have died from torture or the guards' brutality and abuse. This body is substituted for Joan, who then leaves the prison using the dead girl's identity. The corpse is half-dragged, half-carried to the stake and secured there, as if the guards were bringing out an unconscious prisoner.

Another rescue theory arises from one of the alleged "saintly remains" of St. Joan. During the second half of the nineteenth century it was reported that some relics of the Pucelle had been discovered in a glass phial that had been stored along with a range of old medicines, perhaps in a museum, a private collection, or a disused apothecary's storeroom. Inside this phial there were bones and fragments of cloth, along with a label saying that they had been found among the ashes below the execution fire in the old Market Square of Rouen. Careful analysis in the nineteenth century revealed that one of the bones in the phial was human, although two of them were from animals. Is it remotely possible that it was an animal carcass clothed to look like a human being that was chained to the stake and burnt? It might have been easier for Joan's rescuers to obtain the head of some decapitated female criminal and fasten that to a dead animal rather than to obtain an entire human corpse.

Other reports suggest that Joan spoke *at the stake*, indicating that she may have been rescued from the flames rather than the prison cell. Did a rescuer use apothecary's fire powder to free Joan under the cover of smoke and substitute the corpse?

Once the cruel treachery and malicious betrayal of their beloved Pucelle had brought the people of France unequivocally to her side, it would have been relatively safe for her to reappear, to let her brothers know that she was alive and well, to marry Robert des Armoises and settle down to years of the normal, happy, loving family life that she so richly deserved.

Another strange mystery connected with Chinon Castle is that the last grand master of the Templars, heroic Jacques de Molay, was questioned there prior to his execution. Like St. Joan, the gallant de Molay was burnt alive by his evil enemies. Indomitable warrior that he was, however, Jacques roundly cursed both the odious Philip le Bel and the feeble, indecisive Pope Clement V, who had served the malicious French King rather than the God of truth and justice. From the flames, de Molay said that they would both have to answer to God before a year had passed. It is a matter of historical record that King and Pope both died within twelve months of de Molay's curse. The Grand Master's formidable words were also thought to have affected the whole of the remainder of Philip IV's Capetian dynasty — known as the Accursed Kings — *Les Rois Maudits*. All three of his sons died between 1314 and 1328.

Castle Gaillard, built by Richard the Lionheart in 1197 to defend his territory in northern France.

Château Gaillard stands proud and high on a rocky outcrop above the River Seine. Built by Richard the Lionheart — an expert at attacking castles — it was a superb defensive structure, as close to invulnerable as any castle could be in the twelfth and thirteenth centuries. Gaillard offered so much apparently impregnable protection that the medieval town of Les Andelys grew up in its shadow. When Richard died in 1199 there were the usual plots and counter-plots regarding the succession, which ended in Richard's youngest brother, John, taking the throne, although the French had tried to crown Richard's teenaged nephew, Arthur. That unfortunate young man vanished in Rouen castle as grimly and effectively as the two young princes were later to vanish in the Tower of London.

The French King Philip II (1165–1223) decided to attack the formidable Gaillard. Had John been even half the man that Richard the Lionheart had been, Philip would have had no chance at all, but John did little or nothing to assist the garrison at Gaillard, under the command of Roger de Lacy.

The mystery of how Gaillard finally succumbed began with an ingenious French hero, who may well merit the title of the world's first frogman. The problem for Philip's army at that juncture was the fast, broad stream of the River Seine. Then one gallant Frenchman, a fearless warrior and a powerful swimmer, broke the deadlock. This pioneer of underwater attack put white-hot coal into earthenware pitchers and sealed them with tar. Then he swam with them to the bank where Gaillard stood so defiantly — and emptied out his glowing coal where it would do most damage. His daring ruse worked: Les Andelys began to blaze. The townspeople fled to the castle for protection. King Philip took the town and surrounded Gaillard.

Roger de Lacy checked his food supplies, retained every able-bodied fighting man, and then drove the rest of the townspeople out of the castle to conserve what food was left. King Philip promptly drove them back — but de Lacy had locked the gates against them. Caught in the no man's land between the French attackers and the English defenders, the appalling situation of the refugees was desperate. Contemporary accounts said that the starving victims in no man's land ate rats, cats, birds, dogs — and even resorted to cannibalism, so terrible was their hunger.

When Gaillard finally fell, there were scarcely one hundred men left alive out of more than one thousand who had once manned it. Realizing how powerful its position and defences had been, Philip took Gaillard over and rebuilt the castle for himself.

The fortifications at Carcassonne date back to Roman times, perhaps much earlier. It was here that the Celtic Tectosages, literally "the wise builders," once lived — those same Tectosages who had their ingenious hands in the mystery of Rennes-le-Château. The Roman fortifications at Carcassonne seem to have followed the defensive works laid down by the Tectosages. The Visigoths were present in the fifth and sixth centuries, and they were followed by Arabian rulers who held the town for some forty years during the eighth century. There were also

Merovingian and Carolingian influences in the vicinity, and the Trencavel family was prominent in the thirteenth century.

The historic fortifications of Carcassonne that once gave refuge to the persecuted Cathars.

This was a time of terrible, mindless, religious persecution, especially of the Cathars — also known as Albigensians. Their theological and philosophical origins can be traced back via the Bogomils and Paulicians — so-called heretical movements that taught Gnostic dualism — and were accordingly unpopular with the established Orthodox and Catholic churches. The Cathars in turn were in contact with the Templars of the Carcassonne area and were protected by Raymond-Roger Trencavel, ruler of Carcassonne, during the persecution of 1209.

It should also be remembered that it was not far from here in the ancient territory of Septimania that wise old Jewish experts on the magic and mysticism of the Kabbalah were to be found. They, too, would have been known to the Cathars.

The Cathars were truly benign and remarkable people: they helped the poor and healed the sick to a far greater extent than the established churches did. They were also believed to be in possession of mysterious ancient secrets and unique religious artifacts, treasures that the politically powerful and avaricious forces of established religion coveted.

Because of the friendship and protection that Raymond-Roger showed to the Cathars, the forces of the established churches attacked him and laid siege to Carcassonne. With their despicable disregard of truth and fairness, Raymond-Roger's religious enemies treacherously betrayed and imprisoned him. He was assassinated a few weeks later.

Co-author Lionel researching at Carcassonne.

By 1244 the Cathars had taken refuge in their great castle of Montségur — one of a chain of mutually defensive Cathar castles, where a small but highly effective garrison was holding out against the huge army of their religious persecutors.

Queribus — a powerful link in the chain of Cathar mountain castles.

Strange surrender terms were negotiated with the Cathars: provided that no one attempted to leave the castle of Montségur for a week while the garrison thought over the terms of the surrender, they would be more or less allowed to become "nominal" Catholics and return unharmed to their everyday lives. However, if anyone attempted to leave, the garrison survivors would all be burnt alive.

The Cathar stronghold of Montségur high on its massive rock foundation.

Peyrepertuse — another of the Cathar chain of mountain castles.

Another impressive stronghold in the chain of Cathar mountain castles: this one is at Puilaurens.

Despite this Mafia-style, carrot-and-stick, offer-they-can't-refuse situation, four intrepid Cathar mountaineers escaped down the rock under cover of darkness, carrying with them the treasures of their faith (as mentioned in Chapter Three).

What could this treasure have been? In the annals of the Inquisition it is referred to as *pecuniam infinitam* — meaning infinite, or unlimited, money. When we talked with Dr. Arthur Guirdham, the acknowledged world authority on Catharism, he was convinced that the Cathar mountaineers were carrying ancient books full of strange secrets.

This again ties in with the mystery of Rennes-le-Château. One theory concerning the riddle of the priest's treasure there is that Bérenger Saunière somehow got hold of those lost books of Cathar secrets and found a way to turn their esoteric knowledge into money.

The Bastille, once one of the most awesome castles in France, was built in Paris in the late fourteenth century. In the seventeenth century the Bastille, once an important part of the city's defences, became a prison. It consisted of eight towers, each of which was about twenty-five metres tall. There was also a large courtyard and an important armoury. The prisoners were housed in the towers, although at one time there had been unspeakable accommodation for them known as *cachots*. These were subterranean horrors similar to the *clink* in London, as described in Chapter Two.

The Bastille was stormed by the French revolutionaries on July 14, 1789, and demolished shortly afterwards under the leadership of Palloy — who employed one thousand men to help with the work. Among the famous prisoners who had been held there over the years was Nicholas Fouquet, the former finance minister — was it the unfortunate Fouquet who later became the Man in the Iron Mask?

Nicholas Fouquet was the son of a rich ship owner who moved in high political circles close to the French king. Following in his father's footsteps, Nicholas became a powerful financier — tantamount to being the royal banker. He was a loyal supporter of the influential Cardinal Mazarin, and until Mazarin's death in 1661, Fouquet was doing very well indeed. Unfortunately for Fouquet, Mazarin had had a personal assistant named Jean-Baptiste Colbert who now wanted Fouquet's job. With Mazarin dead, there was no way that Fouquet could prove that the financial "irregularities" of which Colbert accused him had been carried out with the late Cardinal's connivance.

After a long trial, Fouquet was incarcerated in Pignerol — a prison fortress in the French Alps — and then in Sainte Marguerite, a fortified island near Cannes on the south coast of France. He was always under the close and careful eye of Saint-Mars, the prison governor, until Fouquet's *supposed* death in 1680. *But was it Fouquet who died?* Did he then become the mysterious masked prisoner, while some other hapless captive filled the grave that was labelled as Nicholas Fouquet's?

The nature of the mask itself is frequently disputed. Some researchers believe that it was only grey cloth, hanging like a curtain from a metal frame resting on the unknown prisoner's head. In other accounts, the mask was made of iron or steel and hinged so that it could be unlocked and opened when the prisoner needed to eat or drink. Yet another version says that it was never hinged back or removed at all, and the unfortunate masked prisoner had to eat and drink as best he could through an aperture at the base which allowed limited access to his mouth. The common denominator of these accounts was that the masked prisoner's face was carefully concealed from the gaze of anyone who might recognize him.

Theories have ranged from the romantic notion that the masked prisoner was the marginally elder twin brother of the King of France to his being an illegitimate son of Louis XIII. However, if the Man in the Iron Mask was Fouquet, the mystery deepens. The state's one-time financial genius had a younger brother who specialized in a form of espionage that was of particular value to Fouquet senior, and this enigma, too, lines up with the mysterious treasure of Rennes-le-Château.

One important strand of the complex Rennes entanglement is attached to a curious painting executed by the gifted seventeenth-century painter Nicholas Poussin. Just outside Rennes, at Arques, are the remains of the Tomb of Pontils. Its most recent tabletop accoutrement was destroyed a few years ago, having been erected at the start of the twentieth century by a family named Lawrence. Strangely, every detail of this early twentieth-century Lawrence tomb had been made to resemble the painted tomb around which the shepherds and their shepherdess are clustering in Poussin's well-known canvas *Bergères d'Arcadie — The Shepherds of Arcadia.* Another of the tangled strands knotted up in Rennes-le-Château refers to a coded manuscript allegedly found in Father Saunière's Church of St. Mary Magdalene. According to this hypothetical manuscript, Poussin and another painter named Teniers "hold the key" to the Rennes treasure mystery. Poussin links up with the Fouquets.

What does seem to be fairly well documented is that Fouquet's younger brother — the lad who was the seventeenth-century James Bond — had gone to Rome to question Nicholas Poussin about something highly secret and very important that the French minister of finance was interested in learning from the painter. Hints in *The Da Vinci Code* reinforce the general theory that painters like Poussin, Leonardo, the Teniers brothers, and their contemporary artists did stick together like a guild, or brotherhood — similar in some ways to the freemasons — and that secrets known to one member of the artists' guild would be known by others. Having met Poussin and gained his confidence and co-operation, young Fouquet wrote a report to his elder brother in Paris. The gist of this enigmatic document was that Poussin was enthusiastic to throw in his lot with the Fouquets and that he was in possession of a profound secret that contained great advantages, which kings would give their all to possess, and which could never be discovered accidentally. *What could it have been?*

One theory suggests that it was something to do with alchemy — not the type of transmutational secret that Augustus the Strong was after — but great longevity, the alchemist's Elixir of Life.

When the situation of the Man in the Iron Mask is analyzed in terms of power politics, there are factors that seem curiously contradictory. First, here is someone in the clutches of a powerful monarch, someone who is in some way a threat to that monarch — such a potent threat, in fact, that he must not be recognized in case his friends get together and release him. The man is too dangerous to live — yet the powerful monarch does not kill him. *Why?* The answer might well be that the mysterious masked prisoner has a secret that the monarch covets ardently.

But secrets yield to torture. So why not apply the sort of exquisite and prolonged pain that guarantees results? The Inquisition's men were consummate experts at it. Devices existed that could induce a saint to confess that he was sleeping regularly with a whole harem of succubae and thoroughly enjoying the experience. A powerful seventeenth-century monarch would have had plenty of dedicated experts in masks and leather aprons working busily in his torture dungeons — men who could make a tortoise confess that it had repeatedly broken the hundred-kilometres-per-hour speed limit. So why not simply torture the masked prisoner until he sang every note the monarch wanted to hear? There wouldn't have been any moral or ethical inhibitions in those days and in those circumstances. So why bother with an iron mask? Why not simply extort the necessary information using the time-honoured inquisitorial techniques? Simply because the victim might die of shock, or heart failure, before all of the beans had been spilled.

If you were the grand inquisitor blissfully torturing what you regarded as just any old heretic who would be executed anyway once you'd wrung the necessary confession out of him, or her, then it didn't matter a jot if the said heretic died before the confession was made: the end result was the same. But the masked prisoner wasn't just any old heretic, who was, in the Inquisition's eyes, totally disposable. The masked captive had a secret that the ruthless monarch wanted *at any cost.*

Now suppose that the Man in the Iron Mask *was* the wily and politically knowledgeable Fouquet. Here was a man who was far more astute than Louis XIV. Fouquet has the situation analyzed perfectly: the minute he tells Louis the secret, Louis will execute him for safety. Power politicians of Louis's type regard coffins as the ultimate silencing mechanism, the safest and most reliable form of security. The stalemate is complete: Louis can't torture the prisoner in case he dies without talking during the proceedings, and the prisoner can't tell Louis the alchemical secret of longevity that he obtained from Poussin because, when he does, Louis will terminate him.

When the masked prisoner finally died of natural causes in 1703, the attention paid to his cell was incredible. Furniture was removed and destroyed and the plaster was scraped off the walls. The question echoes down the ages: what was it that the masked prisoner must never be allowed to disclose — even posthumously? According to some reports, those who laid the Man in the Iron Mask to rest did apparently get a glimpse of that long-hidden face: what they saw surprised them. He was said to have been remarkably youthful looking despite all the long years that he had languished in the Bastille. Was the masked prisoner Nicholas Fouquet, and had he really possessed some strange alchemical secret of longevity that had reached him via Poussin the painter?

The beautiful and romantic old castles of France hold many mysteries and secrets: Catherine's sinister poison cupboards at Blois; its suspected links with the controversial Priory of Sion; the connection with the enigmatic Francis Bacon; and Houdin, the inventor, conjuror, and master of robot technology. Did Joan of Arc really revisit Chinon to challenge the King again after her supposed death? Courage and ingenuity produced the world's first frogman, the French hero whose idea helped to bring down Gaillard. The ponderous defences of the citadel of Carcassonne, and the ring of Cathar mountain castles — Montségur, Queribus, Peyrepertuse, Puilaurens, and the others — all protected a very mysterious Cathar secret. What was it, and where is it now? The grimly confining walls of the Bastille might once have imprisoned Nicholas Fouquet — hidden by an iron mask. Did he know something of unique significance that Louis XIV desperately wanted?

From the secrets of the French castles, we go on to the riddle of Glamis and the enigma of Tintagel: two of the world's strangest castle mysteries.

The mysterious castle of Glamis is said to contain a secret chamber that once concealed a monster.

Chapter 13
Glamis and Camelot: Castles with Legends

KING ROBERT II of Scotland (1316–1390) gave Glamis to his son-in-law, Sir John Lyon, in 1372, and the castle has remained with the family ever since. They are the earls of Strathmore and Kinghorne. Their huge, picturesque castle stands in the vale of Strathmore in Tayside, Scotland, ringed by the villages of Jericho, Padanaram, and Zoar: all three names are biblical in origin, and this may hold historical and geographical clues to the mystery of Glamis itself.

The collapse of the walls of Jericho, when Joshua and the Israelites attacked the city, is often used as a symbol of the triumph of religious forces over their enemies. Padanaram was also highly significant in the story of Jacob, the Hebrew patriarch who went there to find a non-Canaanite wife from the family of Laban, his uncle. Zoar is featured in the biblical accounts of Lot's adventures when Sodom and Gomorrah were destroyed and his wife was transformed into a pillar of salt (Genesis 19). All three locations are associated in different ways with *conflicts*: Joshua versus the Canaanites, Lot versus the men of Sodom and Gomorrah, and the fraternal quarrel between Jacob and Esau. Was it at the back of the minds of the pioneer inhabitants who named their Strathmore villages that there were strange psychic forces of good and evil in conflict in the vicinity of Glamis?

One of the first tragedies that took place at Glamis was the murder of King Malcolm II (1005–1034), who was butchered by rebels wielding claymores. As a result of his appalling injuries, almost all of his blood seeped out around his body, and the stain was said to have remained indelibly on the floor of the room in Glamis where he died. As the assassins retreated across a frozen loch, the ice broke and they were all drowned.

Prior to 1372, the Lyon family had lived at Forteviot, where they were said to be the custodians of a very beautiful and ancient sacred chalice. This chalice, according to legend, was said to bring peace, safety, and good fortune to the Lyon family, provided that it was never moved. After being given Glamis, however, Sir John took the ancient Forteviot chalice with him. Whatever negative influences were supposed to follow the removal of the chalice, Sir John seems to have prospered and lived happily at Glamis for the next ten or eleven years, but he died as the result of a duel in 1383.

Another of the great Glamis tragedies occurred in 1537, when the beautiful young Janet Douglas was burnt at the stake in Edinburgh on charges of witchcraft and trying to murder King James V (1512–1542). Janet had the misfortune of marrying the thoroughly unpleasant sixth Lord of Glamis. He was found dead after eating alone, and Janet was accused of poisoning him. After her trial collapsed because of insufficient evidence, King James V of Scotland, who had a pathological hatred of the Douglas family, extorted evidence under torture that Janet had been part of a conspiracy to murder him. Lady Janet was innocent, but she was condemned and executed all the same.

It is said that the spectral Grey Lady, who has been reported from Glamis on many occasions by reliable witnesses, is the ghost of the brutally wronged and abused Lady Janet. She appears both in the chapel and above the clock tower.

Another horrific spectre appealing for sympathy and justice is the apparition of a woman with a mutilated face who is apparently tongue-less. Little or nothing definite is known about her, but it is conjectured that she may be the ghost of an unfortunate servant who discovered the secret of Glamis, which is traditionally known only to the reigning earl and his chief steward. Rather than kill the woman, her tongue was cut out so that she could never tell what she had seen inside the forbidden chamber. She is occasionally glimpsed looking out from a barred window but has also been reported moving about in the grounds.

The sad little apparition of a young coloured servant boy has also been reported at Glamis. It is thought that he was on the staff in the eighteenth century, when it was considered fashionable in some quarters to have Afro-Caribbean servants. According to the accounts of his appearances, he looks very unhappy and is said to sit silently near the door of the royal bedroom.

The ghost of Beardie is a distinct contrast from that of the unhappy servant boy. He is said to be either one of the earls or an associate who was staying at Glamis as the earl's guest — versions of the legend differ slightly. In any event, a game of cards was in progress when a servant announced respectfully that it was almost midnight, and that as it would soon be the Sabbath, it would be wise for the game to end. Beardie shouted profane abuse and swore that he would rather play with the devil than abandon his game. The devil duly appeared and accepted Beardie's offer of a game — with the gambler's soul as the inevitable stake. Needless to say, Beardie lost, and he has been thumping, banging, and crashing his way around Glamis ever since. Another ghostly noise emanating from the region of the gambling ghost is the rattle of dice.

Glamis also has an emaciated, almost skeletal ghost who was — in life — locked in a dungeon and left to starve to death.

This tale of a victim starved in a dungeon may be related to the tragedy of a group of Ogilvies who reportedly fled to Glamis seeking protection from their traditional enemies, the Lindsays. The then Lord of Glamis took them to a deep hiding place below the castle, secured the doors, and left them there to die.

The main legend of Glamis, however, concerns the occupant of the secret room — if the room and its legendary inhabitant ever existed. One relatively recent version of this secret room saga is that it dates back only as far as 1821, when the first son of the eleventh earl was said to have been born suffering from major deformities. According to this story, it was announced that the boy had died — when in reality he was concealed in a mysterious secret chamber deep within the castle. When another son arrived, his father kept the secret of the hidden elder brother from him until his twenty-first birthday.

Co-author Lionel exploring the interior of Glamis Castle, which is said to contain a mysterious secret chamber.

In one variation of the story, the concealed brother has abnormal strength; in another, this is combined with extreme longevity; in a third version he has both these attributes. By an obscure and convoluted route, the child is said to have been so different from normal human beings because of an experiment with an alchemical elixir that bestowed superhuman strength and longevity — but at a terrible price as far as appearance went. An extension of this hypothesis postulates that the baby had been quite normal at birth but became so ill that he was not expected to live — hence the announcement that he had died. The administration of the mysterious alchemical medicine was then a desperate last resort in a situation that seemed hopeless. According to this explanation it saved the boy's life but turned him into something barely recognizable as human.

Working on the simplest and broadest basic assumptions that at some period in the history of Glamis *something* was concealed in a secret room deep within the castle, seven hypotheses present themselves. First, it was just a sadly malformed but otherwise normal human being, and, for reasons of their own, the family decided to keep his existence secret. Second, as well as his strange appearance, he had attributes such as abnormal strength and longevity that enabled him to survive long enough for several generations of eldest sons to meet him on their twenty-first birthdays. Third, the occupant of the hidden chamber had no biological associations with the family — nor, for that matter, with *Homo sapiens* at all — he, she, or it was an extraterrestrial alien visitor that had somehow reached Glamis from outer space. Fourth, the entity in the secret chamber was a weird-looking visitor from another dimension. Fifth, the mysterious occupant was from another probability track — one of the tantalizing *Worlds of If* — a realm in which evolution had taken a significantly different path so that their equivalent of human beings was far removed from our experiences of terrestrial humanoids. The sixth hypothesis involves time-slips like the ones that J.W. Dunne envisaged in *An Experiment with Time* and *The Serial Universe*. Ever since the bizarre and conflicting reports of the Philadelphia Experiment, a few serious scientists have wondered whether time and space might be more intricately interwoven and more susceptible to warps and slips than was previously recognized. There are well-documented accounts of contemporary observers who *seem* to have moved through time, or who have reported encountering beings who have reached us from another time frame. Is it remotely possible that whatever lies concealed in the secret chamber of Glamis came from a different era via a time portal? Might that, perhaps, account for the *longevity* dimension of the "Monster of Glamis" mystery? The seventh hypothesis centres on the opening decades of the nineteenth century, and Mary Shelley's fateful visit to Castle Frankenstein on the advice of her stepmother, Mary Jane Clairmont. Before writing her magnum opus about a creature constructed from parts of dismembered corpses and hurled back into the realm of the living at the whim of his creator and the power of a lightning flash, Mary had heard of a remarkable eccentric scientist named Johann Conrad Dippel. This strange man had lived in Castle Frankenstein, and, if half the stories about him were true, the real life Dippel had attempted many of the gruesome experiments that Mary laid at the door of the fictional Baron Frankenstein in her epic, which was published in 1818.

Co-author Lionel on the roof of mysterious Glamis Castle.

The tales of the "Monster of Glamis" began circulating at about the same time. Was there another Dippel, an eccentric Scottish surgeon, perhaps, someone like Dr. Knox who was buying murdered corpses from Burke and Hare in Edinburgh in the 1820s? Had a successful version of the Frankenstein experiment been carried out — and then concealed and incarcerated for safety in the secret chamber of Glamis?

Claude Bowes-Lyon, who was the thirteenth earl, died in 1904 at the age of eighty. During his long life, he had been deeply involved with whatever mystery the secret chamber contained. On one occasion, he said with great solemnity and seriousness to an enquirer, "If you knew what the mystery was, you'd thank God that it wasn't yours."

On another occasion, a workman carrying out repairs and refurbishments at Glamis accidentally broke through a partition wall that led to the secret room. Horrified at what he found in there, he spoke earnestly with Earl Claude, who rewarded him generously for his silence and paid for him and his family to start a prosperous new life in Australia.

In the 1920s, a period when rumours of the secret chamber and its mysterious occupant were at their height, a group of light-hearted young people from London were staying at Glamis as house guests. They decided to hang a sheet or towel from every window in the accessible rooms, reckoning that if a window had no indicator then it must be the window of the secret chamber. Perhaps a little more thought would have suggested to them that a genuine secret chamber would be singularly unlikely to have a window! According to reports of this adventure with the marker-linen at the windows, the Earl was absolutely furious and ordered his guests to leave. What did he know about the secret room that was so important to him to conceal? Is it still there? Is its mysterious occupant still there?

The myths and legends that surround Tintagel Castle in Cornwall are the equal of those that surround Glamis in Scotland — but they differ dramatically in style and content. In contention with several other ancient sites, including Glastonbury, Cader Idris in Gwynedd, Wales, and Cadbury Castle, Tintagel in Cornwall claims to be Camelot, the citadel of King Arthur and the Knights of the Round Table.

Although a number of mainstream scholars have suggested that the oldest ruins at Tintagel — dating from the fourth century — were possibly only a Celtic monastery rather than Arthur's Camelot, alternative theories concerning the nature and purpose of those earliest structures are also viable. A different hypothesis may be put forward to the effect that theories of Arthurian ruins and monastic usage are not necessarily incompatible: perhaps there is room for *both* at Tintagel.

It adds to the Tintagel mysteries to trace the origins of the Celtic religious culture that may have been responsible for the monastic work there. Saint Juliot of Tintagel was probably a descendant of King Brychan of Wales and belonged to an ancient Celtic Christian tradition that traced its roots all the way back to the mysterious Theban desert hermits and from them into Britain via Gaul. St. Nectan, associated with Nectan's Glen near Tintagel, would have been a contemporary of Juliot, and the curious thing about Nectan is his burial in the river just below a singular waterfall adjacent to his hermitage. River burials were a Visigothic tradition — yet again associated with the Rennes-le-Château mystery and the possibility that the deepest part of the enigmatic tomb at Pontils is connected to a sepulchre and treasure repository under the River Sals. Was Nectan of Tintagel buried below the Cornish riverbed because his Celtic Christianity was associated with Visigothic Christianity of a type that would have been practised at Rennes?

There is no mention of any monastery at Tintagel in the Domesday Book of 1086. Tintagel was in the hands of Robert of Mortain at this time, but his motte-and-bailey castle was situated at Bossinney, a kilometre farther west, and he would not have seen the need to build another castle on the great rocky headland where the intriguing old Tintagel ruins are located. Robert's son, William, lost his Cornish estates after the Battle of Tinchebrai in 1106. In 1140 the powerful Reginald, Earl of Cornwall, an illegitimate son of Henry I, came to power, and if Geoffrey of Monmouth's record is correct, it was Reginald who built a castle out on the island beyond the rocky Tintagel promontory.

The subterranean mysteries of Tintagel are as intriguing as the castle ruins themselves. According to Dr. Ralegh Radford's scholarly guidebook, there is a tunnel in a fold of the rock facing seawards, approximately five feet wide and five feet high. It dates back at least to the sixteenth century, but its true age and purpose are unknown. Another enigmatic feature is Merlin's Cave near Tintagel Castle, and this is, of course, associated with the Arthurian traditions and legends concerning Merlin the Magician.

Merlin's Cave at Tintagel.

A very important archaeological discovery was made at Tintagel in 1998. It was a slate slab, twenty centimetres by thirty-six centimetres, approximately fifteen hundred years old — and bearing the name Artognov. It was discovered by Kevin Brady, an archaeologist from the University of Glasgow. The inscription reads *Pater Coliavificit Artognov.* One possible translation is *Artognov, father and/or descendant of Coll, has constructed this building.* Was it then a foundation stone, or marker, of some sort that Brady and his team had found? Artognov refers to the Bear Tribe, or Bear Clan — and they go right back into the furthest mists of time.

Whatever it was that Artognov and his people constructed at Tintagel was destroyed in battle, damaged by wind and storm, or simply neglected after his death and allowed to decay. For whatever reason, Artognov's building had vanished by the seventh century, and when new structures were erected on the site, this vitally important slate was demoted to the role of drain cover.

How old are the Arthurian traditions? There were European versions dating back before the thirteenth century, mainly in France, and

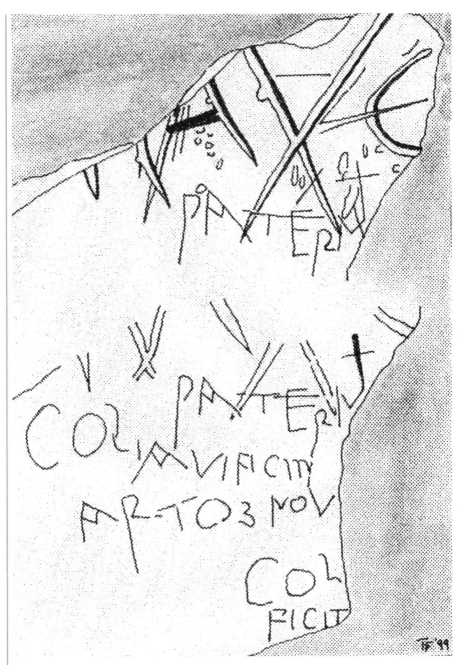

The Artognov stone found at Tintagel in 1998.

Chrétien de Troyes, the poet, flourished during the second half of the twelfth century. He was responsible for writing down at least five of the Arthurian stories: *Erec, Cligès, Lancelot, Yvain,* and *Perceval.* How many were older traditions, rather than his original creative work, is impossible to decide. Of Chrétien's work, the most significant and mysterious is *Perceval* and the quest for the Holy Grail, which percolates through so many other mysteries in various guises — sometimes as the Christianized version of the Cup used by Christ at the Last Supper and brought to Glastonbury by Joseph of Arimathea, and at other times as a much older, magical vessel that worked as a cornucopia.

Geoffrey of Monmouth wrote *Historia Regum Britanniae* (*The History of the Kings of Britain*) during the first half of the twelfth century. In this version, Arthur defeated a Roman army in Europe, but was then seriously — perhaps fatally — wounded by his rebellious nephew, Mordred, in a civil war back in Britain.

One of the most important aspects of the Arthurian romances is that both Chrétien and Geoffrey were writing at a time when the Knights Templar were at their zenith. Detailed analysis of the Arthurian stories has led some researchers to believe that they actually refer to the Templars and contain coded references to important Templar secrets.

The Arthurian legends concerning the love affair between Lancelot and Guinevere seem to illustrate an unfortunate converging of a much older pagan fertility theme with pious modifications made by later Christian writers. In the older theme, Guinevere is seen as a Persephone-type figure, abducted by the forces of evil and darkness as represented by Pluto, god of the underworld. Her freedom, as the daughter of the earth goddess, is essential if crops are to grow, and flocks and herds — as well as people — are to prosper and increase. Lancelot, like the superheroes of Greek mythology, rides to her rescue. The conflation of the two variant traditions ends in tragedy with the devoted and passionate lovers separated by the nonsensical celibacy of a monastery and a convent.

The pre-Christian version with the happy ending has Lancelot delivering his beloved Guinevere from the flames just in time, and riding away with her in triumph to Joyous Garde, where they spend the rest of their lives together. Is there some strange connection here with

King Arthur's throne in the Great Halls at Tintagel.

Co-author Patricia with one of the round tables in King Arthur's Great Halls at Tintagel.

Stained glass window in the Great Halls showing Arthur taking Excalibur, the magic sword, out of the anvil on the stone.

the hypothetical rescue of Joan of Arc and her subsequent life as the wife of Robert des Armoises? Do these two legends of rescue from fire overlap and intertwine?

Another fascinating mystery in Tintagel is the inspiring building known as King Arthur's Great Halls, the headquarters of the Fellowship of the Knights of the Round Table of King Arthur, of which the authors are members.

The Hall of Chivalry here is situated on a ley line (a line of earth energy) known as the Merlin Line. Such lines are also found at Glastonbury and Stonehenge. Their full significance has not yet been totally understood — but there is no doubt that they exist and that they do exert their influence at significant ancient sites. Among the many superb interior decorations, thrones, shields, swords, and magnificent stained glass windows is a round table, of the type associated with Arthur and his knights.

The myths and legends associated with Glamis and Tintagel may lack historicity, but the symbolic truths behind such stories — like the teachings to be found in Aesop's Fables or the New Testament parables — are timeless and of inestimable value in our human efforts to understand the deepest meanings of life.

In the final chapter, we extend this idea when considering the imagery and symbolism of *castles of the mind.*

Chapter 14
Castles of the Mind

ONE GREAT AND valuable legacy bequeathed to us by the castles and fortresses of history is the awareness that the human mind can also be envisaged as a castle, and that we are its castellans.

The link between castles and literature continues with John Bunyan's book *The Holy War*. Bunyan was born in Elstow near Bedford in England in 1628, fought as a Parliamentarian during the Civil War, was imprisoned for preaching without a licence, and spent a dozen years in Bedford jail. He later became a pastor, travelling preacher, and religious writer. His most famous and widely read work was *The Pilgrim's Progress*. In *The Holy War*, which he wrote in 1682, Bunyan describes the fortified city of Mansoul, which is captured by an evil tyrant named Diabolus and eventually liberated by the hero, Emmanuel. Bunyan's own military experiences enrich and enliven the realistic descriptions of the battles for his allegorical city. Despite the passage of more than three centuries, *The Holy War* is as relevant today as when Bunyan wrote it.

Our minds, like medieval castles and fortresses, are all too often attacked by opposing forces that could be described as coming at us from every side. External stresses of this lateral kind take many forms. Our vitally important personal relationships can sometimes go through difficult patches; preparation for exams, study, and academic research can be painfully slow and demanding; business deadlines have to be met and there are too many conflicting demands on our limited time; financial problems worry many of us; health is another source of anxiety; from the moment we are born, the threat of eventual death clouds our lives; and then we worry about our social success — or lack of it — our professionalism, status, and position in our immediate hierarchy and in society as a whole. We can also be stressed by ageism, racism, genderism — and the nonsensical rules and regulations imposed by mindless control freaks saturated in the socially toxic nonsense of political correctness: the obsessive worshippers of trivia and minutiae.

As well as doing the best it can to defend itself against these lateral stresses and pressures, the conscious self, or ego, takes steps to defend itself and its everyday activities from attacks that emanate both from above and below. From the point of view of the ego in its mind-castle, these attacks on its behavioural patterns and decision-making processes can originate from two sources. Attacks from above are referred to in popular language as the promptings of conscience. They come from the superego, the repository of religious ideas, ethics, morals, norms, and mores — whatever has been placed there during the process of socialization that was applied to that particular individual while he, or she, was living in a certain society at a specific time. Such attackers from above are often armed with conceptual weapons based on sexual relationships and practices, food and drink prohibitions, ownership of property, fairness and justice, and religious creeds and dogmas. They can also involve the work ethic, racial differences, ethnicity, perceived social class membership, and related topics.

The "defenders" would like to pursue certain courses of action: to engage in sexual relationships with "forbidden" partners, in "forbidden" ways, to eat prohibited foods and consume banned drinks, to visit taboo locations, or to steal someone else's property. The superego SWAT team parachutes down over the curtain wall of the mind-castle's outer bailey and proclaims such things to be forbidden. The ego in command of its mind-castle then has three choices: it can surrender abjectly to the dictates of the superego and regretfully abstain from alcohol, chocolate, or the inviting smile of a sensually alluring courtesan; it can gallop to counter-attack under the swirling banner of hedonism — drink the whisky, eat the chocolate, and hire the courtesan for an entire weekend; or it can compromise, accepting *some* of the demands of the superego while standing firm on the things it wants to do most: the girl and the chocolate can go their ways, but the ego will have its whisky.

Attackers from below are entirely different. These are no SWAT team heroes trying to overcome the defenders only to help them to be better and stronger than they were before. The superego seeks to conquer only in order to strengthen, maintain, and fortify the ego's castle of the mind. By contrast, slimy *things* from below crawl up from the id like maggots emerging from rotting flesh. Primeval selfishness, coarse appetites, and avaricious greed: these are dangerous enemies indeed, lusting after power, seeking to control others just for the pleasure of controlling and subordinating their victims. The horrors from below undermine the walls. They pick away insidiously at the mortar between the stones, and the ego is hard-pressed to hold the castle against them. Wartime alliances are made: the ego calls on the superego to help it fight against the reptilian menace from the id. Again, there are three possible outcomes: victory, defeat, or compromise.

The value of images of this kind cannot be overstated. The normal, conscious ego, the personality we recognize as "I", defends the mind-castle it has constructed out of the heavy stones of experience and the sturdy timbers of education, interpretation, and an understanding of life — insofar as any of us are able to comprehend where we are and what we are. The rejected, lonely person can identify with the Ugly Duckling in the Hans Christian Andersen story, and, in the course of such ficti-tious self-identification, can go at least some of the way towards finding a solution. The human ego, under constant attack from above and below, can see itself as the castellan defending the fortress — and can find that image extremely helpful psychologically. Images are the lenses through which we scrutinize the mysteries and anomalies of life. Those images also help our decision-making processes, enabling us to improve our quality of life by making the right choices. The man, or woman, who sees himself, or herself, in charge of a mind-castle, with full responsibility for its defence and maintenance, has an improved probability of making positive decisions and choosing the right alternatives.

How else can this image of a mind-castle benefit our survival and success in a world that is often as hostile and hazardous as any threat the

Middle Ages posed? One useful perspective is the idea of sustaining the castle metaphor, extending it and seeing the various parts of it as germane to our sense of personal identity and our life situations.

The location of the castle — on a rocky headland, on an island in a river, at the top of a natural knoll or a laboriously constructed artificial motte — can be seen as our genetic inheritance. We are given the land on which our castle has to be built. The foundations, however, are ours to dig. These are our networks of families and friends, our loyal, loving, and trusted partners, our educational choices both of levels and subject areas, and our chosen careers. Here the analogy is truest of all, and the parallel is closest: if our foundations are not strong, the castle will not stand for long.

Jesus told a very meaningful parable about two houses — one built on rock and the other on sand. When the floods came, only the house that was founded on rock survived. So the human mind-castle must have the strongest foundations we can provide. There are dangerous fallacies associated with this vitally important area. All too often we tell ourselves that it's too late, that we cannot now go back and choose different foundations. The dynamic truth is that we *can*. We can change *anything* at any time. It just takes a will of steel and a determination to succeed that makes a hurricane seem like a gentle spring breeze compared to you. The dynamic, decisive woman, or man, can change and improve anything and everything out of all recognition.

This is tantamount to finding out where your mind-castle foundations have been damaged, or were never installed properly in the first place, and then pumping in the fast-setting liquid concrete of willpower and determination. *The power of the human mind exceeds anything we've done with it yet by a factor of infinity.* Locate your target. Mobilize your forces — and go for it with everything you've got. Never give up. Never take no for an answer. Once you've cracked that, go for the next target.

So much for the foundations. What of the walls? It's a rough, dangerous world out there. When the three little pigs built houses of straw, wood, and bricks, the big, bad wolf destroyed the straw and wood houses with very little difficulty. Your mind-castle has to have massive stone walls — and they need to be indestructibly thick. Remind yourself daily of just how tough and resilient you are — and remember that every battle makes you tougher and more experienced than you were the day before. Concentrate on your many talents and your vast ability to handle things. Get into the habit of seeing yourself as totally superior to every setback. Laugh at each difficulty. Ridicule every obstacle and obstruction. Despise the hurdle. Ask it mockingly, "Do you call yourself a problem? You're pathetic!" You will develop walls that no cannon ball can penetrate, no trebuchet missile can crack. Your mind-castle will be impregnable.

Medieval castles needed high watchtowers. The sooner the defenders could see the enemy approaching, the more effectively the garrison could deal with them. The mind-castle has similar needs. Perspicacity is a watchtower that each of us should build as high as possible. To be able to calculate what is going on in society around us and to calculate accurately how those events are likely to affect our future — and the future of our families and friends — is a great survival aid. Failing to observe that an impending unpleasant event is in the vicinity of our mind-castle reduces our chances of neutralizing it or overcoming it. Ceaseless vigilance from the mind-castle's watchtowers makes as great a contribution to our defences as do the walls themselves.

The medieval castle was equipped with a drawbridge, a portcullis, and sturdy gates. The mind-castle needs the same equipment. Every war in history has begun as a battle of ideas and a conflict of inter-ests. When two implacable adversaries are both convinced of the unique rightness of what each believes to be inviolably true, the world around them is in grave danger. The doors and gates of the mind-castle need to be strong and eminently defensible: drawbridge and portcullis are vital — yet both are movable. When a new idea approaches us in honest friendship, showing its credentials of reason and rationality, the wise castellan will lower the drawbridge and raise the portcullis accordingly. Fresh ideas are always welcome. Life is a dynamic, flexible process that thrives on new ideas. The mind-castle will admit the heralds of avant-garde science and technology with the greatest of pleasure — and will benefit hugely from their company. The drawbridge remains up and the hefty portcullis stays down when prudery, bigotry, prejudice, and hide-bound tradition seek entry.

Despite the hazards and dangers surrounding it, the medieval castle could still be filled with humour and happiness: family and friends, jesters and minstrels, acrobats and dancers, and delicious food and wine all made their beneficent contributions. The mind-castle can serve us in the same way, if we admit the right thoughts and the right people.

Bibliography

Bacon, Francis. *The Essays: The Wisdom of the Ancients and The New Atlantis.* London: Odhams Press Ltd., 1950.

Bradley, Michael. *Holy Grail across the Atlantic.* Toronto: Hounslow Press, 1988.

Chant, Christopher. *Castles.* London: C. Roydon Publishing Co. Ltd., 1984.

Coventry, Martin. *The Haunted Castles of Scotland.* Musselburgh, Scotland: Goblinshead, 1996.

Coventry, Martin. *A Wee Guide to Scottish Ghosts and Bogles* Musselburgh, Scotland: Goblinshead, 2000.

Dupuy, R.E., and T.N. Dupuy. *The Collins Encyclopaedia of Military History.* London: HarperCollins Publishers, 1993.

Dyall, Valentine. *Unsolved Mysteries.* London: Hutchinson, 1954.

Encyclopaedia Britannica Online: http://www.eb.com.

Fanthorpe, Patricia and Lionel. *The Holy Grail Revealed.* California: Newcastle Publishing Co. Inc., 1982.

Fanthorpe, Lionel and Patricia. *Secrets of Rennes le Château.* Boston, MA: Samuel Weiser Inc., 1992.

Fanthorpe, Lionel and Patricia. *The Oak Island Mystery.* Toronto: Hounslow Press, 1995.

Fanthorpe, Lionel and Patricia. *The World's Greatest Unsolved Mysteries.* Toronto: Hounslow Press, 1997.

Fanthorpe, Lionel and Patricia. *The World's Most Mysterious People.* Toronto: Hounslow Press, 1998.

Fanthorpe, Lionel and Patricia. *The World's Most Mysterious Places .* Toronto: Hounslow Press, 1999.

Fanthorpe, Lionel and Patricia. *The World's Most Mysterious Objects.* Toronto: Hounslow Press, 2002.

Fanthorpe, Lionel and Patricia. *The World's Most Mysterious Murders.* Toronto: Hounslow Press, 2003.

Fanthorpe, Lionel and Patricia. *Unsolved Mysteries of the Sea.* Toronto: Hounslow Press, 2004.

Fanthorpe, Lionel and Patricia. *Mysteries of Templar Treasure and the Holy Grail.* Boston, MA: Samuel Weiser Inc. 2004

Fanthorpe, Lionel and Patricia. *Mysteries and Secrets of the Templars: The Story behind the da Vinci Code.* Toronto: Hounslow Press, 2005.

Graves, Robert. "Introduction." In *Larousse Encyclopaedia of Mythology.* London: Paul Hamlyn, 1959.

Guerber, H.A. *Myths and Legends of the Middle Ages.* London: Studio Editions Ltd., 1994.

Hardy, Clive. *Francis Frith's English Castles.* UK: Frith Book Company Ltd. 1999.

Harlech, Lord. *Southern England — Illustrated Regional Guide to Ancient Monuments Number Two.* London: HMSO, 1952.

Henderson, Elaine. *Castles of Scotland.* Glasgow: HarperCollins Publishers, 1997.

Hitching, Francis. *The World Atlas of Mysteries.* London: Pan Books, 1979.

Hook, Jason, and M. Pegler. *To Live & Die in the West.* Oxford: Osprey Publishing, 2001.

Kinross, John. *Discovering Castles in England and Wales.* Princes Risborough, Buckinghamshire: Shire Publications Ltd., 1995.

Knight, Gareth. *The Secret Traditions in Arthurian Legend.* Wellingborough, Northants: The Aquarian Press, 1983.

Michell, John, and Robert J.M. Rickard. *Phenomena: A Book of Wonders.* London: Thames & Hudson, 1977.

Morrissey, Brendan. *Quebec 1775: The American Invasion of Canada.* Oxford: Osprey Publishing Ltd., 2003.

Pott, Mrs Henry. *Francis Bacon and His Secret Society.* London: Sampson Low, Marston & Company, 1891.

Radford, Ralegh. *Tintagel Castle.* London: HMSO, 1971.

Rountree, H.C. & E.R. Turner III. *Before and After Jamestown*. Florida: University Press of Florida, 2002.

Salter, Mike. *Discovering Scottish Castles*. Princes Risborough, Buckinghamshire: Shire Publications Ltd., 1995.

Sharper Knowlson, T. *The Origins of Popular Superstitions and Customs*. London: Studio Editions Ltd., 1995.

Trench, C.E.F. *Slane*. An Taisce Killrian, Slane, Co. Meath: Meath Association., 1987.

Wills, Charles A. *A Historical Album of Texas*. Brookfield, CT: The Millbrook Press Inc., 1995.

Wallace, Anthony F.C. *Jefferson and the Indians*. Cambridge, MA: The Belknap Press, 1999.

Warner, Philip. *The Medieval Castle*. London: Book Club Associations, 1973.

Wise, Leonard F. *World Rulers*. UK: Ward Lock Educational, 1967.